VOLUME 2

Best Practices in Professional Learning and Teacher Preparation

Special Topics for Gifted Professional Development

Edited by Angela M. Novak, Ph.D.,
& Christine L. Weber, Ph.D.

PRUFROCK PRESS INC.
WACO, TEXAS

a service publication

Library of Congress information on file with the publisher.

Copyright ©2019, National Association for Gifted Children

Edited by Katy McDowall

Cover design and layout design by Micah Benson

ISBN-13: 978-1-61821-843-8

No part of this book may be reproduced, translated, stored in a retrieval system, or transmitted, in any form or by any means, electronic, mechanical, photocopying, microfilming, recording, or otherwise, without written permission from the publisher.

For more information about our copyright policy or to request reprint permissions, visit https://www.prufrock.com/permissions.aspx.

Printed in the United States of America.

At the time of this book's publication, all facts and figures cited are the most current available. All telephone numbers, addresses, and website URLs are accurate and active. All publications, organizations, websites, and other resources exist as described in the book, and all have been verified. The authors and Prufrock Press Inc. make no warranty or guarantee concerning the information and materials given out by organizations or content found at websites, and we are not responsible for any changes that occur after this book's publication. If you find an error, please contact Prufrock Press Inc.

Prufrock Press Inc.
P.O. Box 8813
Waco, TX 76714-8813
Phone: (800) 998-2208
Fax: (800) 240-0333
http://www.prufrock.com

Table of Contents

INTRODUCTION 1

SECTION 1: SPECIAL POPULATIONS

CHAPTER 1:
Targeted Professional Learning for Twice-Exceptional Students:
A Double Target 7
BY CLAIRE E. HUGHES

CHAPTER 2:
Professional Learning Standards and Practices for
Educators of Gifted GLBTQ Youth 31
BY TERENCE PAUL FRIEDRICHS AND PJ SEDILLO

CHAPTER 3:
Reframing Professional Learning to Meet the Needs of
Teachers Working With Culturally Diverse Gifted Learners 51
BY JOY LAWSON DAVIS

CHAPTER 4:
Professional Learning Strategies to Develop Creativity
Among Attention Divergent Hyperactive Gifted Students 71
BY C. MATTHEW FUGATE AND JANESSA BOWER

CHAPTER 5:
Professional Learning Strategies for
Teachers of Underachieving Gifted Students 89
BY JENNIFER RITCHOTTE, CHIN-WEN LEE, AND AMY GRAEFE

CHAPTER 6:
Professional Learning for the Parent:
How Educators Can Support Parents 113
BY TRACY FORD INMAN AND LYNETTE BREEDLOVE

SECTION 2: PROGRAMMATIC TOPICS

CHAPTER 7:
Identifying and Supporting Culturally, Linguistically, and Economically
Diverse Gifted Learners: Guiding Teachers Through the Four Zones of
Professional Learning 133
BY KATIE D. LEWIS AND ANGELA M. NOVAK

CHAPTER 8:
Empowering Educators to Implement Acceleration:
Professional Learning Is Essential 159
BY LAURIE J. CROFT AND ANN LUPKOWSKI-SHOPLIK

CHAPTER 9:
Designing Professional Learning Centered on
Social and Emotional Issues for the Gifted. 185
BY ELIZABETH SHAUNESSY-DEDRICK AND SHANNON M. SULDO

CHAPTER 10:
Finding Gifted English Language Learners:
Professional Learning Designed to Change the Lens. 207
BY ANNE K. HORAK, BEVERLY D. SHAKLEE, AND REBECCA L. BRUSSEAU

ABOUT THE EDITORS 237

ABOUT THE AUTHORS 239

Introduction

This book is the second volume of a three-book series related to professional learning and teacher preparation in gifted education. Volume 1 focuses on methods and strategies for gifted professional development. Volume 2 explores professional learning strategies for special topics in gifted education. Volume 3 provides professional learning strategies for teachers of the gifted in the content areas. The purpose of this series is to present various topics supporting strategies and best practices in teacher training, focusing on identifying and meeting the needs of gifted learners, as outlined and required in the Every Student Succeeds Act (ESSA, 2015) for Pre-K–grade 12 administrators and supervisors, coordinators of gifted programs, Pre-K–grade 12 educators and teachers of the gifted, and other stakeholders in the field. These books continue the discussions started in *Using the National Gifted Education Standards for Pre-K–Grade 12 Professional Development* (Johnsen & Clarenbach, 2017) and offer expert suggestions for exemplary practices that maximize professional learning.

In this volume, the first group of chapters explores special populations of gifted learners. The first chapter, crafted by Hughes, crosses into special education, discussing twice-exceptional, or 2e, students. Hughes presents the need to approach professional learning from the eyes of both fields, special and gifted education, recognizing the importance of both pedagogical and literature bases.

Friedrichs and Sedillo overlay the needs of gifted gay, lesbian, bisexual, transgender, and questioning (GLBTQ) youth with professional learning guidelines in the second chapter. The authors discuss topics essential to teachers of gifted GLBTQ students at the elementary and secondary levels, with professional learning topics, strategies, and resources throughout. Needs and standards align with themes such as individualization, safety, and providing effective curricula.

The focus of Chapter 3 is on culturally diverse gifted learners. Davis explores the case study of a teacher who wants to do well but recognizes that she's missing the mark when trying to meet the diverse educational needs of her students. Davis explores three professional learning needs identified as critical for teachers of culturally diverse gifted students in a reframed model, with examples and resources of each embedded throughout the chapter.

Chapter 4 investigates a specific twice-exceptionality: gifted learners with Attention Deficit/Hyperactivity Disorder (ADHD). Fugate and Bower explore how to use professional learning to foster creativity for this group of students, described in this chapter as Attention Divergent Hyperactive Gifted students, or ADHG. The authors walk the reader through a six-step plan for professional learning groups—study, select, plan, implement, analyze, and adjust—that focuses on intensive, job-embedded learning.

Ritchotte, Lee, and Graefe explore underachieving gifted students in Chapter 5. The authors examine the foundations of this often misunderstood topic—if the child isn't achieving, how is she gifted?—and offer specific topic suggestions, individually addressed, for general education professionals and gifted education professionals who have differing levels of knowledge about gifted underachievement, along with best practices in activities and strategies to enhance professional learning.

Chapter 6 outlines how educators can support professional learning for parents by providing strategies to help increase parents' understanding of their children and gifted education as a whole, as well as their understanding of the importance of advocacy. Recognizing the importance of research-based best practices for educators, Inman and Breedlove take the most salient elements and apply them in a practical way that is accessible and realistic for parents. The authors share potential topics, and then walk the reader through several detailed examples of professional learning strategies.

The second section of the book changes gears. Although special populations of gifted students are central to several chapters, the focus shifts to programmatic elements that require targeted support. Chapter 7 describes the Four Zones of Professional Learning. Lewis and Novak identify teachers as frequent gatekeepers to gifted identification, and suggest the use of this model to help identify and support culturally, linguistically, and economically diverse gifted learners.

Chapter 8's focus is the cost-effective, yet often underutilized, strategy of acceleration. Croft and Lupkowski-Shoplik detail a model of professional development created specifically for supporting acceleration, while providing valuable research-related topical suggestions, including essential understandings, tools to enable both objective and informed decisions, and general talking points for the topic.

Shaunessy-Dedrick and Suldo examine the noncognitive aspects of the gifted child in Chapter 9. The authors' focus on professional learning centered on social and emotional issues of gifted learners draws from both gifted research and standards, while also incorporating best practices from the field of positive psychology.

The second volume of the series concludes with a blend of a special population and programmatic topic. Horak, Shaklee, and Brusseau draw on a Jacob K. Javits grant, Project ExCEL, as the foundation of Chapter 10, describing how curriculum emphasizing problem-based learning (PBL), can also be used as a universal screening tool for the identification of gifted English language learners (ELLs). The authors present the grant's professional learning process and implications thereof. Although focused on inquiry-based learning through PBL, the overarching goal of the professional learning was transforming beliefs, perceptions, and practices with regard to teaching and recognizing ELLs, as well as challenging them with meaningful curriculum.

"Special topics" in gifted education is a broad topic, indeed, and chapter authors examine a variety of areas in great need of substantial professional learning experiences. Volume 2 of *Best Practices in Professional Learning and Teacher Preparation* presents an array of topics to explore, with research-based strategies, examples, and resources—all designed to allow a teacher the opportunity to personally explore a chosen topic, a gifted resource leader an outline to coach fellow teachers, an administrator a guide to providing specific professional learning sessions based on the needs of the school, or a gifted coordinator the blueprint to implement districtwide opportunities that also include meeting the needs of parents of gifted children.

References

Every Student Succeeds Act, Pub. L. No. 114–95. (2015).

Johnsen, S. K., & Clarenbach, J. (Eds.). (2017). *Using the national gifted education standards for pre-k–grade 12 professional development* (2nd ed.). Waco, TX: Prufrock Press.

Section 1
Special Populations

CHAPTER 1

Targeted Professional Learning for Twice-Exceptional Students:
A Double Target

Claire E. Hughes

Introduction: Definition and History of Twice-Exceptional

Children who are gifted and have a disability, often known as *twice-exceptional* or *2e*, have been confounding the educational system since schools became institutions. This is due to the lack of knowledge and acceptance of twice-exceptionality among general education teachers and leaders (Kalbfleisch, 2013). The fields of gifted education and special education converge on the educational issues facing twice-exceptional children, but the fields diverge through their separate histories and issues related to how best to educate students who learn differently. Professional learning designed to address the needs of twice-exceptional children must be based upon two areas of understanding—(1) the similarities and differences between the two fields (gifted education and special education) from historical and philosophical perspectives, and (2) the assumptions and misunderstandings that practitioners from each field will have about the other—in order to address the knowledge and lack of knowledge that each field has about twice-exceptional children.

A Brief History of Two Fields

Prior to the 20th century, children with visible or severe disabilities were placed in hospitals, churches, or prisons if their families did not have enough money to care for them at home. Concepts such as autism spectrum disorders (ASD), learning disabilities, and Attention Deficit/Hyperactivity Disorder (ADHD) did not exist in a society in which the one-room schoolhouse provided basic education. Further, education was a luxury. In wealthier families, invisible exceptionalities were easily accommodated through private tutoring or career paths that did not require education (Spielhagen, Brown, & Hughes, 2015). Children with gifted and advanced learning abilities either moved through the basic curriculum faster or were provided more advanced schooling opportunities, depending on their families' financial status. Talents were often found in families, either through similar nurturing environments and/or genetics (Robinson & Jolly, 2013). However, talent alone has been recognized as not being enough. Stories abound regarding individuals who were in high-achieving families, but not performing at expected levels; the story of Branwell Brontë, who had similar writing gifts to those of his Brontë sisters but coupled with mental health issues, is a tragic tale. Zac Lachey, who has ASD, is often cited as an inspiration by his more famous brother, Nick Lachey, a member of the boy band 98 Degrees (McNeil, 2014). There are also examples of successful adults misunderstood as children; Thomas Edison was said to be "addled" by his teachers (Betts, 1987, p. 11), while Hans Christian Andersen struggled with dyslexia.

In the 1930s and 1940s, students with limited financial backgrounds often dropped out of school or went to work, and the wealthy often elected private schooling, so public schools became the embodiment of the middle class (Spielhagen et al., 2015). Special education became a dumping ground for those children who came from poor or immigrant backgrounds, while the advent of gifted and advanced education provided opportunities for those who were wealthier and/or more culturally successful. Children with disabilities were served through a medical model that sought to identify, treat, and cure disabilities as though they were a disease; children were warehoused, separated from their age-mates in educational settings similar to quarantine (Osgood, 2008). Gifted children were also identified using test measures, such as IQ tests, that sought to identify successful thinking abilities within a Western cultural context, but were often then either placed in a separate classroom or ignored within a general education classroom. During this time of school reorganization and increased academic rigor, psychologists and educators became aware of invisible disabilities. New labels were conceptualized to explain observable specific patterns of behavioral characteristics that lack physical markers. At the time, several researchers—including Leo Kanner and Hans Asperger, who helped formulate the field of ASD, and William Cruikshank, who helped originate the field of learning disabilities—noted that that children could have high IQs, but still have problematic behavioral and learning issues (Baldwin, Baum, Pereles, & Hughes, 2015).

In 1954, the Supreme Court determined that separate schools could not provide equal opportunities for all children in the landmark case *Brown v. Board of Education*. Thus, special education began a push for access to both inclusive classrooms and curriculum. With the advent of Sputnik in the 1950s, gifted education began to emphasize acceleration and enrichment of public education. Both fields became more organized through the formation of the National Association for Gifted Children (NAGC) in 1954 and the creation of the Handicapped Children Office at the federal level in 1963. Such organizations led quickly to federal action. In 1972, the Marland Report published an official definition of gifted children and led to the passing of the Gifted and Talented Children's Education Act (1978). In 1975, the landmark Public Law 94-142 was passed, defining special education and the rights of children with disabilities. Neither law specifically noted that some children could be gifted and have a disability, but in 1977, C. June Maker first conceptualized the twice-exceptional child in her work *Providing Programs for Gifted Handicapped* (Baldwin et al., 2015).

Educational programs and organizational support soon followed in the 1980s. In Westchester County, NY, a program was started for the "gifted-handicapped child." A "Gifted Underachiever" program was started in Cupertino, CA, in 1980. The Twice-Exceptional Child Project was started in the late 1980s in Albuquerque, NM, using the term "2x." Connecticut, Maryland, and Colorado started programs (Baldwin et al., 2015). NAGC formed its Special Populations Division, while the Council for Exceptional Children (CEC) formed The Association for the Gifted (CEC-TAG) Division. Public Law 94-142 was renamed in 1990 and reauthorized in 2004 as the Individuals with Disabilities Education Act, and the general education classroom was specified as the starting place for inclusive activity. In 2013, the "Letter to Jim Delisle," from the U.S. Department of Education Office of Special Education Programs (OSEP), specifically stated the term *twice-exceptional* and specified that being gifted and having a disability is possible (Musgrove, 2013). However, the emerging field of twice-exceptionality has found itself caught between the force for inclusion of special education and the desire for identification and service of gifted education because of these opposing histories.

A Definition of Twice-Exceptional

The Twice-Exceptional National Community of Practice (Baldwin et al., 2015), a collaboration of individuals representing numerous organizations, including NAGC and CEC, released a definition of twice-exceptional that states:

> Twice exceptional (2e) individuals evidence exceptional ability and disability, which results in a unique set of circumstances. Their exceptional ability may dominate, hiding their disability; their disability may dominate, hiding their exceptional ability; each may mask the other so that neither is recognized or addressed.
>
> 2e students, who may perform below, at, or above grade level, require the following:
> - Specialized methods of identification that consider the possible interaction of the exceptionalities
> - Enriched/advanced educational opportunities that develop the child's interests, gifts and talents while also meeting the child's learning needs
> - Simultaneous supports that ensure the child's academic success and social-emotional well-being, such as accommodations, therapeutic interventions, and specialized instruction.
>
> *Working successfully with this unique population requires specialized academic training and ongoing professional development.* (emphasis added, p. 4)

The emerging field of twice-exceptionality intersects two fields that developed along parallel and opposing lines. It incorporates both the push for access of special education and the pull of acceleration of gifted education. It must take into consideration the issues of poverty and overrepresentation that haunt special education and the mirror issues of elitism and underrepresentation with which gifted education struggles.

Even the terms used within the two fields are laden with differences in meanings. Gifted education may talk about "regular" education (VanTassel-Baska & Little, 2016), whereas special education, aware of the perceived insult of "irregular," uses the term "general" education (Kirk, Gallagher, &

Coleman, 2015). Gifted education describes the "gifted child" (VanTassel-Baska & Little, 2016), implying the integral nature of giftedness. In contrast, special education describes the "child with disabilities," using person-first language that emphasizes the person, not the disability, because of the dehumanizing history of the field. However, particularly in the areas of deafness and ASD, there is an emerging concept of "neurodiversity" in which the emphasis is on changing society's understanding of disability to be more inclusive (Kirk et al., 2015). The potential landmines of the educational terminology, emphases, and concerns of the different fields have to be considered when providing professional learning.

The emerging field of twice-exceptionality is young, and many of the original founders, writers, and teachers are still actively engaged (Hughes, 2018). However, as the field grows in impact, the concepts of dual services and needs meld into the understanding of unique services and needs for these remarkable children.

Overview: Two Fields, but Three Goals

The need for professional learning in twice-exceptionality is critical because it is an area that is rarely addressed in general training of teachers, leaders, or counselors, and only briefly touched on in gifted and special education. Not understanding the interactions of talents and disabilities can lead to misunderstanding, miseducation, and misdiagnoses (Webb et al., 2016). When a child's ability is neither recognized nor developed because of educators' lack of understanding, there is a tremendous loss of potential. In-depth understanding of twice-exceptional students often comes from personal experience that is reactive instead of proactive. Proactive educational identification and intervention can only come from comprehensive professional learning.

However, professional learning in twice-exceptionality is not simply a matter of providing gifted and special education information. When providing professional learning for schools on twice-exceptional students, there are three intertwined goals:
1. identifying and developing strengths,
2. identifying and mediating issues related to disability, and
3. understanding the issues that occur as a result of the interaction of the talent and the disability.

The first goal originates in gifted education and focuses on identifying and developing the talents of a child who may not be displaying standard characteristics of giftedness, such as high verbal memory and achievement (Assouline, Foley-Nicpon, & Dockery, 2012; Berninger & Abbott, 2013). Identification of strengths views student behavior positively, focusing on what the student can do, and asks the question about what a child does well and often. Gifted education strategies often include an emphasis on providing enriched and advanced opportunities within a particular content area that encourage critical and creative thinking (VanTassel-Baska & Little, 2016). The emphasis on meeting a gifted student's needs originates in the general education curriculum and extends the concepts and content, allowing the student to learn and develop beyond what is expected of agemates. Such an emphasis on growth in an academic area is critical for twice-exceptional students, because they have the ability to manipulate information and grasp concepts in manners similar to their gifted peers. Twice-exceptional students must also have their educational experience emphasize their strengths to ensure the development of their future careers and directions, as well as reduce negative self-image issues (Baum, Schrader, & Hébert, 2014).

In contrast, the second goal, originating from special education, is how to mediate the area of challenge. Hugh Herr, who heads the biomechatronics research group at the MIT Media Lab, stated that, "There is no such thing as a disabled person, there are only disabled technologies—there is only poor design" (Fanning, 2014, para. 9). Mediation is a concept rooted in Vygotsky's sociocultural connection to learning and implies the interaction between learner, content, and teacher, while remediation is a process that is less dependent on the resolution and more focused on closing the gap through a focus on the discrepancies (Kozulin & Gindis, 2007). The role of a teacher is critical in focusing on commonalities and growth for mediation, rather than emphasizing deficits.

A strengths-based approach to special education is a paradigm shift (Department of Education and Early Childhood Development, 2012) that values the skills, knowledge, and potential of individuals (Pattoni, 2012), and encourages a focus on self-management, self-advocacy, and the mitigation of disabilities. Often, teachers focus on what a twice-exceptional child cannot do—and, as a result, the system focuses on raising skills that are problematic (Besnoy et al., 2015). In contrast, a strengths-based approach focuses on student assets and what they contribute to the learning process (Weishaar, 2010).

Good professional learning in special education will often focus on providing means for the student to access curriculum, often using the concept of Universal Design for Learning (UDL) as the cornerstone for strategic instruction. UDL uses the brain as the foundational architecture of intervention (Rose, Meyer, Strangman, & Rappolt, 2002). UDL "is a framework to improve and optimize teaching and learning for all people based on scientific insights into how humans learn" (CAST, 2019, para. 1), and focuses on providing multiple strategies for students to engage with content, representations to create understandings, and expressions of skill and knowledge. What both gifted education and special education have in common is a focus on growth; however, the starting points are different.

Professional learning in twice-exceptionality is unique, not just because of the learning that can take place with a combination of special and gifted education strategies that might be created by having two separate professional learning opportunities, but also because of the interaction between these two fields. This interaction results in a distinctly unique third type of learning—understanding the impacts of the disability on the development of the talent and the impact of the gift on the disability. As Eleonoor vanGerven (personal communication, August 13, 2018) said, "1+1=3!" See Figure 1.1.

The issue of educating twice-exceptional students is the development and expression of talent that is impacted by the areas of skill and speed related to the disability. A student with a prodigious interest in geology may be able to understand the formation, type, and geologic era of rocks, but may be limited by his or her difficulty with reading and organization. Often, social-emotional and self-esteem issues emerge from the child's inability to perform in ways similar to his or her gifted peers, causing an impediment to creativity, problem solving, and academic achievement (Preuss, Baum, & Sabatino, 2009).

Some curricular approaches that have been developed include an integrated historical study of phonics and zero in order to better learn reading and math skills (Hughes, 2017), arts as a primary medium of instruction (Baska & VanTassel-Baska, 2018; Weiner, 2016), and a significant use of technology (Leppien & Thomas, 2016). By understanding how curriculum can be designed to meet this intersection of ability and disability, and how effects of disability can be mediated for the development of ability, teachers and school leaders would be better able to provide appropriate instructional interventions.

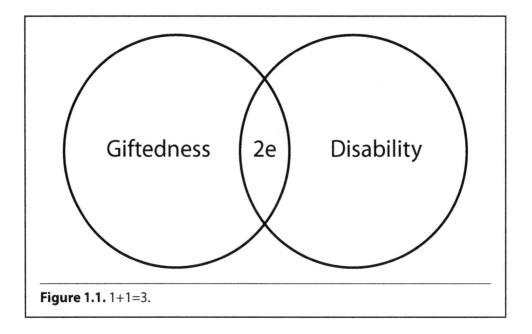

Figure 1.1. 1+1=3.

Strategies: Dual Audiences

The success of any professional learning lies in, of course, understanding the needs and backgrounds of the involved participants. When delivering professional learning to various audiences, leaders must understand the differences and similarities in the training and perspectives, building on the understandings from the participants' backgrounds, challenging the assumptions each may have about the other group, and filling in missing information. In other words, the leaders are modeling the process of building on strengths and mediating areas of challenge.

Teachers and administrators of twice-exceptional children will likely come from a special or gifted education background, but rarely will they have an understanding of both. Although teachers in general education may have had limited experience, they are more likely to have received exposure to and limited awareness of special education needs because of the legal requirements of inclusion.

Noting the similarities between special education and gifted education is worthwhile. Both fields are focused on students who are outside of the "norm" of typical age-grade progressions. There is a significant focus on adapting the curriculum and the instructional approaches; in fact, "differentiation" first appeared in gifted education literature and was quickly adopted by special education (Spielhagen et al., 2015). Both fields often use a Response to Intervention (RtI; Coleman & Hughes, 2009) process to determine if the child's academic development needs attention beyond what is provided in the general education classroom; both are concerned with issues related to diversity; and both support assessment that focuses on growth, as opposed to meeting age-based standards. Both fields fall under the concept of "exceptional," and both are addressed in some organizations, such as the CEC. Boredom, frustration, and resultant social issues are all factors that teachers face when working with children whose needs are not met by the standard curriculum. Finally, both special education and gifted education focus on meeting the individual needs of children who may be different from their same-age peers.

The audience for professional learning in twice-exceptionality should be comprised of both gifted and special education professionals. This will allow them to hear and learn the same information in the context of working with a twice-exceptional child, as well as have an opportunity to engage with each other. Working with a twice-exceptional population requires a multidisciplinary team (Coleman & Gallagher, 2015) that can focus on content adaptations, counseling needs, and behavioral modifications to help a child identify the strengths and mediate the challenges.

Gifted Education Professionals

If the audience is formed of gifted education professionals, they will likely have a background in identification and services that focus on children whose performance and aptitude are significantly above the norm. If they have had teacher training with the NAGC-CEC Teacher Preparation Standards in Gifted and Talented Education (NAGC & CEC-TAG, 2013; Johnsen et al., 2015), they probably have information regarding positivistic views of behavior, recognizing talent, and potential, and they probably have knowledge of creative and critical thinking strategies. They also have some understanding that giftedness can be found across economic and cultural groups, and are aware of the need to look for diverse ways in which talent can be expressed.

However, gifted education professionals will probably not have information regarding specific disability areas. The most commonly cited disability areas in twice-exceptionality include ASD, specific learning disabilities, and ADHD (Foley-Nicpon & Assouline, 2015). Information that would be helpful to cover with gifted education professionals includes:

- characteristics and needs of high-incidence disabilities,
- legal guidelines and cautions,
- strategies to attract and keep students' attention,
- strategies to help students with memory issues organize information,
- strategies to help students with reading challenges acquire information,

- strategies to provide information in meaningful ways that build on prior knowledge,
- social skill development strategies,
- positive emotional and behavioral support strategies, and
- alternate ways to assess students so that a disability does not negatively affect the performance of a child.

The focus of special education is often not on the nature of curriculum experiences, but on providing supports for students to access the curriculum. Inclusion and access are significant themes in special education. A gifted educator can learn to provide supports so that a twice-exceptional student can access the gifted education experiences that are provided.

Special Education Professionals

In contrast to gifted education professionals, special education professionals have had extensive education regarding federal laws and training on how to write an Individualized Education Plan (IEP). Their training provides them with a means of identifying how students can be integrated into a particular setting and how to normalize a setting so that a child with disabilities is not singled out, but can participate in the activities of the classroom. They are also trained in ways to work with parents and other professionals so that the needs of the child can be met (Brownell, Ross, Colón, & McCallum, 2005).

However, when regarding twice-exceptional students, special education professionals need to include training in the following topics (Johnsen et al., 2015):

- characteristics and needs of gifted individuals that challenge the myths and misconceptions of being gifted,
- supportive environments for talent development,
- instruction and assessments strategies particularly suited for gifted children,
- curricular experiences for gifted children,
- ethical issues related to working with gifted children,
- acceleration strategies,
- enrichment techniques,
- management techniques such as compacting and higher order questioning strategies,
- definitions of and strategies to develop creativity and critical thinking, and
- social and emotional issues related to giftedness.

Special educators are experts at designing and creating inclusive environments. However, their training has not led them to look for strengths. Oftentimes, the same behavior or characteristic is apt to be misunderstood by different teachers. For example, a child may ask the question "Why do we have to do this?" A special educator may make the assumption that the child is challenging authority or trying to distract the teacher from an undesired task. In contrast, a gifted educator might assume that the child wants to know the meaning and purpose behind the activity and is looking for a connection to goals and interests. In another instance, a child might be particularly talkative, and the special educator might assume the child is impulsive and needs positive reinforcement to take time to think, whereas the gifted educator might understand the child to have a high level of verbal skills and need an alternative means of expression. A general educator is apt to think in more general classroom management terms and provide incentives to behave "correctly." In both of these cases, either or all of the educators may be correct. Through professional learning, educators can begin to understand that other fields may make very different assumptions about the function of a behavior and the nature of a child.

Implications: Dual Professional Learning Needs for Both Audiences

Although both special and gifted educators will have specialized knowledge within their sphere of interest and both may have been briefly introduced to the concept of twice-exceptional students, either group of educators is unlikely to have encountered significant understanding about twice-exceptional students except through experience. Studies have found that up to 9.1% of the special education population qualifies as also being potentially gifted, but only one percent of children in special education are also served under gifted and talented (Barnard-Brak, Johnsen, Pond Hannig, & Wei, 2015). Initial teacher training and most professional learning are primarily focused on either one of the exceptionalities, not the combination.

When working with a set of teachers, in addition to the missing elements of either gifted or special education, twice-exceptional professional learning topics should include:

- collaboration and coteaching training to enable professionals to work together more effectively;
- strengths-based educational approaches;
- mediation approaches to lessening the impact of a disability;
- characteristics and needs of twice-exceptional students—both academic and social-emotional;
- identifying the "masked" twice-exceptional child, whose gifts hide the disability and whose disability obscures the talent;
- integrated curricular approaches, so that areas of strength and passion can be incorporated into areas of challenge; and
- programmatic models that do not require separate provisions for services, but collaborative integrative services (i.e., models such as the ones in Montgomery County, MD, Albuquerque, NM, Westchester County, NY, and Bridges Academy in Los Angeles should be highlighted).

Collaborative Professional Development/Professional Learning

Deciding whom to present the professional learning experiences is a very appropriate concern. Although having someone with a dual background in gifted and special education lead the professional learning is preferable, there are very few people with that combination of experience and formal knowledge. In the absence of such qualified leaders, the professional learning team should consist of someone with deep experience and knowledge of special education and someone with deep experience and knowledge of gifted education, and time and resources be provided for the two (or more!) professionals to develop integrated and cohesive professional learning opportunities. There is a legitimacy that can be found when a professional in a field hears about the issue from other professionals in that same field. As noted by Satterly (2015),

> It is important for special educators to hear from other special educators about the existence and needs of twice-exceptional students. Gifted educators and general educators have their areas of expertise, but special educators need to learn about twice-exceptional children from the shared experiences of a special educator. (p. 238)

In this era of shifting from one-shot professional learning models to engaged models of professional learning (Western Governors University Teachers College, 2014), educators need to be "active partners in determining the content of their learning, how their learning occurs, and how they evaluate its effectiveness" (Learning Forward, 2011), while respecting their own professional training and ethos.

Also important is that, if an organization undertakes professional learning to help teachers develop the talents and mediate the impacts of a disability, enough time is spent conducting the professional learning. The traditional 2-hour lecture or presentation is appropriate for overall theoretical development, but to make significant changes in how teachers engage with students, 10+ hours of practice and instruction are recommended (Dixon, Yssel, McConnell, & Hardin, 2014).

Because the provision of professional learning is a model for the teaching that is desired, the professional learning leaders should model the skills that will be needed by the teachers with whom they are working. These skills include the 4 C's of:
- collaboration,
- communication,
- coteaching, and
- connections.

Collaboration

Collaboration can be defined as a "recursive pedagogical approach in which educators actively coordinate instruction to impact student learning" (Pellegrino, Weiss, & Regan, 2015, p. 191). Such skills involved in collaboration include not just pleasant exchanges between presentation leaders, but a willingness to learn from each other through clear communication and exchange of information (Stepans, Thompson, & Buchanan, 2002). In addition, leaders must be prepared to develop shared new understandings that emerge from their areas of expertise and communicate these with the participants. Modeling this process of collaboration with the participants is important because few, if any, of the teachers receiving the training will have deep knowledge of twice-exceptional students, and they will need to collaborate extensively with each other and other school-based experts.

Communication

Copresenters should be able to communicate effectively with each other to find commonalities so that they present a cohesive experience for teachers, rather than fragmented instruction. Communication skills that are necessary include:
- active listening;
- finding common ground and common goals, while respecting philosophical and historical differences;
- ability to focus on the task, rather than taking things personally;
- brainstorming of possible solutions;
- summarizing conclusions and ideas; and
- contributing and following up (Scruggs & Mastropieri, 2017).

Coteaching

Coteaching is a strategy that can be employed to provide models of instruction that allow both experts to share their areas of knowledge, as well as provide an opportunity to engage with participants in meaningful manners. Friend and Cook (2017) identified five different models of coteaching that can help facilitate multiple perspectives and the inclusion of varied expertise among presenters:
- **One teach, one support:** A lead teacher presents material, and a supporting teacher either documents behaviors or provides visual supports, such as writing on the board or taking notes. Topics such as special education legal information or teaching critical and creative thinking could be presented by the different experts, with them taking turns demonstrating expertise.
- **Parallel instruction:** The group is divided into two equal halves, and each presenter teaches the same material to half of the class. Such an activity is particularly good for discussion. Topics regarding twice-exceptionality might include school-based options or workshops in which participants design lessons and activities appropriate for twice-exceptional children.
- **Center-based instruction:** Participants move from presenter to presenter to learn different ideas or techniques. Content might include the topic of characteristics of twice-exceptional students, and participants would move from the gifted education expert to the special education expert to a research resources center to learn about the different characteristics and needs of twice-exceptional children.

- **Alternative teaching:** One presenter works with the large group, and one presenter works with a smaller group. This model allows participants to ask questions and receive targeted instruction if their needs are different than those of the larger group. One idea is for the large group to be focused on elementary issues, while a smaller group focuses on secondary issues. Or one group can focus on science, technology, engineering, and math (STEM) issues, while the larger group focuses on arts and humanities issues.
- **Team teaching:** Both instructors are engaged with each other and the class. Team teaching is not a case of taking turns, because that is a form of one teach, one support. Team teaching can incorporate ideas, such as role-playing, brainstorming, and debates—there are many ways to actively engage both presenters at the same time.

Connections: Professional Learning Resources

Considering the role that technology and resources will play when working with teachers of twice-exceptional children is important. Although individual school districts and states may have local resources, there are extensive resources online that can be accessed and adapted for local use. Professional learning opportunities must provide participants access to some of these for two reasons: (1) Participants do not feel that they are alone in understanding and adapting for twice-exceptional students, and (2) there is an efficient use of time where teachers and educators do not "reinvent the wheel." There are many very useful books and online resources available for ideas and strategies for twice-exceptional learners. Appendix 1.1 describes some of the school-based and state-based resources that would be particularly appropriate to share with teachers and leaders, while Appendix 1.2 provides a broad outline of a possible professional learning experience.

Summary

Teachers and educational leaders should receive professional learning and professional learning opportunities about the needs of twice-exceptional children because they likely will not receive such information in their education training programs. Because of its relative youth as a field, the lack of research and publications (Hughes, 2018), and the lack of knowledge among professionals (Foley-Nicpon, Assouline, & Colangelo, 2013), there are very few places where there will be experts in twice-exceptionalities.

There is certainly information from each field (gifted education and special education) that various audiences can learn from the other. Gifted education audiences need to learn about the legal framework, the characteristics, the Universal Design for Learning for planning lesson modification, and the positive behavior management strategies that special education is expert in. However, care should be taken so that that the gifted education aspects of talent development, critical thinking, and creative thinking are also highlighted as particular strengths of the field. Take care to note how these aspects of gifted education do not contradict the needs and rights inherent within special education.

Although sharing information from the fields of special and gifted education is important, the focus of the professional learning should be on understanding the impacts on a child when these aspects of programming and characteristics are combined. This can be accomplished by not only sharing information between fields, but also examining commonalities and differences in approach. Presenters and facilitators need to be from both fields, not only sharing information, but also modeling collaboration and communication for the participants.

References

Assouline, S. G., Foley-Nicpon, M., & Dockery, L. (2012). Predicting the academic achievement of gifted students with autism spectrum disorder. *Journal of Autism and Developmental Disorders, 42*, 1781–1789.

Baldwin, L., Baum, S., Pereles, D., & Hughes, C. (2015). Twice-exceptional learners: The journey toward a shared vision. *Gifted Child Today, 38*, 206–214.

Barnard-Brak, L., Johnsen, S. K., Pond Hannig, A., & Wei, T. (2015). The incidence of potentially gifted students within a special education population. *Roeper Review, 37*, 74–83.

Baska, A., & VanTassel-Baska, J. (2018). *Interventions that work with special populations in gifted education.* Waco, TX: Prufrock Press.

Baum, S. M., Schrader, R. M., & Hébert, T. P. (2014). Through a different lens: Reflecting on a strengths-based, talent-focused approach for twice-exceptional learners. *Gifted Child Quarterly, 58,* 311–327.

Berninger, V. W., & Abbott, R. D. (2013). Differences between children with dyslexia who are and are not gifted in verbal reasoning. *Gifted Child Quarterly, 57,* 223–233.

Besnoy, K., Swoszowki, N. C., Newman., J. L., Floyd, A., Jones, P., & Byrne, C. (2015). The advocacy experiences of parents of elementary-age, twice-exceptional children. *Gifted Child Quarterly, 59,* 108–123.

Betts, L. (1987). *Thomas Edison: The great American inventor.* Hauppauge, NY: Barron's Educational Series.

Brown v. Board of Education of Topeka, 347 U.S. 483 (1954).

Brownell, M. T., Ross, D. D., Colón, E. P., & McCallum, C. L. (2005). Critical features of special education teacher preparation: A comparison with general teacher education. *Journal of Special Education, 38,* 242–252.

CAST. (2019). *About universal design for learning.* Retrieved from http://www.cast.org/our-work/about-udl.html

Coleman, M. R., & Gallagher, S. (2015). Meeting the needs of students with 2e: It takes a team. *Gifted Child Today, 38,* 252–254.

Coleman, M. R., & Hughes, C. E. (2009). Meeting the needs of gifted students within an RtI framework. *Gifted Child Today, 32*(3), 14–17.

Department of Education and Early Childhood Development. (2012). *Strength-based approach: A guide to writing transition learning and development statements.* East Melbourne, Victoria, Australia: State of Victoria.

Dixon, F. A., Yssel, N., McConnell, J. M., & Hardin, T. (2014). Differentiated instruction, professional development, and teacher efficacy. *Journal for the Education of the Gifted, 37,* 111–127.

Education for All Handicapped Children Act of 1975, Pub. Law 94-142 (November 29, 1975).

Fanning, P. (2014). How biomechanic prosthetics are changing the face of disability. *Eureka!* Retrieved from http://www.eurekamagazine.co.uk/design-engineering-features/technology/how-biomechatronic-prosthetics-are-changing-the-face-of-disability/60092

Foley-Nicpon, M., & Assouline, S. G. (2015). Counseling considerations for the twice-exceptional client. *Journal of Counseling and Development, 93,* 202–211.

Foley-Nicpon, M., Assouline, S. G., & Colangelo, N. (2013). Twice-exceptional learners: Who needs to know what? *Gifted Child Quarterly, 57,* 169–180.

Friend, M., & Cook, L. (2017). *Interactions: Collaboration skills for school professionals* (8th ed.). Boston, MA: Pearson.

Gifted and Talented Children's Education Act of 1978, §901, 20 U.S.C. 3311.

Hughes, C. E. (2017). Dual differentiation for twice-exceptional students. In J. VanTassel-Baska & C. A. Little (Eds.), *Content-based curriculum for high-ability learners* (3rd ed., pp. 79–92). Waco, TX: Prufrock Press.

Hughes, C. E. (2018, November). *Diversity of viewpoint?: Preliminary findings of a content analysis of twice-exceptional literature.* Paper presented at the Council for Exceptional Children-Teacher Education Division annual conference, Las Vegas, NV.

Individuals with Disabilities Education Act, 20 U.S.C. §1401 et seq. (1990).

Individuals with Disabilities Education Improvement Act, Pub. Law 108-446 (December 3, 2004).

Johnsen, S., VanTassel-Baska, J., Robinson, A., Cotabish, A., Dailey, D., Jolly, J., . . . Adams, A. (2015). *Using the national gifted education standards for teacher preparation* (2nd ed.). Waco TX: Prufrock Press.

Kalbfleisch, M. L. (2013). Twice-exceptional students: Gifted students with learning disabilities. In C. M. Callahan & H. L. Hertberg (Eds.), *Fundamentals of gifted education: Considering multiple perspectives* (pp. 358–368). New York, NY: Routledge.

Kirk, S., Gallagher, J., & Coleman, M. R. (2015). *Educating exceptional children* (14th ed.). Stamford, CT: Cengage Learning.

Kozulin, A., & Gindis, B. (2007). Sociocultural theory and education of children with special needs: From defectology to remedial pedagogy. In H. Daniel, M. Cole, & J. V. Wertsch (Eds.), *The Cambridge companion to Vygotksy* (pp. 332–358). London, England: Cambridge University Press.

Learning Forward. (2011). *Standards for professional learning.* Oxford, OH: Author.

Leppien, J. H., & Thomas, T. M. (2016, May). Revealing the strengths of 2e students by using technology. *2e Newsletter.* Retrieved from http://www.2enewsletter.com/subscribers_only/arch_2016_5_UsingTechnology_Leppien.html

Maker, C. J. (1977). *Providing programs for the gifted handicapped.* Reston, VA: Council for Exceptional Children.

Marland, S. P., Jr. (1972). *Education of the gifted and talented: Report to the Congress of the United States by the U.S. Commissioner of Education and background papers submitted to the U.S. Office of Education,* 2 vols. Washington, DC: U.S. Government Printing Office. (Government Documents, Y4.L 11/2: G36)

McNeil, L. (2014). Nick Lachey opens up about brother with Asperger Syndrome. *People.* Retrieved from https://people.com/celebrity/nick-lachey-opens-up-about-brother-with-asperger-syndrome

Musgrove, M. (2013, December 20). [Letter to Jim Delisle]. Retrieved from https://www2.ed.gov/policy/speced/guid/idea/memosdcltrs/13-008520r-sc-delisle-twiceexceptional.pdf

National Association for Gifted Children, & The Association for the Gifted, Council for Exceptional Children. (2013). *NAGC-CEC teacher preparation standards in gifted education.* Retrieved from http://www.nagc.org/sites/default/files/standards/NAGC-%20CEC%20CAEP%20standards%20%282013%20final%29.pdf

Osgood, R. L. (2008). *History of special education: A struggle of equality in American public schools.* Westport, CT: Praeger Press.

Pattoni, L. (2012). *Strengths-based approaches for working with individuals.* Retrieved from https://www.iriss.org.uk/resources/insights/strengths-based-approaches-working-individuals

Pellegrino, A., Weiss, M., & Regan, K. (2015). Learning to collaborate: General and special educators in teacher education. *The Teacher Educator, 50,* 187–202.

Preuss, L., Baum, S., & Sabatino, C. (2009, July/August). Understanding the connection for twice-exceptional students: Academic and emotional readiness. *2e Newsletter,* 16–19.

Robinson, A., & Jolly, J. (Eds.). (2013). *A century of contributions to gifted education: Illuminating lives.* New York, NY: Routledge.

Rose, D., Meyer, A., Strangman, N., & Rappolt, G. (2002). *Teaching every student in the digital age: Universal Design for Learning.* Alexandria, VA: Association for Supervision & Curriculum Development.

Satterly, D. (2015). Special education coordinator: Learning lessons from all our students. *Gifted Child Today, 38,* 237–238.

Scruggs, T. E., & Mastropieri, M. A. (2017). Making inclusion work with co-teaching. *Teaching Exceptional Children, 49,* 284–293.

Spielhagen, F., Brown, E. F., & Hughes, C. E. (2015). Policy implications and directions in special populations. In B. S. Cooper, J. G. Cibulka, & L. Fusarelli (Eds.), *Handbook of educational politics and policy* (2nd ed., pp. 716–750). New York, NY: Routledge.

Stepans, M. B., Thompson, C. L., & Buchanan, M. L. (2002). The role of the nurse on a transdisciplinary early intervention assessment team. *Public Health Nursing, 19,* 238–245.

VanTassel-Baska, J., & Little, C. A. (Eds.). (2017). *Content-based curriculum for high-ability learners* (3rd ed.). Waco, TX: Prufrock Press.

Webb, J. T., Amend, E. R., Beijan, P., Webb, N. E., Kuzujanakis, M., Olenchak, F. R., & Goerss, J. (2016). *Misdiagnosis and dual diagnoses of gifted children and adults: ADHD, bipolar, OCD, Asperger's, depression, and other disorders* (2nd ed.). Tucson, AZ: Great Potential Press.

Weiner, W. H. (2016, July). Using the arts to reach twice-exceptional learners. *2e Newsletter*. Retrieved from http://www.2enewsletter.com/article_2016_07_UsingArts%20to%20Reach2eLearners_Weiner.html

Weishaar, P. M. (2010). Twelve ways to incorporate strengths-based planning into the IEP process. *The Clearinghouse: A Journal of Educational Strategies, Issues and Ideas, 83*, 207–210.

Western Governors University Teachers College. (2014). *Professional development vs. professional learning* [Web log post]. Retrieved from https://www.wgu.edu/blogpost/professional-development-vs-professional-learning-teachers#

Appendix 1.1
School-Based and State-Based Resources for Twice-Exceptional Students

2e: Twice exceptional. Retrieved from http://2emovie.com

Bridges Academy. (2016–2018). *2e resources.* Retrieved from http://www.bridges.edu/resources.html

Colorado Department of Education. (1999–2019). *Twice-exceptional (2e).* Retrieved from https://www.cde.state.co.us/gt/twice-exceptional

Idaho Department of Education. (2010). *Twice-exceptional: Students with both gifts and challenges or disabilities.* Retrieved from https://sde.idaho.gov/academic/gifted-talented/files/manuals/Twice-Exceptional-Students-Both-Gifts-Challenges-or-Disabilities.pdf

Montgomery County Public Schools. (1995–2019) *Twice exceptional students and services.* Retrieved from http://www.montgomeryschoolsmd.org/curriculum/enriched/gtld

Montgomery County Public Schools, Office of Curriculum and Instructional Programs and Office of Special Education and Student Services. (2015). *Twice exceptional students: A staff guidebook for supporting the achievement of gifted students with special needs.* Retrieved from http://www.montgomeryschoolsmd.org/uploadedFiles/curriculum/enriched/programs/gtld/0470.15_TwiceExceptionalStudents_Handbook_Web.pdf

Ohio Department of Education. (2017). *Twice exceptional guide: Preparing Ohio schools to close the achievement gap for gifted students with disabilities.* Retrieved from https://education.ohio.gov/getattachment/Topics/Special-Education/Students-with-Disabilities/Educating-Students-with-Disabilities/Educating-Gifted-Students-with-Disabilities/Twice-Exceptional-Guide.pdf.aspx

Virginia Department of Education. (2010). *Supporting the identification and achievement of the twice-exceptional student: Frequently asked questions.* Retrieved from http://www.doe.virginia.gov/instruction/gifted_ed/twice_exceptional.pdf

Appendix 1.2
Suggested Daylong Plan for Initial Overview of Twice-Exceptionality

Recommendations:

- Two presenters: one from gifted education, one from special education
- Teacher teams should consist of general education, special education, and gifted education
- Keep the pace active and enthusiastic; this general outline can be broken up into more time if the needs of learners require it
- Ensure that there is follow-up for ongoing planning time and support within the team; future sessions could delve deeper into any of the topics or incorporate district initiatives

Time	Objective(s)	Topics
:00–:30	Determine prior knowledge; introduce speakers; form a group identity	Introductions; preassessment; group activities; discussion of strengths and challenges within individuals
:30–1:00	Why 2e?	Clip of *2e* movie
1:00–1:30	Introduce special education	Special education labels and rights; state level laws; identification issues
1:30–2:00	Legal protections of special education	Individualized Education Program (IEP) elements and areas of focus
2:00–2:30	Awareness of giftedness	Gifted education characteristics and identification; state-level laws
2:30–3:00	Create knowledge of 2e	2e definition and characteristics
3:00–3:30	Overview of special education instructional strategies	Universal Design for Learning (UDL); learning strategies; visual learning
3:30–4:00	Overview of gifted education instructional strategies	Creativity; critical thinking; enrichment; advanced and conceptual content
4:00–4:30	Overview of what teaching 2e students could be like	Clip from *2e2* movie
4:30–5:00	Behavioral and teaching recommendations for 2e	Recommendations from resources
5:00–5:30	Planning time for teacher teams	Discussion and plans for what could happen
5:30–6:00	Conclusion and future plans	Next steps and resources

CHAPTER 2

Professional Learning Standards and Practices for Educators of Gifted GLBTQ Youth

Terence Paul Friedrichs and PJ Sedillo

Gay, lesbian, bisexual, transgender, and questioning (GLBTQ) youth and their advocates have long struggled for recognition and basic safety within U.S. schools and gifted programs (Council for Exceptional Children GLB Caucus, 1993; Griffin, 1998; Katz, 1976). Over the past 25 years, professional gifted education organizations have gradually striven to advocate for that recognition and safety through various publications and professional presentations (National Association for Gifted Children [NAGC], 2015; NAGC Gay, Lesbian, Bisexual, and Transgender [GLBT] Task Force, 2002). Recently, these organizations have attempted to more fully recognize the strengths and safety needs of gifted GLBTQ youth, their educators, and their parents, and to more fully engage the responsibilities of their respective organizations for the progress of these students and their advocates (Manzella, 2017; NAGC, n.d.; Seney, 2017). Given a progressive perspective, both elementary and secondary administrators and gifted coordinators need to understand:

1. high-potential GLBTQ youths' strengths and needs;
2. home, community, and school safety barriers to demonstrating strengths;

3. approaches for addressing needs, especially with regard to youth safety;
4. planning social-emotional practices for these students;
5. positive and negative terms that envelop these youth in both safety and academic efforts;
6. implementation of effective curricular and instructional strategies; and
7. existing barriers and facilitators to implementing educators' professional learning.

Along the way, we can recommend new professional guidelines—a combination of the NAGC-CEC Teacher Preparation Standards in Gifted Education (NAGC & The Association for the Gifted, Council for Exceptional Children [CEC-TAG], 2013) and the Professional Development Workshop Objectives from the Gay, Lesbian, and Straight Education Network (GLSEN, 2017b)—as approaches for professional learning within each of these seven areas. Each standard can be adapted for gifted facilitators and their educators, at both the elementary and secondary levels, with learning that is timely, ongoing, and empowering (Novak & Weber, 2018).

Professional GLBTQ-Related Learning for Elementary and Secondary Educators

At the elementary level, students may identify as GLBTQ or, more often, may be thinking about the ways in which they may be "different" in sexual orientation and/or gender identity. Further, many straight students may begin to think of themselves as allies, and others may begin to consider ways in which these seemingly "new" youth fit into their worlds (Sears, 2005). All of these students can benefit, in their present and future lives, from knowing about the nature, needs, and issues of GLBTQ students and adults.

Although middle and high schools also engage students' growing awareness of GLBTQ identities, they increasingly become places of academic learning, as well as miniature societies. In these diverse climates, gifted GLBTQ youth must learn and interact well with their peers. Although some secondary gifted coordinators, educators, and administrators already work hard toward safe and inclusive settings, some youth who are—or who are perceived as—GLBTQ continue to face harsh realities. In a recent Human Rights Campaign (HRC, 2017) study of harassment, 10,000 GLBTQ teens (ages 13–17) experienced twice the rate of this harassment as a similar group of straight students. GLBTQ students' harassment and lack of role models has long led to negative academic and social outcomes, such as student absenteeism, lower grades, dropping out of school, substance use, and homelessness (Ray, 2006).

As both elementary and secondary gifted facilitators and their teachers and administrators address the seven critical GLBTQ youth professional development areas, they have powerful daily opportunities to create supportive settings. They can do so through first enhancing their critical understanding of gifted GLBTQ student *needs* (as discussed in the first part of each guideline below), and then taking actions to address those needs, based on *standards* to create more supportive settings (as explained in the second section on each guideline). The following are the seven needs and related standards that can significantly enhance K–12 educators' professional learning on gifted GLBTQ youth issues:

- **Need 1 and Standard 1:** *Individualization.* K–12 gifted facilitators' professional learning for their administrators and teachers must focus on knowledge of individual gifted GLBTQ students' strengths, needs, and outcomes (adapted from NAGC-CEC [2013] Standard 1 and GLSEN [2017b] Standard 1).
- **Need 2 and Standard 2:** *Understanding Safety Needs.* In designing effective, accessible professional development sessions, K–12 gifted facilitators should learn from existing research about settings for gifted GLBTQ students that are—and are not—safe, inclusive, and culturally responsive (adapted from NAGC-CEC [2013] Standard 2 and GLSEN [2017b] Standard 3).
- **Need 3 and Standard 3:** *Providing Safety.* Elementary and secondary gifted facilitators' professional learning sessions on providing school-based GLBTQ student safety should be informed by surrounding family, school, and community settings (adapted from NAGC-CEC [2013] Standard 7 and GLSEN [2017b] Standard 4).
- **Need 4 and Standard 4:** *Community Consciousness.* K–12 gifted facilitators should gather multiple forms of assessment data and resources on how well their educators are addressing gifted GLBTQ students' difficulties and joys, and on how effectively educators' approaches work with these youth, in homes, schools, and communities (adapted from NAGC-CEC [2013] Standard 4 and GLSEN [2017b] Standard 7).

- **Need 5 and Standard 5:** *Providing Supportive Language.* Gifted facilitators' professional learning efforts should involve collaborative educators' reflections and feedback on selecting, using, and adapting school language and associated instructional practices that assist gifted GLBTQ students and their allies (adapted from NAGC-CEC [2013] Standard 5 and GLSEN [2017b] Standard 2).
- **Need 6 and Standard 6:** *Conveying Effective Curricula.* The educational system is responsible, through its gifted facilitators, for educators' individual and collective professional learning about gifted GLBTQ students' thinking, content, and materials. Through this demonstration of systemic responsibility, K–12 educators may implement specific and general curricula to teach these youth (adapted from NAGC-CEC [2013] Standard 3 and GLSEN [2017b] Standard 5).
- **Need 7 and Standard 7:** *Understanding and Dealing With Barriers.* Elementary and secondary gifted facilitators should understand systemic GLBTQ-related obstacles and should work toward GLBTQ-supportive educational systems. Supportive systems include school buildings, school districts, states, and national entities, so that educators have ongoing, fully integrated, ethically-infused professional learning opportunities regarding gifted GLBTQ students (adapted from NAGC-CEC [2013] Standard 6 and GLSEN [2017b] Standard 6).

Need 1: Individualization

K–12 administrators and teachers should understand, from the start of their professional learning, the range of gifted GLBTQ students' unique strengths in intelligence, achievement, creativity, arts, and leadership (NAGC, 2015; Whittenburg & Treat, 2009). These strengths, apparent to many parents, community leaders, and educators at a young age (Manzella, 2017), include cognitive excitability about matters of the mind, as well as insight into daily intellectual challenges (Peterson & Rischar, 2000; Treat, 2006). Educators certainly need to learn about these youths' early potential for high academic achievement, so that their scholastic strengths can be nurtured. Such nurturance can serve as important self-esteem, as well as instructional, support for sometimes-harassed gifted GLBTQ students (Peterson & Rischar, 2000). Despite advances (NAGC, 2015), however, advocates have only been marginally successful in getting into elementary classrooms the language arts materials that tell the stories of GLBTQ youth and families. Blocked GLBTQ informational access, both in university-level preparation and in elementary classrooms, has partially frustrated hopes that sexual minority and straight students can easily attain secondary learning on topics in GLBTQ history, government, health, and literature (Hutcheson & Tieso, 2014; Sleeter & Owour, 2011).

Secondary educators need to understand the increasing importance, to older gifted GLBTQ students, that schools address not just their strengths, but also several other aspects. These elements include these youths' geographical and cultural backgrounds (Kumoshiro, 2000; Parmenter, 2017), their intense excitement about specific creative phenomena (Treat, 2006), their extensive involvement in the arts (Manzella, 2017), and their application of creative problem solving to daily life (Piirto, 2004). Secondary educators also should learn the reasons that peers give for persecuting gifted GLBTQ youth (Kumoshiro, 2000), so that these educators may better grasp these students' struggles to be who they are (Hutcheson & Tieso, 2014).

***Standard 1* (K–12 gifted facilitators' professional learning for their administrators and teachers must focus on knowledge of individual gifted GLBTQ students' strengths, needs, and outcomes).** Given the highly individualized needs of K–12 gifted GLBTQ students and their educators' need to address those needs, gifted facilitators' action-oriented professional learning modules should address several factors. Elementary educators' learning should draw on various data sources, in their students' own school settings, so that these educators can create goals and activities that truly enhance learning and performance for young, gifted GLBTQ students (GLSEN, 2017b). Elementary gifted facilitators should clearly outline what their educators must know about these youths' strengths and needs, focus on individual students' school-based outcomes, and base their work on existing best practices and resources (NAGC & CEC-TAG, 2013). As with other professional learning in gifted education, goals of professional learning for educators of elementary gifted GLBTQ students should be comprehensible to educators and be differentiated in content and approach for different gifted student subgroups and their individual members (Hilt, 2011).

Secondary educators need to be able to individualize student interpersonal and academic treatment, according to the wide range of intellectual development shown by gifted GLBTQ students, as those youth move from concrete to abstract thought (Clark, 2013). This transition makes it possible for these students, at highly individualized rates, to question ideas, formulate new hypotheses, and project about their future lives (Fenwick, 1987). As these youth continue to convey different modes of thinking and continue to spend much time committed to their intellectual interests and sexual and gender identities, they may begin to feel very different from their peer groups. Accordingly, educators who design learning environments for these gifted GLBTQ students should individualize those settings to align with students' diverse intellectual development, identities, and self-esteem needs. Teachers, counselors, and administrators may personalize both instruction and one-on-one talks about these youths' high abilities and sexual/gender diversity (Cohn, 2002; Sowell, 2000). Even in long-GLBTQ-supportive schools and communities, these multifaceted individuals are best served by continued educator knowledge and support (NAGC, 2015). Similarly, secondary gifted educators need, from their facilitators, ongoing professional learning that encourages them to adjust classroom goals and outcomes based on varied student settings, changing circumstances within those sites, and individual students' intellectual, identity, and self-esteem growth. For example, secondary teachers and administrators must adjust to rapid changes that may be seen in some gifted classroom dynamics when GLBTQ youth begin to think that they might be more open in class discussions about GLBTQ topics—and be more supported by peers and educators as those discussions unfold (GLSEN, 2017b).

Need 2: Understanding Safety Needs

In addition to elementary and secondary gifted GLBTQ youths' school-related individual strengths, administrators and coordinators also must understand these students' needs. Among these many needs in our "progressive" era, safety probably comes first. External anti-GLBTQ pressures still lead to significant safety concerns across much of the country for both students and their allies (Munoz-Plaza, Quinn, & Rounds, 2013). From a very early age, high percentages of GLBTQ youth may experience verbal and physical harassment (Sears, 2005). Schools and communities may raise questions about the necessity of professional learning to achieve elementary-age GLBTQ student safety, considering students' supposedly "young ages," so elementary administrators and coordinators must prepare themselves for possibly contentious GLBTQ-related school debates on school district policies and state laws (Mazza, 2009). The outcomes of these important discussions may determine the ease with which facilitators conduct their gifted GLBTQ-related professional development sessions (GLSEN, 2017b).

If unchecked, occasional teasing has a way of growing, as the years go by, into more consistent and violent bias (Sears, 2005). Among secondary school respondents, high percentages of students recently self-reported various types of victimization (GLSEN, 2017a). Seventy percent were verbally harassed based on sexual orientation, while 59% were verbally harassed due to gender expression. Twenty-nine percent were physically harassed on account of sexual orientation, and 24% were physically harassed based on gender expression. Twelve percent were physically assaulted due to sexual orientation, while 11% were physically assaulted on account of gender expression. In two other areas for which GLSEN (2017a) records statistics for the varied sexual orientation and gender expression groups, 57% and 49% of GLBTQ youth were sexually and electronically harassed, respectively. To effectively address these pressing problems faced by many of their individual gifted GLBTQ students, educators first need to know the patterns of harassment and assault in their own settings, in terms of type, frequency, place, duration, and current educator responses (GLSEN, 2017a). With such knowledge, educators are better able to design on-target professional learning for their administrators and teachers.

***Standard 2* (In designing effective, accessible professional development sessions, K–12 gifted facilitators should learn from existing research about settings for gifted GLBTQ students that are—and are not—safe, inclusive, and culturally responsive).** Elementary and secondary gifted facilitators should convey to their fellow educators, in professional learning sessions, the ways in which certain school settings nationally contribute to the safety challenges that gifted GLBTQ students are subjected from the earliest years. That is, educators need to understand the specific, ongoing forms of verbal, physical, and sexual harassment and even assaults that these youth face (HRC, 2017). Educators also should learn about school-based, district, state, and national forces that oppose campaigns for interpersonal and curricular safety (GLSEN, 2015; NAGC, 2015). Facilitators should research school building, school district, and broader home and community trends on safety, inclusivity, and cultural responsiveness, so that their research leads to educators' best possible professional learning and decisions for gifted GLBTQ students (NAGC & CEC-TAG, 2013). Facilitators must know how documented gifted GLBTQ student needs can lead—through school, community, and home involvement—to youth safety rules and supportive student learning (GLSEN, 2017b; Saint Paul Public Schools Out for Equity, 2013).

At the elementary and secondary levels, gifted coordinators should also be careful to list patterns of bias and support that are most often seen in specific schools, classrooms, hallways, and playgrounds in the district (GLSEN, 2015). This effort should be especially specific at the secondary level, in which one building in a district may be especially different from another and, therefore, may need different student and professional development approaches (Saint Paul Public Schools Out for Equity, 2013). Training sessions should include educators' reasons why bias and support are so high or low in each of the discussed settings, as gifted GLBTQ support discussions move from discussing problems to creating solutions (NAGC & CEC-TAG, 2013; GLSEN, 2017b).

Need 3: Providing Safety

Safety-minded, solution-oriented administrators and teachers need to understand that gifted youth can benefit, from a young age, from the GLBTQ-related social-emotional support of others, including peers (Hutcheson & Tieso, 2014), educators (Peterson & Rischar, 2000), and parents (Manzella, 2014, 2017). Greater safety for elementary gifted GLBTQ youth tends to occur more rapidly when peers, educators, and parents all speak up about these youths' safety needs. Elementary educators and administrators must learn, in some persuasive detail, about GLBTQ youths' ample existence, the harmful and supportive terms that envelop these students, organized efforts to teach and support helpful terms, and ways to heal these youth from negative words (Ratts et al., 2013; Time Out Youth, n.d.). Educators should understand that professional learning at the elementary level needs to be frequent enough to create a GLBTQ-positive impression, offer ample enough materials with which to teach, and involve follow-up, supportive help with which to make a difference for young students in a multicultural, multi-issue context (Kumoshiro, 2000; Sapon-Shevin, 2008).

Middle and high school gifted GLBTQ adolescents and young adults need a supportive environment and positive language, as do elementary youth. In addition, secondary youth need educated and encouraged allies, as well as an abatement of verbal and physical harassment (HRC, 2017). Creating educational, encouraging, and supportive environments for gifted GLBTQ students can improve educational outcomes for *all* students, not just those who may identify as GLBTQ (NAGC GLBTQ Network, 2015). Thus, being GLBTQ-supportive is not really about politics, but rather, supporting the overall classroom mission. Therefore, gifted facilitators and educators, regardless of their personal beliefs, can be tremendous, multilateral resources to all supporters of gifted GLBTQ students. Educators can learn about the group encouragement and support offered through Safe School Zones and Gay Straight Alliances (otherwise known as Gender-Sexuality Alliances, or GSAs). Safe Zone Programs, common on some middle and high school campuses, provide organized systems of training campus faculty, staff, and student allies about GLBTQ students' safety (GLSEN, 2017b). Safe Zone allies have placards outside their offices, classrooms, or meeting spaces to show that they preside over confidential and safe havens. GSAs allow socialization among sexual and gender minorities and straight students; in addition, GSAs and similar GLBTQ community-based youth groups may provide valuable encouragement for individual GLBTQ students to educate teachers and other students on the nature and needs of sexual and gender minorities (Colson-Price, 2019). Finally, verbal and physical harassment can be prevented by discovering the sites of harassment;

by learning about the effectiveness of a balanced program of education, consequences, and restitution for harassers; and by learning about wise rules that guarantee privacy and gender-neutral facilities (Minnesota State Department of Education, 2017).

Standard 3 (**Elementary and secondary gifted facilitators' professional learning sessions on providing school-based GLBTQ student safety should be informed by surrounding family, school, and community settings**). Elementary and secondary administrators' and teachers' professional learning should be based on, and built into, the day-to-day work of educating their elementary gifted GLBTQ students. Powerful learning experiences can occur within existing elementary educational settings when gifted facilitators instruct their colleagues about positive and negative terms, when facilitators make plans to address generally supportive or unsupportive conditions affecting these young students, and when facilitators address immediately any specific gifted GLBTQ student safety and related social-emotional challenges (GLSEN, 2017b; NAGC & CEC-TAG, 2013).

Working closely with gifted GLBTQ students, and with colleagues in elementary and secondary environments, enables gifted facilitators to identify student difficulties and to collaboratively progress toward student safety and healing (GLSEN, 2017b; NAGC 2013). Secondary facilitators should work toward establishing rules against verbal and physical harassment and toward establishing Safe Zones and GSAs (Ratts et. al., 2013). Further, in the increasingly fast-paced environment facing gifted GLBTQ youth, facilitators should look for outside opportunities for enhancing their educators' professional knowledge and skills in gifted-conscious and GLBTQ-supportive student homes, schools, and communities (Manzella, 2017). Gifted facilitators need to arrange for frequently updated visits, and for reflections and empowering feedback on those visits for their administrators and educators (Hilt, 2011; McIntosh, 2017).

Need 4: Community Consciousness

K–12 gifted facilitators and their administrators and teachers benefit when they see gifted GLBTQ students as more than just a collection of safety needs. These educators need to learn broadly—from gifted GLBTQ students, their families, local GLBTQ rights organizations, and nearby universities—about a full range of gifted GLBTQ youths' challenges, joys, and preferred methods of support (Cohn, 2002; Flores, 2014). Especially at the elementary level, facilitators can draw on the general challenges and joys of gifted GLBTQ youths' family lives through positive, instructive readings and videos that show the humanity of those lives. Works for gifted GLBTQ-supportive students, such as *Heather Has Two Mommies* (Newman, 2014) and *Daddy's Roommate* (Willhoite, 1991), show how constructive family qualities, such as adults' dedication to children and children's dedication to each other, are similar for GLBTQ and other families.

Other affirming, secondary-level literature, which can be covered in class or recommended for individual bibliotherapy (Seney, 2017), can reach beyond the family unit to address the increasingly complex extended families, schools, universities, and overall communities in which older gifted GLBTQ students live. (University educators in less-than-GLBTQ-accepting communities might particularly learn critical information from these works.) Recommended books, which show the varying types of acceptance and nonacceptance that GLBTQ youth may face, include two works by Genta Sebastian: *A Man's Man* (2015)—a coming-of-age tale about grief, homophobia, and GLBTQ family members who live in a small, rural Midwestern town—and *Riding the Rainbow* (2016)—the story of a lesbian who deals resiliently with bullying. M. G. Hennessey's *The Other Boy* (2016) deals with a nonconformist, transgender middle school student, and Justin Sayre's *Husky* (2015) is the coming-of-age story of a middle grades adolescent questioning both his sexual orientation and his family's supportiveness. Short stories, history lessons, and videos can also show the humanity of GLBTQ youth in various communities and classrooms (GLSEN, 2015; Lipkin, 2000). Elementary and secondary educators and their administrators benefit when they are aware of the different kinds of progress that students can make, using various materials and methods, and when these educators encourage pro-GLBTQ classroom activities and make adjustments based on the outcomes (NAGC & CEC-TAG, 2013).

Standard 4 **(K–12 gifted facilitators should gather multiple forms of assessment data and resources on how well their educators are addressing gifted GLBTQ students' difficulties and joys, and on how effectively educators' approaches work with these youth, in homes, schools, and communities).**

Elementary and secondary gifted facilitators should collect data from different home, school, and community resources to determine not just student safety but the broad effectiveness of educators' gifted GLBTQ approaches (GLSEN, 2017b; NAGC & CEC-TAG, 2013; Ryan, 2009). Learning materials and methods can then be adapted, designed, implemented, and validated to further hone the professional learning of facilitators—and their administrators and educators—in GLBTQ and other underrepresented areas (Sleeter & Owour, 2011). At the elementary level, data must be collected regularly to measure how well educator approaches are addressing student interests and challenges related to GLBTQ issues (Saint Paul Public Schools

Out for Equity, 2013). At this level, GLBTQ and other diversity issues are sometimes combined; through these combined assessments, frequent and constructive formative evaluations can guide improvement of diversity-related professional learning on practices, knowledge, and learning regarding gifted GLBTQ and similar students (Sleeter & Owour, 2011). Formative evaluations allow teachers to make diversity-related modifications and corrections.

In secondary school, data should be collected on increasingly diversified and rapidly changing student needs and on available resources, so that educators can design both professional and student learning. Specific GLBTQ student interests in various settings should be ascertained through surveys and yearly updates on gifted GLBTQ youth in schools, homes, and communities (GLSEN, 2017b; NAGC & CEC-TAG, 2013). From these ongoing studies (in which secondary educators can learn much through their participation), facilitators can direct administrators and teachers to seek libraries, theaters, historical exhibits, GLBTQ teen centers, GLBTQ family support groups, and many other resources that make positive difference in these youths' lives. These educators can then provide valuable reactions on how those sites should (or should not) be used instructionally (Hilt, 2011; Manzella, 2017).

Need 5: Providing Supportive Language

Because language very much affects the overall performance and self-perception of gifted GLBTQ youth of various ages, K–12 educators need to know both the positive and negative language facing gifted GLBTQ youth in communities, schools, and homes (Manzella, 2014; Ryan, 2009). Even in the early elementary years, gifted teachers and their administrators should also learn exactly why positive terms are preferable (Pallotta-Chiarolli, 2000). Working in collaborative problem-solving groups, elementary educators can also become aware of how GLBTQ-related cultural distinctiveness and humanity can be learned early by youth, how this distinctiveness and humanity distinguishes ongoing pro-GLBTQ school movements, and how today's educators can further these movements (McIntosh, 2017).

At the secondary level, opportunities for professional learning should extend beyond generic discussions of GLBTQ terms, cultural differences, and humanity, to gifted students' needs for specific, situational types of language, culture, and empathy (Seney, 2017). Facilitators should structure their sessions with colleagues around collaborative problem solving, regarding the learning of pro-GLBTQ language to further human relations at school and beyond (Pace, 2009). In flexible learning groups, colleagues share knowledge, expertise, and experience in order to deepen learning about school- and community-based language, student differences, and humanitarianism. Such deeper learning, in turn, fosters a common understanding of an effective classroom (McIntosh, 2017). Facilitators' flexible groups create conditions for colleagues' reflections and feedback to gifted facilitators or mentors. Subsequently, these facilitators can provide follow-up information for their administrators, their teachers, and, indirectly, their gifted students (GLSEN, 2015).

Standard 5 **(Gifted facilitators' professional learning efforts should involve collaborative educators' reflections and feedback on selecting, using, and adapting school language and associated instructional practices that assist gifted GLBTQ students and their allies).** K–12 gifted facilitators' professional learning sessions on gifted GLBTQ students' needs for supportive language and related practices at school, home, and community should flow from fellow educators' gifted GLBTQ-related collaborative problem solving. Facilitators' flexible learning groups with elementary educators should share general knowledge, expertise, and experience about gifted-GLBTQ-related language and practices, on an ongoing basis, to deepen all participants' learning and inspire their own confidence in their work (GLSEN, 2017b; NAGC & CEC-TAG, 2013). Such professional exchanges, in turn, should foster a common understanding of how to design classrooms that will use language to deepen all teachers' (and students') empathy and knowledge of GLBTQ culture (Lind, 2000). Similarly, elementary educators' own flexible groupings to address GLBTQ issues should create conditions for ample gifted student reflection and feedback (Villanueva, 2016).

Professional learning about gifted GLBTQ youth needs to be ongoing, long-term, and frequently practiced by both elementary and secondary educators (GLSEN, 2017b; NAGC & CEC-TAG, 2013). Changes in language may occur especially quickly at the secondary level (Saint Paul Public Schools Out for Equity, 2013). And, at both levels, trial-and-error learning—including performance, reflection, and enhancement—must be a sustained process (Phelps, 2014). Secondary gifted facilitators need support from both administrators and flexible teacher groups so that professional learning practices regarding language and other necessary areas are well-funded, innovative, continuous, and effective (NAGC, 2015).

Need 6: Conveying Effective Curricula

Educators of children and young adults should learn that these students need more than just GLBTQ-supportive language. They need a wealth of information, which they are cognitively and emotionally ready to acquire, related to GLBTQ issues. From their earliest years, GLBTQ youth need to know as much as possible about themselves and their worlds so that they may better live their lives (Peterson & Rischar, 2000; Ryan, 2009). Specifically, these students need to be exposed on a regular basis to GLBTQ-focused discussions and materials, in various subjects and in teachable moments (Kumoshiro, 2000). In these lessons, gifted youth might learn to initially and respectfully consider, in various subjects, differences and similarities that might occur among straight people and sexual and gender minorities (Seney, 2017).

Secondary facilitators can introduce, to their educators, different aspects of GLBTQ students' lives and how GLBTQ issues might affect those lives. Educators may learn about lesson possibilities for various subjects, such as English, social studies, health, and biology (Letts, 2000; Lipkin, 2000; Seney, 2017). Secondary staff, like their elementary colleagues, can benefit from arranged learning time, in these relatively new areas of curricula, so that they can exchange in-person and cyber perspectives with educators from other buildings and districts (GLSEN, 2017b; NAGC & CEC-TAG, 2013).

Standard 6 (**The educational system is responsible, through its gifted facilitators, for educators' individual and collective professional learning about gifted GLBTQ students' thinking, content, and materials. Through this demonstration of systemic responsibility, K–12 educators may implement specific and general curricula to teach these youth**). Professional learning on elementary/secondary gifted GLBTQ matters occurs best when it happens at all levels of the educational system and when it can be practiced through collective and individual measures (NAGC, 2015). This learning, frequently ignored in the past in the elementary grades, should include building, district, state, and national information to truly meet professional learning needs in a highly mobile and quickly changing society (GLSEN, 2017b; NAGC & CEC-TAG, 2013). Through such broadly based sharing, educators can be prepared for a society that experiences frequently changing types of student thinking, content, and materials on gifted GLBTQ issues, even at the elementary level (Letts, 2000). Regarding the GLBTQ-associated knowledge and skills of elementary gifted youth, performance goals should be set for various key stakeholders, including elementary gifted teachers, administrators, facilitators, and young students themselves (NAGC GLBTQ Network, 2015).

For secondary educators, there is a growing body of gifted and GLBTQ-related group and individual knowledge for supporting gifted GLBTQ students in classrooms (Jennings, 1994; Whittenburg & Treat, 2009). These educators may need to piece together a more diverse and supported system of building on, dialoguing about, and delivering the knowledge that now exists at the local, state, and national levels (GLSEN, 2017b; NAGC &

CEC-TAG, 2013). For complex environments—in which a middle or high school student might see varying support at the home, school, neighborhood, and state levels—secondary curricular and instructional goals may need to be more individualized than at the elementary stage (Hutcheson & Tieso, 2014).

Need 7: Understanding and Dealing With Barriers

There are both barriers and facilitators to implementing GLBTQ curriculum and instruction and to engaging the other preceding steps of professional learning regarding K–12 gifted GLBTQ youth and issues (GLSEN, 2015). Although these barriers and facilitators can be different at the elementary and secondary levels, they are often the same (NAGC GLBTQ Network, 2015). First, researchers who wish to investigate effective professional learning may face continued barriers from kindergarten level onward (Cohn, 2002). Secondly, in some locations, if administrators even marginally enhance educator learning about GLBTQ pupil strengths, these leaders may be viewed as morally "perverse" (Sears, 1992; Swan, 2016). Third, if administrators and educators wish to learn about safety barriers, they may be perceived as admitting that their schools have security problems. Further, if these educators do provide more safety, they may be viewed by anti-GLBTQ forces as challenging the primacy of straight students (Pace, 2009). Fourth, if these educators acquire a large amount of home, school, and community knowledge about how to deal sensitively with GLBTQ students, they may be dismissed as being "gay" themselves (Jennings, 1994). Fifth, as educators learn about negative and preferred terms for gifted GLBTQ students, they may be seen with some suspicion as speaking a language that is foreign to the school establishment (Jennings, 1994). Sixth, if they provide lessons related to the GLBTQ experience, they may be viewed as promoting the rights of GLBTQ people, an act that is technically against some states' education laws (GLSEN, 2018).

Although there are clearly some daunting barriers in the six professional learning areas, there are also strong facilitators toward K–12 gifted GLBTQ progress in each area (Russell, Koskiw, Horn, & Saewyc, 2010). Eventually, these six facilitative factors may strongly impact the education of gifted GLBTQ youth. First, according to NAGC (2015), educators already are expected to know about the strengths and needs of gifted GLBTQ youth at all ages. Second, educators are increasingly producing professional tool boxes to address both younger and older children's safety and other needs (NAGC, n.d.). Third, for legal reasons, many educators have already been made aware of, and must act on, harassment patterns facing elementary and other gifted GLBTQ students (e.g., Minnesota Safe and Supportive Schools Act, 2014; *Nabozny v. Podlesny*, 1996). Fourth, in response to legal problems, many states have general GLBTQ-related reporting guidelines and rules that cover schools, community agencies, and homes. Fifth, in some states, teachers are made aware that they can be proactive in providing GLBTQ-supportive language, utilizing guides such as the Minnesota Department of Education's (2017) *Toolkit for Supporting Transgender and Gender Non-Conforming Students*. This guide builds understanding of pro-transgender terms, as well as protective locker room and bathroom rules. Sixth, some districts already mandate educator training on an array of pro-GLBTQ teaching techniques and materials, using the best of local, state, and national resources (GLSEN, 2017b). With those diverse resources, facilitators can create short- and long-term goals, design action plans, engage outside agencies (if needed), and make revisions based on plan outcomes.

***Standard 7* (Elementary and secondary gifted facilitators should understand systemic GLBTQ-related obstacles and should work toward GLBTQ-supportive educational systems. Supportive systems include school buildings, school districts, states, and national entities, so that educators have ongoing, fully integrated, ethically-infused professional learning opportunities regarding gifted GLBTQ students).**

Professional learning on K–12 gifted GLBTQ youth needs to be both mission-driven and directed toward short- and long-term goals, to deal effectively with systemic barriers and facilitative factors (GLSEN, 2017b; NAGC & CEC-TAG, 2013). Facilitators need to understand the perspectives of those citizens who criticize educators for moving too fast or too slow on districts' chosen professional learning paths, as well as those citizens who distrust modern educational research, dislike administrator certainty, and undervalue pro-GLBTQ safety, knowledge, language, and advocacy (Cohn, 2002; Kumoshiro, 2000).

Gifted GLBTQ-related professional learning can be successful if it is informed about these barriers and not frightened by them. Facilitators can avoid challenges by successfully researching the strengths and needs of their gifted GLBTQ youth, making sure that existing toolboxes are available to teachers, fighting everyday harassment with ever-more-effective systems of protection, providing support to youth and teachers under fire, being proactive in educating about supportive language, and providing GLBTQ-supportive curriculum (NAGC, 2015). As they make their way on their supportive journeys, K–12 gifted facilitators may need local, state, and national support for their educators' professional, broadly based learning, because those new and innovative practices may require outside resources (GLSEN, 2017b; NAGC & CEC-TAG, 2013). Support for these facilitators should be immediate and continuous, just like the professional learning that they are trying to enact (Novak & Weber, 2018).

Conclusion

Elementary and secondary gifted GLBTQ students increasingly present themselves as a group worthy of gifted facilitators' professional learning. Through addressing the seven presented needs and professional learning standards, facilitators can assist these students in various ways: by educating their school administrators and gifted coordinators on these pupils' strengths and safety needs; by training these educators on how to provide safety and how to utilize the educational resources of home, community, and school; and by learning about the positive effects of using pro-GLBTQ language and curricula. Although there are some professional barriers to implementing such techniques through effective professional learning modules in schools, online sites, or community-based experiences, there are, nonetheless, convincing reasons for such implementation. In moving toward understanding, safety, curricular and professional growth, through working toward the seven standards presented in this chapter and in other ways, gifted facilitators acknowledge that elementary and secondary students, their teachers, and their administrators deserve GLBTQ-related support.

References

Clark, B. (2013). *Growing up gifted: Developing the potential of children at home and at school* (8th ed.). Upper Saddle River, NJ: Pearson.

Cohn, S. J. (2002). *Gifted students who are gay, lesbian, or bisexual: A summary of the research*. Unpublished manuscript, National Association for Gifted Children Gay, Lesbian, Bisexual, and Transgender Task Force, Washington, DC.

Colson-Price, P. (2019). The talk. *Georgia Voice*. Retrieved from https://thegavoice.com/feature/the-talk

Council for Exceptional Children GLB Caucus. (1993). CEC GLB caucus begins. *Exceptional Pride, 1*(1), 1–2.

Fenwick, J. J. (1987). *Caught in the middle: Educational reform for young adolescents in California's public schools* (Report of the Superintendent's Middle Grade Task Force). ERIC Document ED 289246.

Flores, M. T. (2014). Teachers working cooperatively with parents and caregivers when implementing LGBT themes in the elementary classroom. *American Journal of Sexuality Education, 9*, 114–120.

Gay, Lesbian, and Straight Education Network. (2015). *National school climate survey of GLBTQ students*. New York, NY: Author.

Gay, Lesbian, and Straight Educators Network. (2017a). *National school climate survey of GLBTQ students*. New York, NY: Author.

Gay, Lesbian, and Straight Education Network. (2017b). *Professional development workshops: Objectives*. New York, NY: Author.

Gay, Lesbian, and Straight Education Network. (2018). *Laws prohibiting "promotion of homosexuality" in schools: Implications and impacts*. New York, NY: Author.

Griffin, P. (1998). *Strong women, deep closets: Lesbians and homophobia in sport*. Champaign, IL: Human Kinetics.

Hennessey, M. G. (2016). *The other boy*. New York, NY: HarperCollins.

Hilt, L. (2011). *Out with professional development, in with professional learning* [Web log post]. Retrieved from https://plpnetwork.com/2011/08/18/out-with-professional-development-in-with-professional-learning

Human Rights Campaign. (2017). *Growing up LGBT in America: HRC youth survey report key findings*. Retrieved from https://assets2.hrc.org/files/assets/resources/Growing-Up-LGBT-in-America_Report.pdf

Hutcheson, V. H., & Tieso, C. L. (2014). Social coping of gifted and LGBTQ adolescents. *Journal for the Education of the Gifted, 37*, 355–377.

Jennings, K. (1994). *One teacher in ten: Gay and lesbian educators tell their stories*. Los Angeles, CA: Alyson.

Katz, J. N. (1976). *Gay American history: Lesbians and gay men in the U.S.A*. New York, NY: Crowell.

Kumoshiro, K. K. (2000). Toward a theory of anti-oppressive education. *Review of Educational Research, 70*, 25–53.

Letts, W. J., IV. (2000). Introduction. In W. J. Letts IV & J. T. Sears (Eds.), *Queering elementary education: Advancing the dialogue about sexualities and schooling*. Lanham, MD: Rowman & Littlefield.

Lind, S. (2000). Overexcitability and the highly gifted child. *The Communicator, 31*(4), 19, 45–48.

Lipkin, A. (2000). *Understanding homosexuality, changing schools.* Boulder, CO: Westview.

Manzella, T. R. (2014). Home for the holidays: Reducing the stress for your GLBTQ kid. *Parenting for High Potential, 4*(2), 2–3.

Manzella, T. R. (2017). Parental support. In T. P. Friedrichs, T. R. Manzella, & R. W. Seney (Eds.), *Needs and approaches for educators and parents of gifted gay, lesbian, bisexual, and transgender students.* Washington, DC: National Association for Gifted Children.

Mazza, M. J. (2009). *This fierce geometry: Uses of the Judeo-Christian Bible in the anti-abolitionist and anti-gay rhetoric of the United States.* Ann Arbor, MI: UMI.

McIntosh, J. (2017). *A progressive educator's toolbox on gifted LGBTQ issues: Review comments.* National Association for Gifted Children Annual Convention, Charlotte, NC.

Minnesota Safe and Supportive Schools Act (School Student Bullying Policy), 121A.031 (2014).

Minnesota State Department of Education. (2017). *Toolkit for supporting transgender and gender non-conforming students.* Roseville, MN: Author.

Munoz-Plaza, C., Quinn, S. C., & Rounds, K. R. (2013). Lesbian, gay, bisexual, and transgender students: Perceived social support in the high school environment. *High School Journal, 85*(4), 52–63.

Nabozny v. Podlesny, 92 F.3d. 446 (7th Cir. 1996).

National Association for Gifted Children. (n.d.). *Diversity toolbox.* Retrieved from https://www.nagc.org/resources-publications/resources/timely-topics/including-diverse-learners-gifted-education-program-1

National Association for Gifted Children. (2015). *Supporting gifted students with diverse sexual orientations and gender identities* [Position statement]. Retrieved from http://www.nagc.org/sites/default/files/Position%20Statement/GLBTQ%20%28sept%202015%29.pdf

National Association for Gifted Children, & The Association for the Gifted, Council for Exceptional Children. (2013). *NAGC-CEC teacher preparation standards in gifted education.* Retrieved from http://www.nagc.org/sites/default/files/standards/NAGC-%20CEC%20CAEP%20standards%20%282013%20final%29.pdf

National Association for Gifted Children Gay, Lesbian, Bisexual, Transgender, and Questioning Network. (2015). *Application for NAGC Network status.* Washington, DC: Author.

National Association for Gifted Children Gay, Lesbian, Bisexual, and Transgender Task Force. (2002). *Task force report to the NAGC board.* Washington, DC: Author.

Newman, L. (2014). *Heather has two mommies* (25th anniversary ed.). Los Angeles, CA: Alyson.

Novak, A., & Weber, C. (Eds.) (2018). *Professional learning and teacher preparation in gifted education: Methods and strategies for gifted professional development* (Vol. 1). Waco, TX: Prufrock Press.

Pace, N. J. (2009). *The principal's challenge. Learning from gay and lesbian students*. Charlotte, NC: IAP.

Pallotta-Chiarolli, M. (2000). Learning experiences for elementary children on lesbian, gay, and bisexual themes. In W. J. Letts IV & J. T. Sears (Eds.), *Queering elementary education*. Lanham, MD: Rowman & Littlefield.

Parmenter, J. (2017). An artist and his gifted, gay, and Mormon roots. *National Association for Gifted Children GLBTQ Network Newsletter, 5*(2), 5–8.

Peterson, J. S., & Rischar, R. (2000). Gifted and gay: A study of the adolescent experience. *Gifted Child Quarterly, 44*, 231–245.

Phelps, C. (2014). Introduction. *Catalyst* [NAGC Professional Development Network Newsletter], *4*(1), 1.

Piirto, J. (2004). *Understanding creativity*. Scottsdale, AZ: Great Potential Press.

Ratts, M. J., Kaloper, M., McReady, M., Tighe, L., Butler, S. K., Dempsey, K., & McCullough, J. (2013). Safe space programs: Creating a visible presence of LGBTQ allies. *Journal of LGBTQ Issues in Counseling, 7*, 387–404.

Ray, N. (2006). *Lesbian, gay, bisexual, and transgender youth: An epidemic of homelessness*. New York, NY: National Gay and Lesbian Task Force Policy Institute and the National Coalition for the Homeless.

Russell, S. T., Koskiw, J., Horn, S., & Saewyc, E. (2010). Safe schools policies for LGBT students. *SRCD Social Policy Report, 24*(4), 1–17.

Ryan, C. (2009). *Helping families support their LGBT children*. San Francisco, CA: San Francisco State University Family Acceptance Project.

Saint Paul Public Schools Out for Equity. (2013). *Safe schools manual*. Retrieved from https://www.spps.org/cms/lib/MN01910242/Centricity/Domain/125/2013_safe_school_manual_2.pdf

Sapon-Shevin, M. (2008). Gender, sexuality and social justice education. In W. Ayers, T. Quinn, & D. Sowall (Eds.), *Handbook of social justice in education* (pp. 279–284). New York, NY: Routledge.

Sayre, J. (2015). *Husky*. New York, NY: Random House.

Sears, J. T. (1992). Educators, homosexuality, and homosexual students: Are educators' feelings about homosexuality and homosexual students related to professional beliefs? *Journal of Homosexuality*, 3–4.

Sears, J. T. (2005). Introduction. In J. T. Sears (Ed.), *Youth, education, and sexualities: An international encyclopedia*. Westport, CT: Greenwood.

Sebastian, G. (2015). *A man's man*. New York, NY: Shadoe.

Sebastian, G. (2016). *Riding the rainbow*. New York, NY: Shadoe.

Seney, R. S. (2017). Curriculum for gifted GLBTQ students. In T. P. Friedrichs, T. R. Manzella, & R.W. Seney (Eds.), *Needs and approaches for educators and parents of gifted gay, lesbian, bisexual, and transgender students.* Washington, DC: National Association for Gifted Children.

Sleeter, C. E., & Owour, J. (2011). Research on the impact of teacher preparation to teach diverse students: The research we have and the research we need. *Action in Teacher Education, 33,* 524–536.

Sowell, T. (2000, May 7). In hoops of life, achievers deserve praise, not attack. *Mercury News.*

Swan, W. (Ed.). (2016). *Gay, lesbian, bisexual, and transgender civil rights: A public policy agenda for uniting a divided America.* Boca Raton, FL: CRC Press.

Time Out Youth. (n.d.). *School staff and administration.* Retrieved from http://www.timeoutyouth.org/trainings

Treat, A. R. (2006). Overexcitabilities in gifted sexually diverse populations. *Journal of Secondary Gifted Education, 17,* 244–257.

Villanueva, M. (2016). We are artists, out and proud: My experiences at a visual and performing arts high school supportive of LGBTQ youth. *NAGC GLBTQ Network Newsletter, 4*(1), 17–27.

Whittenburg, B., & Treat, A. R. (2009). *Shared characteristics of gifted and sexually diverse youth.* In N. L. Hafenstein & J. A. Castellano (Eds.), *Perspectives in gifted education: Diverse gifted learners* (Vol. 5). Denver, CO: University of Denver.

Willhoite, M. (1991). *Daddy's roommate.* Los Angeles, CA: Alyson.

CHAPTER 3

Reframing Professional Learning to Meet the Needs of Teachers Working With Culturally Diverse Gifted Learners

Joy Lawson Davis

Introduction

Twenty-first century classrooms are challenged by the norms of society to become more sensitive to the diverse cultures and ethnic groups of students attending our schools. In order to do this, school personnel must arm themselves with resources and, in many cases, change their own attitudes regarding teaching and learning. Culturally diverse gifted learners comprise a wide variety of students from a range of ethnic and income backgrounds. These students bring a unique set of intellectual and academic strengths to the classroom, as well as psychosocial needs that teachers and other academic professionals must be cognizant of in order to enable these learners to meet their full potential. Unfortunately, most classroom teachers are ill-prepared to meet the needs of culturally diverse learners as a result of teachers' personal experiences and a lack of relevant professional training. This chapter will provide insights into critical professional learning needs and resources for teachers that will encourage them to teach in a holistic and culturally responsive manner as they provide services to gifted learners from diverse backgrounds. The resources listed include some of the most prominent books in use by contemporary equity educators.

Overview

Equity in and access to gifted education and advanced learner programs has become the clarion call drawing attention to a more inclusive approach to educating our nation's best and brightest. To enable classroom teachers to meet the academic, intellectual, and socioemotional needs of this broader and more inclusive group of learners, the focus must shift from enhanced academic content to professional learning content that is defined by the interconnectedness of culture, learning, relevancy, and academic outcomes. This is a complex and multilayered process. The intersection of culturally relevant pedagogy, high-end curriculum, and the affective needs of diverse gifted learners will be addressed in the following fictitious case study of a classroom teacher, her students, and recommended professional learning that will enhance her capacity to serve her students in the most effective manner possible. For purposes of this chapter, culturally diverse students are defined as those students who are members of the following ethnic/racially identifiable groups: Black/African American, Latino/Hispanic, and Native American/First Nation.

Among the issues plaguing our schools and acknowledged in the following case is the cultural mismatch between our predominately White, female, middle-class teaching force and our increasingly culturally diverse population of students, whose backgrounds differ to such an extent that the mismatch is detrimental to student performance, thus limiting students' chances of reaching their highest potential through the teaching and learning experience. Cultural mismatch can be mediated when teachers are culturally aware and sensitive to the behavioral norms, traditions, and values that diverse gifted learners bring to the learning experience (Villegas & Lucas, 2002). This mediation, coupled with teachers' value for the intellectual potential of diverse gifted learners, can enable teachers to create dynamic, engaging, and positive classroom environments in which all students reach high expectations.

Sarah M., identified in this case, is one such teacher. She is a White female from a middle-class background, whose primary schooling experience has been in a predominately White community, attending predominately White suburban schools and universities. Absent any community engagement with cultural groups outside of her own, this teacher's sole educational experience has been from the views of the middle-class White community. Without cultural competency training and immersion in diverse cultural experiences, she is unprepared to teach students from culturally diverse urban communities. The following section describes her experience with her students in more detail and how specific training and crossing cultural boundaries can enhance her abilities to work more effectively with her students and provide a more dynamic, engaging, and culturally responsive classroom environment.

Case Study: Sarah M.

Sarah M., a new teacher, took a position in a middle school in Brooklyn, NY. In a school designed for high-ability and gifted students from diverse cultures, 50% percent of her students are African American, 40% Hispanic/Latino, and 10% from a variety of other diverse ethnic groups. Sarah earned her teaching degree from a liberal arts university in the Midwest, with a major in mathematics and a minor in science. Her practical and student teaching experiences were in predominately White schools with high populations of identified gifted students. Sarah also holds certification as a teacher of the gifted; for this program, she took four courses in gifted education that addressed general knowledge of the field, identification practices, how to modify general education curriculum for gifted students, and socioemotional needs of the gifted. In her view, Sarah felt she was well-prepared to teach these gifted learners. In this new assignment, Sarah was the math, science, and history teacher, with students traveling to another teacher for English language arts. Over the course of the previous year, Sarah had the opportunity to participate in a few gifted education workshops that focused on high-end curriculum and the characteristics of giftedness in general.

Sarah's students were cluster grouped for instruction. She was assigned to teach the highest potential group. Most of her students were participants in a Talent Pool program in elementary school or were formally identified as gifted in the primary grades. The Talent Pool program identified high-potential students in grades 2–3 and exposed them to enrichment experiences through a pull-out model in which a trained gifted education teacher taught them using critical thinking skills curriculum. The Talent Pool students also had opportunities to participate in problem-solving competitions after school; during the summer they participated in a summer enrichment program. The performance-based curriculum allowed teachers to work with students and measure responses, as teachers also added valuable content experiences that would challenge students and prepare them for gifted education and advanced learning experiences in upper elementary and middle school. As a result of participation in their district's Talent

Pool program, Sarah's students were well on their way to taking Algebra I and honors middle school science and English (the only offerings in their school for high-potential students).

During the first week of class, Sarah recognized that there appeared to be a disconnect between her teaching style and prior training and her students' learning styles and interests. When teaching American history, for example, Sarah used the textbook provided and found that the students were disinterested in the material, and as bright students often do, they questioned the legitimacy of the historical facts presented. She was also taken aback by the high level of activity and noise, as well as the tendency of the students to cluster together to work, even when they were asked to work independently. After a few weeks of school, she realized that she knew very little, if anything, about the students' daily lives and experiences. More so, because of her own training and life experience, she was limited in her knowledge of the history of her students' cultures, their communities, and examples of gifted men and women who originated from their communities and cultural groups.

Sarah had a dilemma. Although she loved teaching, she seemed unable to transmit her love of teaching and learning to her students. She became a teacher because of her love of children; she thought that would be enough to help her be able to teach any child in the classroom. Prior to entering the classroom, Sarah was like many teachers who go into teaching expressing a belief that they can and will treat all children the same because of their love and passion for teaching. Such teachers are described as being colorblind. Colorblindness is an ideology that posits that the best way to end discrimination is to treat individuals as equally as possible, without regard to race, culture, or ethnicity. Colorblindness, however, has been described as a form of racism (Williams, 2011). For Sarah, colorblindness meant that she would not be able to reach all of her students and teach them important content without being aware of their ethnic, cultural, or family background. Further, she had no understanding of the rich resources created by people from the same cultural groups as her students that she could bring into the classroom. As the weeks went on, Sarah continued to lose confidence in her ability to meet the needs of her students in a meaningful way.

Although Sarah was a creative teacher, allowing students product options so that they could respond to an instructional unit in their own learning style, she found that students were not always interested in the materials and option choices she provided. Her limitations as a teacher were accentuated by the lack of culturally relevant reading materials, authentic historical documents, and connections to the rich resources available in the community. Sarah found herself challenged by the lack of these resources and the ability to connect with her students' communities; this challenge became overwhelming. She began to realize that the gifted education training she received did not fully prepare her to teach her culturally diverse gifted students. She was deficient in how to build relationships with her students because she had never worked with Black and Hispanic learners before and, thus, did not clearly understand her students' strengths, interpersonal traits, and cultural backgrounds, which were so very different from her own personal and professional background.

Sarah realized that she needed help.

Three Key Critical Professional Learning Needs of Teachers of Culturally Diverse Gifted Students

Culturally responsive teaching and learning has become a hallmark of educating our nation's increasingly diverse student population (Gay, 2010; Ladson-Billings, 2009). As educational policymakers and scholars are more engaged in adapting curriculum to meet the needs of all students, they must be able to ensure that the cultural norms and traditions of all ethnic groups are integrated into curriculum and programming. Gay (2010) suggested that schools exercising the ability to use the cultural characteristics, experiences, and perspectives of the diverse learners can create more effective learning environments. Although the number of children of culturally diverse backgrounds identified for gifted and talented and other advanced learner programs remains a deep concern and the task of providing a remedy for this situation appears daunting, it is imperative that developing teachers have the skill set and commitment to creating socially just and culturally responsive classrooms. Teachers like Sarah M. are responsible for teaching gifted students around the nation. The differences in her personal background from those of her students can be mediated by professional training that includes a comprehensive view of the culture, norms, and traditions of diverse cultures, as well as an increased insight into how she can create and sustain classroom environment conditions in which her bright diverse students can thrive and grow. Accepting the importance of culture to learning in order to develop a trustful, mutually beneficial learning environment is critical in moving schools forward to tackle the enormous task of nurturing and developing the gifts of all high-potential learners.

In order to ensure that teachers of the gifted are more fully prepared to identify, serve, and nurture culturally diverse high-ability and gifted students, the following are recommended professional learning needs. Teachers should:

1. understand the gifted traits, intellectual strengths, and unique psychosocial needs of diverse gifted students;
2. know and be able to implement culturally responsive curriculum and instruction in their gifted education classes and specialized programs; and
3. understand the cultural norms and traditions of culturally diverse families and communities.

These professional learning needs and suggested strategies are addressed in the following sections.

Understanding the Gifted Traits, Intellectual Strengths, and Unique Psychosocial Needs of Diverse Gifted Learners

Successful teachers understand their students' strengths and needs, and have the capacity to build trustful relationships with their students. Building trustful relationships starts with a clear understanding of who students are as learners, individuals, and contributors to the learning community (Ladson-Billings, 2009; Scott, 2012). Gifted children of color generally demonstrate the same traits of giftedness that all gifted learners exhibit: They are curious and sensitive, and have enhanced capacities in one or more domains. They may demonstrate leadership and be driven to connect their learning with real-life situations, and they rapidly learn and apply new concepts. Many of these students may also demonstrate visual-spatial strengths and artistic (visual and performing) strengths.

Additionally, diverse gifted children may also demonstrate an additional layer of cultural norms that, in some ways, may distinguish them from other gifted students. Many of these students may also demonstrate remarkable resilience, persistence, and more creativity than other gifted students (Davis & Moore, 2016). Further, diverse gifted students have internal and external challenges gifted students from the majority culture will not have to address

because of their position in society (Davis, 2010). Being Black or Brown and gifted comes with a unique set of psychological challenges that can impact performance in the classroom (Davis & Moore, 2016). The following topics are important to cover in any training to improve teachers' understanding of the traits, strengths, and psychosocial needs of diverse gifted students:
- the duality of being culturally diverse and gifted,
- racial identity and its impact on academic performance,
- stereotype threat and how to teach students to overcome it, and
- sense of isolation within a larger group of gifted learners.

Narratives by Black historians and sociologists share the dilemma of being a minority in an intellectual environment designed for majority culture students (Coates, 2015; DuBois, 1903). DuBois (1903) noted the following: "One ever feels his twoness,—an American, a Negro; two souls, two thoughts, two unreconciled strivings; two warring ideals in one dark body, whose strength alone keeps it from being torn asunder." This infamous quote about double consciousness speaks strongly to the duality of being a gifted student of color in a gifted education program. Testimonies by parents of diverse gifted students share similar concerns of belonging, overcoming isolation, and feeling the dilemma of being a member of an oppressed group and being gifted (Davis, 2016). Teachers who have not had to experience this duality in their own lives need to have an opportunity to read and discuss this literature to become more sensitive to the experiences their students have and how these experiences can impact students' self-esteem and achievement. The strategies indicated in Table 3.1 will improve teacher understandings of their gifted students' psychosocial needs. The strategies recommended are designed for implementation in small groups of professional learning communities with teachers with similar training needs.

Table 3.1
Training in the Characteristics, Strengths, and Unique Psychosocial Needs of Diverse Gifted Students

Need/Objective	Professional Learning Strategy
To learn more about the strengths of gifted children of color in contemporary situations	View the movie *Akeelah and the Bee*. Take notes of unique traits and challenges faced by Akeelah and other characters in the film. In small groups, teachers can discuss how Akeelah's gifts and her challenges may resemble that of their own students. They may also consider how they may modify instruction and/or relationships with families to enhance their students' experiences.
To be sensitive to the duality of being culturally diverse and gifted	Discuss/analyze the quote "One ever feels his twoness" (DuBois, 1903; see pp. 66–68, this volume). Discuss other "twoness" experiences that students and/or adults may have (female scientists, actors, artists). Examine how the experience of DuBois in the late 19th century parallels that of diverse gifted students in schools today.
To gain insight from stories written by families of diverse gifted students	Read *Talent in Every Community*. Discuss family stories.
To understand stereotype threat and how to teach students to overcome it	Complete a book study on *Whistling Vivaldi* (see Resources list, pp. 66–68). Pose questions to discuss during each session; share personal experiences in similar settings in which readers felt lesser than others (due to gender, income, ethnicity) and how that impacted their behavior.

Case Study: Sarah M.

On her own, Sarah decided to select a few books to read about gifted children of color (such as those in the Resources section of this chapter; see pp. 66–68). Her goal was to read at least one book each semester to help expand her knowledge base of the research most relevant to understanding the strengths and unique challenges of culturally diverse gifted children. In addition to her reading, Sarah rented the movie *Akeelah and the Bee*. While viewing, she wrote down remarkable comments made by the main characters. She learned that even when Black gifted children have high potential, they face many challenges. She also learned, however, that with support and understanding, such students can be very successful, just as Akeelah was in the movie. Sarah decided to bring the movie to class and have her students view it and be prepared to discuss the most important segments of the movie, when they believed that Akeelah was having the most difficult time, and why. She also asked the students to talk about personal situations or challenges they had that were similar to those of Akeelah. Sarah recognized that she was just beginning to learn the full scope of the potential and challenges that her students could face. She accepted this and looked forward to continuing opportunities to learn and share her new knowledge with other teachers.

Implementing Culturally Responsive Curriculum Instruction in Gifted Education Classes and Specialized Programs

Across the nation, many gifted education programs serve students in the regular classroom through push-in models or cluster grouping models. As such, it is critical that all classroom teachers be engaged in professional development that strengthens their cultural competency skills while simultaneously teaching them the pedagogy of gifted education. To do anything less is an injustice to the many students that they teach in K–12 classrooms, who will need them to be culturally sensitive and understand the unique needs of students who are gifted and who differ from their agemates and grade-level peers. To accomplish this, immersion in cultural competency training and engaging in crosscultural experiences are essential. Additionally, classroom teachers will need a stronger understanding of how diverse gifted students see themselves as intellectual beings who are members of a family and community that may differ significantly from the environment at school. For example, communal groups characterize the "spaces" that many culturally diverse students originate from; thus, students may thrive in busy, noisy classrooms, as they interact with each other to exchange information, ideas, and emotions regularly. The classroom environment that mirrors this setting provides a more familiar environment for children of color, one in which they are more likely to excel, flourish, and feel a sense of belonging (Boykin, Tyler, Watkins-Lewis, & Kizzie, 2009; Gay, 2010).

Teachers who understand the culture and daily experiences of their students will be more successful in engaging them in high-level instruction and producing the desired results (Ford & Grantham, 2003; Ladson-Billings, 2009). Materials that are historically authentic and representative of all cultures within the community will be more engaging and have the potential to increase student self-esteem (Ford & Milner, 2013; Gay, 2010). Increased self-esteem is likely to lead to higher achievement. When and where students and teachers have better relationships, positive engagement with classroom experiences and performance outcomes improve (Ladson-Billings, 2009). Integrating more culturally responsive teaching (CRT) practices into gifted education training and, therefore, classrooms in which all gifted students are served, will enable teachers to see giftedness more clearly as it manifests itself across populations. Training teachers to understand the worldview of diverse learners is key to advancing the cause of CRT in schools, and teachers can be more proactive in searching for talent in diverse students, while simultaneously delivering curriculum to meet with their strengths and learning needs (Ford & Milner, 2013). Table 3.2 includes recommended strategies to improve the understandings teachers have of culturally responsive teaching and learning. It is important to engage teachers in collecting, developing, and utilizing representational literature and authentic historic documents across content areas, while emphasizing materials and strategies that demonstrate and applaud the intellectual genius of individuals across cultures and genders to serve as models and mentors in all classrooms.

Table 3.2
Training in Culturally Responsive Teaching and Learning

Need/Objective	Professional Learning Strategies
Understand and value the need for classroom environments that are engaging and bring out the strengths of diverse learners	Enroll in a graduate or undergraduate cultural competency course, such as "Teaching in a Diverse Society or Multicultural Competency." (Content should cover critical race theory, White privilege, microaggressions, reaching diverse students through their strengths, systemic racism, and other barriers to school success.) Listen to a TED Talk, such as "The Danger of a Single Story" by Chimamanda Adichie (or other TED Talks related to race and culture). Discuss critical moments in Adichie's life, as expressed in the talk, when she discovered the dangers of a single story. Follow up with writing down similar single-story narratives the teachers may have expressed or experienced.
Use materials using authentic history, "mirror books"	Read and analyze articles discussing the importance of representational literature, such as *Mirrors, Windows, and Sliding Glass Doors* (Bishop, 1990) and *The Unbearable Whiteness of Literacy Instruction* (Gangi, 2009). Collect and analyze selected books from https://diversebooks.org/resources/where-to-find-diverse-books.

Case Study: Sarah M.

Sarah recognized almost immediately that her understanding of her students' cultural differences was a barrier between herself and the students. She would witness her students clustering together to have discussions, and when she approached them, they would get quiet, suggesting that she could not be a part of their conversations. After doing some independent research, she discovered that perhaps the students' response was due to the cultural differences between herself and the students. In short time, she was able to locate a course in cultural competency offered by a local university in the evenings. She enrolled in the course and began learning so much more about her students' intellectual and social-emotional needs. For example, she now understood why her Black and Hispanic students sat together in the cafeteria away from the White students and sometimes sat with other students in the school who were not in the gifted program. Her students' needs for comfortable peers became more apparent to her when her course instructor covered duality of consciousness and the need for school programs to mediate the isolation felt by diverse students in majority culture schools. She also learned about microaggressions, White privilege, and other topics relevant to teaching in a diverse school environment. The course assignments, reflections, and discussions enhanced Sarah's understanding of the experiences that her students had daily, in and outside of school, that could negatively or positively impact their education.

Additionally, Sarah began watching TED talks related to race and diversity in the classrooms. The TED talks served to enlighten Sarah's understanding of race and privilege in ways that she had not previously considered. Over time, Sarah became more sensitive to how her students might experience schooling and society as culturally diverse students. As a result, she was able to develop better relationships with her gifted students. The improved relationships, in turn, improved the classroom environment and students' engagement with the teaching and learning process. Sarah realized that she had a great deal more to learn about race and the way it impacted teaching and learning; she shared her concerns with her district supervisor for gifted programs and recommended that some of her experiences be integrated into the district's professional learning plan in the upcoming school year.

Understanding the Cultural Norms and Traditions of Culturally Diverse Families and Communities

Black and Hispanic students originate from cultures that are communal in nature (Boykin et al., 2006; Vega & Moore, 2016). Therefore, it is critical for educators to understand that in these communities, each child is important to the whole family unit. To gain the trust and respect of families of Black and Hispanic students, one must understand that the child is only one part of the whole unit. The whole unit is the family or la familia, which includes parents, extended family, and even community members and faith leaders who may play a role in the nurturing and upbringing of the child (Davis, 2010). To gain the trust and interest of families in the Black and Hispanic community, school personnel must show themselves trustworthy with positive and respectful attitudes demonstrated through communications sent home and invitations to informational meetings and in face-to-face meetings. Far too often, these families have been left out of conversations regarding gifted education and know very little about the policies and practices used by the school district (Davis, 2016). The historical accusations of elitism against gifted programs have unfortunately been earned, as program information has not been as widely distributed across communities of color. A comprehensive training program to engage educators and families of diverse learners as copartners in their education is key to the success of the students and school programs, in general. Table 3.3 delineates the components of a comprehensive training model for families, community leaders, and educators.

A recommended family/schools professional learning model for educators should include:
- understanding of the cultural norms and traditions of each diverse ethnic group,
- developing collaborative advocacy programs to allow parents and educators to work together,
- understanding how families become advocates for their gifted children and how to access resources outside of the school for enrichment and funding, and
- having crosscultural experiences to engage in community experiences and reflection of each experience via discussion with other professional peers.

Case Study: Sarah M.

To extend her understanding of the communities her students originated from, Sarah took advantage of opportunities to visit her students' communities by making home visits, attending recreational events, going to worship services, and even taking time to go the local grocery store where her students' families shopped. Upon visiting these places, she experienced the ambience of their world. At cultural and recreational events, she experienced the communication styles of the families, somewhat different from her own. She heard the music and eventually engaged in dancing with the students and their family members. On Sundays, she began attending church services, first in the Black community and later in the Hispanic/Latino community. During the worship experiences, she felt welcome and engaged in singing and praying in a way that was different from her own worship experiences as a youngster. Their churches were livelier; there were more outward expressions of spirituality in the music from the choirs to the congregation. In the Black Baptist church, the minister used a call-and-response preaching style that she had not experienced. Members of the congregation were expected to respond with "Amen" or another affirmative response when they were moved or agreed with the minister's viewpoint. In Sarah's church experience, no one spoke aloud during the sermon, except the minister. She was later able to integrate the call-and-response style as a

Table 3.3
Training to Understand, Value, and Respect Norms and Traditions of Culturally Diverse Families and Communities

Need/Objective	Professional Learning Strategy (for Teachers)
Value families as cultural agents	Invite families and community leaders to serve as panelists to discuss cultural traditions and values norms, as well as serve as cultural "agents" to inform schools and be liaisons in the community for school programs.
To have a crosscultural experience	Visit churches, beauty shops, barber shops, or other community gatherings. Write a reflection paper about how you felt, what you observed, and how you had conversations with other adults in the diverse environments; what activities you participated in; and how the experience affected your previously held views of the diverse communities. Conclude by discussing instructional strategies or classroom environment modifications you may consider to bring "community norms" into the classroom.

formative assessment strategy to ensure that students retained information from a particular teaching unit. She began to use it more frequently across content areas and saw how engaging the call-and-response style was for all of her students. While in the community, she met a number of civic leaders whom she invited to come to her class to share information about culture and careers, and have discussions with the students on a number of topics. She also referred these leaders to her school principal and district office to serve on advisory panels and to help disseminate information about gifted programming in the Black and Hispanic communities. Crossing cultural boundaries strengthened Sarah's commitment to helping the school district increase access to gifted programs for all communities. The experiences she had enhanced her opinion of the Black and Hispanic communities that she knew so little about until she immersed herself in their environments.

Note that engaging with families may require the involvement of other school personnel, including counselors, social workers, and school psychologists, who have a different level of relationship and specialized skills to help with parent and family collaboration. Ideally, these specialists can become part of the school-home team, working together to nurture, develop, and support the academic, intellectual, and socioemotional needs of diverse gifted students.

Implications

Sarah's experiences with becoming more familiar with her students' communities, taking a cultural competency course, and watching relevant TED talks were self-selected. Due to her concern and her discomfort with her relationship with her students, she decided to take the initiative to improve her understandings with the hope that new insights would improve her classroom environment. Translating Sarah's case study into a school or district approach is possible, and new insights into the nature and needs of culturally diverse gifted learners will result from the recommended professional learning strategies. As buildings and districts engage in the implementation of the three areas of professional learning described in this chapter, culturally responsive classrooms will be developed, creating stronger partnerships with families and communities, and improving teachers' understandings of the unique psychosocial challenges of their diverse gifted students.

Gifted education leaders at the school level and district level should integrate these recommendations into their annual professional learning plans to ensure that all teachers of gifted students have access to these culturally responsive training experiences. First, teachers and other educators involved will begin to view their diverse gifted learners in a more holistic manner and hopefully embrace the entire community involved in the nurturance and development of talent. Second, new insights will be gained as teachers and other personnel have crosscultural experiences as they begin to spend time with the students and their families outside of the school, attending community organized events, attending worship services, hosting informational meetings at churches or community centers, and intentionally bringing parents and extended family members in to engage them as "cultural agents." Finally, an unintended consequence of these new experiences and interactions will be that teachers may begin to see the giftedness that exists in communities typically underrepresented and, thus, underserved in gifted education programs overall. Thus, the "single story" myth of communities of color may finally be dispelled.

These dynamic and interrelational engagements hold great promise for transforming gifted education classrooms, schools, and specialized services across our communities over time. It is imperative that these same types of professional learning opportunities be made available to school-level administrators, central office administrators, and, where they exist, district-level diversity and inclusion committee members to increase their level of understanding and support for teachers.

Summary

This chapter gives a glimpse at what a reframed professional learning model in gifted education can do to help classroom teachers working with diverse gifted students create more engaging learning environments. Reshaping professional learning to enable educators to gain a better understanding of cultural groups typically not as involved in gifted programs will open new doors for educators and the students they serve. As one of the most diverse nations in the world, we have an obligation and responsibility to seek and serve intellectual giftedness from all communities, respect and value the communities as they exist, and enable their exceptionally talented students to reach their full potential. With this new model of professional learning as a goal, everyone benefits—schools, students, communities, and our nation.

Resources

Castellano, J. A., & Frazier, A. D. (Eds.). (2010). *Special populations in gifted education: Understanding our most able learners from diverse backgrounds*. Waco, TX: Prufrock Press.

This comprehensive volume provides a range of topical, research-based discussions to inform educators, researchers, and families about ethnic groups that are underrepresented in programs across the country. The authors provide specific recommendations for working with linguistically different students and their families, and what strategies have been most effective in meeting student academic and intellectual needs.

Coates, T. (2015). *Between the world and me*. New York, NY: Random House.

In this critically acclaimed book (framed as a letter to his son), the author defines his view and what he believes to be the viewpoint of many African Americans in contemporary time—that of a citizen living in a world that is designed not to lift him up but to oppress and destroy. The story chronicles the author's journey from the mid-Atlantic as a college student attending a historically Black college in the South, to a time of reuniting with his family in New York City. An experience by a childhood friend who is murdered by a police officer is interwoven with that of a young Black male coming of age, trying to find his place in America on the dawn of the 21st century. Ta-Nehisi Coates is a 2015 winner of a MacArthur Genius Grant.

Davis, J. L. (2010). *Bright, talented, and black: A guide for families of African American gifted learners.* Scottsdale, AZ: Great Potential Press.

This seminal guidebook provides a historical context for the concept of giftedness in the Black community, as well as advocacy strategies for families and educators working with Black gifted students. Each chapter of the book is constructed to focus on important subtopics that give readers an enhanced understanding of what it means for Black students to be identified as gifted and how families can advocate for them to access appropriate educational services. The internal and external challenges of being gifted are addressed and program resources provided. A helpful glossary of gifted education terms provides vocabulary for families to become familiar with the language of gifted education.

Davis, J. L., & Moore, J. L., III. (Eds.). (2016). *Gifted children of color around the world: Diverse needs, exemplary practices, and directions for the future* (Vol. 3, Advances in Race and Ethnicity in Education). Bingley, England: Emerald.

In this special volume, national and international experts provide current research and topical discussions of how giftedness manifests itself in children of color in varied communities and what services are being provided to nurture their strengths. Counseling, twice-exceptionality, biracial gifted, and narratives from families of gifted students are among the special topics included in this groundbreaking text.

Ford, D. Y., & Milner, R. H. (2013). Teaching culturally diverse gifted students. In F. A. Karnes & K. R. Stephens (Series Eds.), *The practical strategies series in gifted education.* Waco, TX: Prufrock Press.

In this practical guidebook, the authors demonstrate the importance of using cultural knowledge of African American, Hispanic, and other ethnically diverse groups to shape advanced instruction. The authors contend that such instruction is critical not only for inclusion or recruitment, but also for retention of diverse students in gifted and advanced learner programs.

Ladson-Billings, G. (2009). *The dreamkeepers: Successful teachers of African American children* (2nd ed.). Indianapolis, IN: Wiley.

In the second edition of this award-winning book, the author shares conversations with the teachers who appeared in the first edition as part of her study. These teachers exhibited many powerful traits that distinguished them as successful teachers of African American students. Among the traits discussed are the importance of embracing each student as an individual, creating a family atmosphere in the classroom, and knowing how to push, encourage, and bring out the best in students despite their demographic conditions, while maintaining strict disciplinarian practices. Characteristics of exemplary teachers, school culture, and implications for the profession of teaching are discussed throughout.

Steele, C. M. (2011). *Whistling Vivaldi: How stereotypes affect us and what we can do*. New York, NY: Norton.

This book shares an extended illumination of Steele's groundbreaking stereotype threat research. In this volume, the author discusses a Black college student's experience as a victim of stereotyping when he has a nonconfrontational interaction with a White couple. This text discusses the deeply ingrained societal disease called stereotyping and how it affects students of color—in particular, those who have been most marginalized in every system and institution of society.

References

Boykin, A. W., Tyler, K. M., Watkins-Lewis, K., & Kizzie, K. (2006). Culture in the sanctioned classroom practices of elementary school teachers serving low-income African American students. *Journal of Education for Students Placed at Risk, 11*, 161–173.

Coates, T. (2015). *Between the world and me*. New York, NY: Random House.

Davis, J. L. (2010). *Bright, talented, and black: A guide for families of African American gifted learners*. Scottsdale, AZ: Great Potential Press.

Davis, J. L. (2016) Talent in every community: A glimpse into the world of parenting gifted children of color. In J. L. Davis & J. L. Moore, III. (Eds.), *Gifted children of color around the world: Diverse needs, exemplary practices and directions for the future* (Vol. 3, Advances in Race and Ethnicity in Education, pp. 71–85). Bingley, England: Emerald.

Davis, J. L., & Moore, J. L., III. (Eds.). (2016). *Gifted children of color around the world: Diverse needs, exemplary practices, and directions for the future* (Vol. 3, Advances in Race and Ethnicity in Education). Bingley, England: Emerald.

DuBois, W. E. B. (1903). *The souls of black folk.* New York, NY: Simon & Schuster.

Ford, D. Y., & Grantham, T. C. (2003). Providing access for culturally diverse students: From deficit to dynamic thinking. *Theory Into Practice, 42,* 217–225.

Ford, D. Y., & Milner, R. H. (2013). Teaching culturally diverse gifted students. In F. A. Karnes & K. R. Stephens (Series Eds.), *The practical strategies series in gifted education.* Waco, TX: Prufrock Press.

Gay, G. (2010). Culturally responsive teaching: Theory, research, and practice (2nd ed.) In J. A. Banks (Series Ed.), *Multicultural education series.* New York, NY: Teachers College Press.

Ladson-Billings, G. (2009). *The dreamkeepers: Successful teachers of African American children* (2nd ed.). Indianapolis, IN: Wiley.

Scott, M. F. (2012). Socio-emotional and psychological issues and needs of gifted African-American students: Culture matters. *Interdisciplinary Journal of Teaching and Learning, 7*(1), 23–33.

Vega, D., & Moore, J. L., III. (2016). Where are all the Latino males in gifted programs? In J. L. Davis & J. L. Moore, III (Eds.), *Gifted children of color around the world: Diverse needs, exemplary practices and directions for the future* (Vol. 3, Advances in Race and Ethnicity in Education, pp. 87–103). Bingley, England: Emerald.

Villegas, A. M., & Lucas, T. (2002). *Educating culturally responsive teachers: A coherent approach.* New York, NY: SUNY Press.

Williams, M. T. (2011). *Colorblind ideology is a form of racism* [Web blog post]. Retrieved from https://www.psychologytoday.com/us/blog/culturally-speaking/201112/colorblind-ideology-is-form-racism

CHAPTER 4

Professional Learning Strategies to Develop Creativity Among Attention Divergent Hyperactive Gifted Students

C. Matthew Fugate and Janessa Bower

> The thing has already taken form in my mind before I start it. The first attempts are absolutely unbearable. I say this because I want you to know that if you see something worthwhile in what I am doing, it is not by accident but because of real direction and purpose.
>
> —Vincent van Gogh

Aristotle believed that creativity came from an outside source, from a daemon or a special power conferred by the gods (Becker, 2000). While watching his teacher write poetry, Plato described Socrates as being under the influence of a divine madness that carried him out of his senses. This idea morphed into what ancient Greeks eventually interpreted as the individual artist's daemon, a mystical and external source of inspiration (Starko, 2014).

Although research exists on creativity (see Batey & Furnham, 2006, for a review), Attention Deficit/Hyperactive Disorder (ADHD), and giftedness (e.g., Mullet & Rinn, 2015; Nelson, Rinn, & Hartnett, 2006), and students who manifest combinations thereof (e.g., Fugate & Gentry, 2016; Fugate, Zentall, & Gentry, 2013), a distinct dearth exists in the training and implications of professional learning on these topics, particularly when considering them in tandem. In this age of globalized competition for academic prowess, educators need access to professional learning concerning the potentially mitigating power of creativity (Carson, 2011; Simonton, 2010) for students of this ilk.

Often, teachers see only an ADHD label hovering over the heads of children who ought to be identified as both gifted and ADHD. We propose that teachers require tools to see the creative sparks as they fly from students' swirling minds, to catch those sparks, to amalgamate them, and to return them to students in a package that they can use to their benefit. From here, educators need to teach students to grab the sparks themselves and to harness and organize thoughts on their own, because the sparks are where beautiful thoughts are born.

Overview

Moon and Reis (2004) asserted that because it is outside the norm, giftedness is, by definition, an exceptionality. For students to be twice-exceptional, they must display the characteristics associated with giftedness and those associated with one or more learning or behavioral disorders (Baum & Olenchak, 2002; Baum, Olenchak, & Owen, 1998; Moon & Reis, 2004). Estimates have shown that there may be more than 385,000 twice-exceptional children in schools throughout the United States (Assouline, Colangelo, VanTassel-Baska, & Lupkowski-Shoplik, 2015). However, this number can be difficult to determine because problems arise for many of these students when teachers, special education professionals, and administrators focus on children's weaknesses rather than on their strengths, using the presence of disorders as evidence that children could not also be gifted (Assouline, Foley Nicpon, & Huber, 2006; Baum, Cooper, & Neu, 2001; Schultz, 2012). To this end, educators require professional learning that addresses specific identification practices, as well as academic interventions and extensions for this special population.

Gifted students with ADHD face unique academic challenges. A normal distribution of IQ scores has been found in children with ADHD (Kaplan, Crawford, Dewey, & Fisher, 2000), suggesting that there is no reason to think that there are any more or less instances of ADHD in the gifted population. However, due to cognitive processing problems often found in students with ADHD, their IQ scores can typically be 5–10 points lower than their non-ADHD peers of similar ability (Castellanos, 2000; Hughes, 2011). Because these scores do not reflect the true potential of these students, educators often fail to recognize gifted potential in students with ADHD, particularly in school districts that rely on IQ scores for identification (Hughes 2011; Moon, 2002; Silverman, 2002). Other common characteristics affecting the academic performance of gifted students with ADHD are a lack of organizational skills (Nielsen, 2002), poor working memory (Fugate et al., 2013), the inability to maintain attention (Zentall, Moon, Hall, & Grskovic, 2001), and poor metacognitive skills (Davis, Rimm, & Siegle, 2018). Further, gifted students with ADHD may also face many social-emotional difficulties that result from feelings of inadequacy and low self-esteem related to their achievement in school when compared with their peers (Baum & Owen, 1988). This may manifest through displays of emotional intensity (Olenchak & Reis, 2002) and frustration that lead to a general lack of motivation (Baum & Owen, 1988). All of these factors combine to highlight the sensitivity with which identification processes must address potential candidates for gifted programs who may also have ADHD. Educators need training to ensure appropriate considerations are given during the testing process.

Once these students are identified, professional learning is also required for specific academic interventions that address this group through a strengths-based approach. Although children with ADHD experience varying degrees of difficulty in the school environment, there is evidence of greater potential for creativity and creative achievement than in the non-ADHD population (e.g., Abraham, Windmann, Siefen, Daum, & Güntükün, 2006; Carson, Peterson, & Higgins, 2003; Fugate et al., 2013; White & Shah, 2006). Consequently, Fugate et al. (2013) noted that "alternative approaches to education that focus on developing creativity could be implemented, thus reducing negative outcomes for students in the ADHD population" (p. 235). Certainly, there is a long history of research focused on creativity and its importance in education (e.g., Davis, 2004; Guilford, 1967; Lewis, 2009; Renzulli, 1999). Although there are varying definitions, creativity is often seen as the generation of a product that is original and task-appropriate within a certain cultural context or domain of expertise (e.g., Beghetto, 2013; Starko, 2014) and has been documented as a predictor of future success (e.g., Tierney, Farmer, & Graen, 1999; Torrance, 1972, 1981). Specifically, creativity has been found to be a factor in healthy emotional development, interpersonal relationships (e.g., Russ, 1998), and career advancements in science, technology, engineering, art, and mathematics (Plucker, Beghetto, & Dow, 2004; Sternberg, 1999). Yet, despite the value placed on creativity in education and in the workplace, it is simultaneously misunderstood, as many people associate creativity with wildly divergent or impractical out-of-the-box thinking (Proudfoot, Kay, & Koval, 2015). Thus, specific training for educators ought to focus on methods for linking creative tendencies with academic expectations.

Creativity is sometimes identified as a fixed trait, leading students and teachers to view it as something that one can be capable of in one domain, but not in others (see Kozbelt, Beghetto, & Runco, 2010 for a review). These beliefs can be changed when educators are provided with proper professional learning opportunities that support student-centered, growth feedback that validates the idea that creative competence comes just as much from failure as it does from success (Beghetto, 2013; Beghetto & Dilley, 2016; Kamins & Dweck, 1999). This means viewing creativity as a set of skills rather than a discrete trait (Kozbelt et al., 2010), with explicit instruction in strategies that develop creativity and creative thinking, such as in analytical writing (Olthouse & Sauder, 2016).

This distinction can be especially important for those gifted students with ADHD who have been found to score higher on tests of creative thinking (Cramond, 1994; Fugate et al., 2013); tell more creative stories with novel themes (Zentall, 1988); use more visual imagery strategies in response to periods of high states of arousal, such as when watching and playing videos and games (Lawrence et al., 2002; Shaw & Brown, 1999); and contribute to higher percentages of correct problem solving in cooperative groups (Kuester & Zentall, 2011) when compared with their same-age peers. Additionally, White and Shah (2016) found these students to be more innovative, reporting higher levels of creative achievement among this population than students without ADHD (White & Shah, 2011). Therefore, it has been suggested that these students be viewed as Attention Divergent Hyperactive Gifted (ADHG; Fugate, 2018; Fugate & Gentry, 2016). This paradigm shift alters the focus from the challenges that these students face and instead highlights their potential for creativity, innovation, and motivation—a difference that is paramount for teachers to understand as they seek training avenues that address the classroom instruction required to meet the unique needs of these students who are ADHG. In order to rise up to this challenge, teachers need opportunities for sustained and supported professional learning that goes above and beyond traditional means of professional development.

Professional Learning to Meet the Needs of Students Who Are ADHG

Students who are ADHG must be seen as gifted first; therefore, teachers must incorporate a variety of strategies that address and enhance students' strengths. Only after strengths have been highlighted can teachers truly address the challenges that students face (Fugate, 2018). Because these students often have co-occurring disabilities related to ADHD, including but not limited to oppositional defiant disorder, conduct disorder, or anxiety (Zentall, 2006), teachers must have opportunities for professional learning that address both students' giftedness and students' disabilities. Ultimately, the goal is to create classroom environments in which "creativity is emphasized as a pathway to learning as well as an outcome of learning" (Fugate et al., 2013, p. 242). This means fashioning an environment in which students are encouraged to ask questions and make connections with the goal of moving beyond simply finding the correct answers (Fugate, 2018).

Nielsen (2002) stressed the importance for schools to create a multidisciplinary task force of gifted, general, and special education professionals whose primary goal is to advocate for twice-exceptional students. To this end, professional learning is necessary in order to raise the awareness educators have about issues related to best practices for meeting the needs of students who are ADHG. To do this, schools should implement a variety of strategies that support the sustained growth of all educators within the learning community. Therefore, a plan must be developed that focuses on intensive, job-embedded learning that includes six steps for professional learning groups—study, select, plan, implement, analyze, and adjust (see Figure 4.1; Southwest Educational Development Laboratory, 2008).

Study

This first step involves teachers working in collaborative teams to study and build their knowledge and understanding of students who are ADHG. Book studies are a low-cost option that give teams the opportunity to explore topics in detail. An excellent option for a book study for teachers is *To Be Gifted and Learning Disabled: Strength-Based Strategies for Helping Twice-Exceptional Students With LD, ADHD, ASD, and More* by Baum, Schader, and Owen (2017). This book provides practical suggestions that teachers can use for self-guided professional learning; it also is a good resource for administrators who are looking to provide guidance to their teachers.

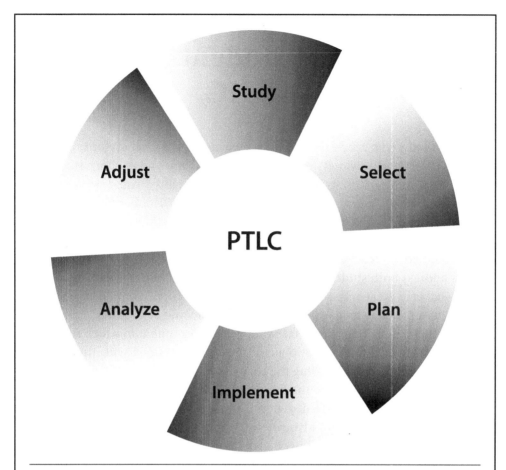

Figure 4.1. The six steps for professional learning. Adapted from *The Professional Teaching and Learning Cycle: Introduction* (2nd ed., p. 3), by Southwest Educational Development Laboratory, 2008, Austin, TX: Author. Copyright 2008 by Southwest Educational Development Laboratory. Adapted with permission.

Donohue, VanTassell, and Patterson (1996) developed a framework for educators to follow for effective book study. Each week, members of the professional learning group read the chapter or chapters assigned prior to coming together. At the beginning of the study group, time is allotted for members to discuss how they have applied the knowledge that they have gained from previous chapters in their classrooms. Then, each person is given the opportunity to discuss what he or she felt to be one of the most significant ideas from that week's reading, why it stood out, and the connections he or she made with the text, either personally or professionally. Next, the group members reflect and discuss the implications of that week's readings for how they interact with, and teach, their students. Finally, time is provided for each person to journal his or her thoughts about what he or she learned that day and brainstorm ideas of how he or she will use the new knowledge in the future.

Select

The next step in the professional learning process is to select research-based resources that will allow teachers to most effectively address students' strength areas and tap into their creativity and creative thinking. For example, an effective framework for establishing a creative classroom environment is Weisberg's (2010) CHOICES (see Figure 4.2). This view presents creativity not as a unique, spontaneous moment only attainable by few, but rather as a deliberate, learned cognitive process. The first "C" stands for Creativity itself. Under this heading, creativity is Habitual, which means that creative processes require access to a deep knowledge base. The next part of this framework is Ordinary: Creative thinking is not the result of a singular, specific cognitive process; rather, it is an outpouring of the same processes that are responsible for other thought activities. The "I" stands for Incremental. This highlights that epiphanies are not spontaneous, but are in fact borne of small, deliberate steps. They are neither delivered in bursts of divine intervention nor in leaps or flashes. The second "C" is Conscious because creativity is gained through intentional effort; it is not bestowed mystically from the gods. The "E" is Evolutionary, describing how creative breakthroughs do not emerge in isolation; each is built upon previous discoveries. The final component of the CHOICES framework is Sensitive—creativity acting within, and reacting to, the cultural zeitgeist.

Plan

Working within their professional learning groups, teachers then create a plan that outlines how they will infuse creative thinking into their classroom practice. It is also important that the group works collaboratively to decide what student products they intend to collect during the implementation phase (Southwest Educational Development Laboratory, 2008). In her book *Sparking Student Creativity: Practical Ways to Promote Innovative Thinking and Problem Solving*, Drapeau (2014) highlighted several ways to nurture creativity. First, she suggested that students need to be presented with work that is interesting and challenging and that can be completed within a reasonable period with attainable goals. The creative classroom requires that students understand that feelings of disequilibrium may exist. When this occurs, the teacher must work with students to embrace that

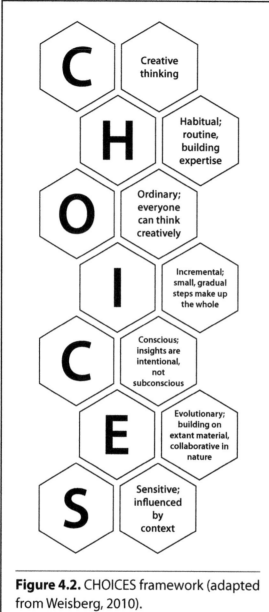

Figure 4.2. CHOICES framework (adapted from Weisberg, 2010).

discomfort and see it for what it is—a moment of possibility. It is in these times that students can begin to muse, "What if?" These musings require teachers to give students time to think. To this end, Drapeau (2014) further emphasized the importance of providing students with appropriate scaffolding when necessary. The goal, then, is not to rescue students when they are faced with challenges, but to empower them as creative thinkers through constructive feedback, the facilitation of discussions, and an exchange of ideas in the classroom. Teachers can infuse the ideas in Drapeau's book into their extant lesson plans to demonstrate that they value different types of creativity, to promote teamwork, and to create a safe and positive environment.

Implement

Next, teachers implement the plan they created in the professional learning group within their individual classrooms. During this phase, the teacher must make note of those things that worked well and those things that presented some challenge, either for his or her students or for him- or herself. Because students who are ADHG are unique in their needs, teachers must also consider which strategies might be most effective to support student learning. Mullet and Rinn (2015) discussed specific strategies that teachers can use with twice-exceptional students that will help to mitigate their challenges associated with ADHD, while allowing them to explore their creativity. One strategy is to model how to break larger, more challenging tasks into manageable chunks. As students learn to successfully complete these subtasks, their self-efficacy will grow, and they will feel more confident in their ability to take on large-scale projects in the future (Hayes, 2016). For instance, a teacher can take a large project that other students are expected to complete in a self-paced manner and break it into smaller chunks with several specific due dates. Other strategies include providing students with examples of how they can begin to self-monitor their progress through the use of timers, checklists, and graphic and/or technology-based organizers. During the implementation step, teachers should provide support through positive reinforcement as students become more self-aware and competent in the use of these strategies, ultimately allowing students to have a deeper sense of independence (Mullet & Rinn, 2015).

Additionally, because students who are ADHG tend to have a reverse hierarchy of learning, focused on the "big picture" as opposed to discrete skills, these students should be provided with authentic learning experiences that "emphasize applied content knowledge over the process of acquisition of knowledge" (Fugate, 2018, p. 198). This type of authentic learning can be accomplished through project-based learning, which can yield a variety of interest-based student products (e.g., cartoons, blogs, videos). These products can then be revised for different audiences, thereby deepening and broadening the learning experience (Fugate, 2018; Fugate et al., 2013).

A final example can be found in Hayes's (2016) "Teaching 2e Children." Much like typical students, students who are ADHG thrive when engaging in authentic learning experiences. However, for these experiences to be successful for students who are ADHG, Hayes offered a process for teachers to consider (see Table 4.1). First, it is important to keep in mind the intended outcome—the necessary demonstration of learning. In order to achieve this first step, teachers need to identify the specific cognitive skills (e.g., communication through written expression), affective skills (e.g., presentation skills), and metacognitive skills (e.g., reflections that address the What? So What? Now What? writing cycle) that they want students to develop. Additionally, teachers can create a list of mastery areas (e.g., cause-and-effect relationships). Once this is complete, teachers should prompt students with specific resources, topics, or questions. Teachers who are working with students who are ADHG should determine an allowable amount of time for project completion. Teachers must understand that these students often require extended "think time" to fully develop their ideas. Furthermore, they need to be allowed the freedom, or sometimes given a built-in structure, to take breaks. Taking time for reflection allows for synectic, or metaphoric, thinking (Gordon, 1981). This synectic thinking takes place when thinkers combine the familiar with the strange to solve a problem or gain

Table 4.1

Process for Authentic Learning Engagement

Demonstration of understanding	Cognitive skills, affective skills, metacognitive skills
Create a list of mastery areas	Specific questions to answer, topics to explore, online resources
Give plenty of time	Extended thinking time to develop ideas
Build in breaks	Take time for reflection
Focus on process over product through project-based learning	Use project exemplars to spark creativity
	Give students opportunities to engage with peers or combine group and individual work
	Time management through checklists
	Presentation opportunities

Note. Adapted from Hayes, 2016.

new insights. Students who are ADHG may be especially appreciative of the opportunity to connect vast ideas together into one project. To this end, when teachers present project-based learning experiences to students who are ADHG, they must clearly convey that the objective is the means to the end, not merely the end in itself. This focus on process over product dispels the myth of creativity as a fixed trait, encouraging a growth mindset perspective by giving students the freedom to demonstrate their learning based upon individualized pacing, crosscurricular connections, and areas of interest.

The prospect of choosing individualized learning processes and products may be new to learners who are ADHG. Therefore, Hayes (2016) suggested providing them with project exemplars to spark their creativity (e.g., find and solve a community problem, design and develop a park with all elements based on the Fibonacci sequence). Additionally, students require occasions to engage with peers in partners, groups, or combinations of individual and joint activities (Hayes, 2016). To promote organization and time management, teach students to create self-checklists. These lists need to include breaking the project into smaller parts and periodic check-in times to obtain teacher support as needed. This will help students learn to self-regulate and stay on task while building their self-efficacy. Additionally, presentation opportunities are important to strengthen these skills as well as to allow students to share and learn from their classmates.

Analyze and Adjust

Finally, once teachers have implemented their plans, the learning teams need to come together to collaboratively analyze student work products and to reflect upon their implications of this analysis to identify areas where they may need to adjust and modify their plan moving forward (Southwest Educational Development Laboratory, 2008). During analysis, teachers should revisit the expectations outlined for the student work that they are going to review and assess, as well as discuss evidence of student strengths, areas in which students may still be struggling, and how teachers can then modify their approach in a way that leverages those identified strengths as they continue to address challenge areas. This is also a time for the team to collaboratively reflect on their experience throughout this process, both individually and as a group. This will allow teachers to identify common and disparate experiences in the teaching process. Recognition of these experiences will then inform teachers' decision making as teachers identify areas in which adjustments to instructional strategies can be made in the future to ensure further student success.

New Insights

In recent years, the data-driven movement in education has tied teacher assessment and compensation to student achievement. Although the use of data to inform educational practice is a positive step, the connection to the livelihood of educators has had an unintended effect—the loss of creativity in the classroom. Despite, or perhaps because of, this high-stakes push to drive specific content into the minds of students, it is imperative to incorporate creative endeavors into daily lessons. Historically, creative activities were merely culminating projects conducted, or even earned, only after content had been mastered. Such "tacked-on" methods of student assessment are no longer effective in addressing the caliber of creative thinking that students are expected to possess upon high school graduation. With the current need for schools to graduate creative thinkers, and, thus, for teachers to create paced, structured, yet open-ended creative opportunities for students who are ADHG, educators ought to seek chances to work together in professional learning communities that break the bounds of traditional professional development models.

In order for teachers to reflect on their teaching strategies and seek professional learning for effective methods in unlocking and simultaneously harnessing creativity within students who are ADHG (Fugate, 2018; Fugate

& Gentry, 2016), they must first consider the pathway they desire to guide these students. If teachers desire deliberate practices, perhaps they should seek Weisberg's (2010) CHOICES framework. If they desire goal-oriented creativity, they should check out Drapeau (2014). Additionally, educators need clear guidance in how to break large, challenging tasks into organized pieces (Mullet & Rinn, 2015).

Conclusion

Educators must incorporate professional learning in order to study, select, plan, implement, analyze, and adjust their classroom environments to meet the needs of students who are ADHG. Because these students tend to have a reverse hierarchy of learning, focused on the "big picture" as opposed to discrete skills, these students should be provided with authentic learning experiences that "emphasize applied content knowledge over the process of acquisition of knowledge" (Fugate, 2018, p. 198). Through study, educators can increase their efficacy to recognize gifted potential in students with ADHD, which can mitigate some of the unique academic challenges these students sometimes face.

Further, educators ought to select research-based resources before they create a plan to foster creativity in the classroom. When creativity is called a fixed trait, it hinders students and teachers from implementing creative content, processes, and products across disciplines. To mitigate these fixed mindsets, educators ought to implement plans that both validate creativity as an outpouring of failure and success, as well as encourage specific student-centered development (Beghetto, 2013; Beghetto & Dilley, 2016; Kamins & Dweck, 1999). An effective method when working with students who are ADHG is focusing on generating original, culturally relevant, and task-appropriate products (Beghetto, 2013; Starko, 2014).

Because White and Shah (2011) found that students with ADHD report higher levels of creative achievement than students without ADHD, it is imperative to analyze and adjust the creative atmosphere in order to provide opportunities for these students to explore creative outlets through structured yet open-ended academic experiences. Students who are ADHG must be seen as gifted first; therefore, it is important for teachers to incorporate a variety of professional learning strategies that address and enhance students' strengths.

Resources

Baum, S. M., Schader, R. M., & Owen, S. V. (2017). *To be gifted and learning disabled: Strength-based strategies for helping twice-exceptional students with LD, ADHD, ASD, and more* (3rd ed.). Waco, TX: Prufrock Press.

Cash, R. M. (2017). *Advancing differentiation: Thinking and learning for the 21st century.* Minneapolis, MN: Free Spirit.

Drapeau, P. (2014). *Sparking student creativity: Practical ways to promote innovative thinking and problem solving.* Alexandria, VA: ASCD.

Gentry, M., Paul, K. A., McIntosh, J., Fugate, C. M., & Jen, E. (2014). *Total school cluster grouping: A comprehensive, research-based plan for raising student achievement and improving teacher practices* (2nd ed.). Waco, TX: Prufrock Press.

Heacox, D. (2009). *Making differentiation a habit: How to ensure success in academically diverse classrooms.* Minneapolis, MN: Free Spirit.

Kennedy, D. M., Banks, R. S., & Grandin, T. (2011). *Bright not broken: Gifted kids, ADHD, and autism.* San Francisco, CA: Jossey-Bass.

Reis, S. M., Renzulli, J. S., & Burns, D. E. (2016). *Curriculum compacting: A guide to differentiating curriculum and instruction through enrichment and acceleration* (2nd ed.). Waco, TX: Prufrock Press..

Trail, B. A. (2010). *Twice-exceptional gifted children: Understanding, teaching, and counseling gifted students.* Waco, TX: Prufrock Press.

Zentall, S. S. (2006). *ADHD and education: Foundations, characteristics, methods, and collaboration.* Upper Saddle River, NJ: Pearson.

References

Abraham, A., Windmann, S., Siefen, R., Daum, I., & Güntükün, O. (2006). Creative thinking in adolescents with attention deficit hyperactivity disorder (ADHD). *Child Neuropsychology, 12,* 111–123.

Assouline, S., Colangelo, N., VanTassel-Baska, J., & Lupkowski-Shoplik, A. (Eds.). (2015). *A nation empowered: Evidence trumps the excuses that hold back America's brightest students* (Vol. 2). Iowa City: University of Iowa, The Connie Belin & Jacqueline N. Blank International Center for Gifted Education and Talent Development.

Assouline, S. G., Foley Nicpon, M., & Huber, D. H. (2006). The impact of vulnerabilities and strengths on the academic experiences of twice-exceptional students: A message to school counselors. *Professional School Counseling, 10,* 14–24.

Batey, M., & Furnham, A. (2006). Creativity, intelligence, and personality: A critical review of the scattered literature. *Genetic, Social, and General Psychology Monographs, 132,* 355–429. doi:10.3200/MONO.132.4.355-430

Baum, S. M., Cooper, C. R., & Neu, T. W. (2001). Dual differentiation: An approach for meeting the curricular needs of gifted students with learning disabilities. *Psychology in the Schools, 38,* 477–490.

Baum, S. M., & Olenchak, F. R. (2002). The alphabet children: GT, ADHD, and more. *Exceptionality, 10,* 77–91.

Baum, S. M., Olenchak, F. R., & Owen, S. V. (1998). Gifted students with attention deficits: Fact and/or fiction? Or, can we see the forest for the trees? *Gifted Child Quarterly, 42,* 96–104.

Baum, S., & Owen, S. (1988). High ability/learning disabled students: How are they different? *Gifted Child Quarterly, 32,* 226–230.

Becker, G. (2000). The association of creativity and psychopathology: Its cultural-historical origins. *Creativity Research Journal, 13,* 45–53.

Beghetto, R. A. (2013). *Killing ideas softly? The promise and perils of creativity in the classroom.* Charlotte, NC: Information Age.

Beghetto, R. A., & Dilley, A. E. (2016). Creative aspirations or pipe dreams? Toward understanding creative mortification in children and adolescents. *New Directions for Child and Adolescent Development, 151,* 79–89.

Carson, S. H. (2011). Creativity and psychopathology: A shared vulnerability model. *Canadian Journal of Psychiatry, 56,* 144–153.

Carson, S. H., Peterson, J. B., & Higgins, D. M. (2003). Decreased latent inhibition is associated with increased creative achievement in high-functioning individuals. *Journal of Personality and Social Psychology, 85,* 499–506.

Castellanos, X. (2000, November). *ADHD or gifted: Is it either/or?* Paper presented at the annual meeting of the National Association for Gifted Children, Atlanta, GA.

Cramond, B. (1994). Attention-deficit hyperactivity disorder and creativity—what is the connection? *Journal of Creative Behavior, 28,* 193–210.

Davis, G. A. (2004). *Creativity is forever* (5th ed.). Dubuque, IA: Kendall Hunt.

Davis, G. A., Rimm, S. B., & Siegle, D. (2018). *Education of the gifted and talented* (7th ed.). Upper Saddle River, NJ: Pearson Education.

Donohue, Z., VanTassell, M. A., & Patterson, L. (1996). *Research in the classroom: Talk, texts, and inquiry.* Newark, DE: International Reading Association.

Drapeau, P. (2014). *Sparking student creativity: Practical ways to promote innovative thinking and problem solving.* Alexandria, VA: ASCD.

Fugate, C. M. (2018). Attention divergent hyperactive giftedness: Taking the deficiency and disorder out of the gifted/ADHD label. In S. B. Kaufman (Ed.), *Twice exceptional: Supporting and educating bright and creative students with learning difficulties* (pp. 191–200). New York, NY: Oxford University Press.

Fugate, C. M., & Gentry, M. (2016). Understanding adolescent gifted girls with ADHD: Motivated and achieving. *High Ability Studies, 27,* 83–109.

Fugate, C. M., Zentall, S. S., & Gentry, M. (2013). Creativity and working memory in gifted students with and without characteristics of attention deficit hyperactive disorder: Lifting the mask. *Gifted Child Quarterly, 57,* 234–236.

Gordon, W. J. J. (1981). *The new art of the possible: The basic course in synectics.* Cambridge, MA: Porpoise Books.

Guilford, J. P. (1967). *The nature of human intelligence.* New York, NY: McGraw-Hill.

Hayes, M. (2016, September/October). Teaching 2e children. *2e Newsletter,* 3–6.

Hughes, C. E. (2011). Twice-exceptional children: Twice the challenges, twice the joys. In J. A. Castellano & A. D. Fraizer (Eds.), *Special populations in gifted education: Understanding our most able students from diverse backgrounds* (pp. 153–173). Waco, TX: Prufrock Press.

Kamins, M. L., & Dweck, C. S. (1999). Person versus process praise and criticism: Implications for contingent self-worth coping. *Developmental Psychology, 35,* 835–847.

Kaplan, B. J., Crawford, S. G., Dewey, D. M., & Fisher, G. C. (2000). The IQs of children with ADHD are normally distributed. *Journal of Learning Disabilities, 33,* 425–432.

Kozbelt, A., Beghetto, R. A., & Runco, M. A. (2010). Theories of creativity. In R. J. Sternberg (Ed.), *The Cambridge handbook of creativity* (pp. 20–47). New York, NY: Cambridge University Press.

Kuester, D. A., & Zentall, S. S. (2011). Social interaction rules in cooperative learning groups for students at risk for ADHD. *Journal of Experimental Education, 80,* 69–95.

Lawrence, V., Houghton, S., Tannock, R., Douglas, G., Durkin, K., & Whiting, K. (2002). ADHD outside the laboratory: Boys' executive function performance on tasks in videogame play and on a visit to the zoo. *Journal of Abnormal Child Psychology, 30,* 447–462.

Lewis, T. (2009). Creativity in technology education: Providing children with glimpses of their inventive potential. *International Journal of Technology and Design Education, 19,* 255–268.

Moon, S. (2002). Gifted children with attention deficit/hyperactivity disorder. In M. Neihart, S. Reis, N. Robinson, & S. Moon (Eds.), *The social and emotional development of gifted children: What do we know?* (pp. 193–204). Waco, TX: Prufrock Press.

Moon, S. M., & Reis, S. M. (2004). Acceleration and twice-exceptional students. In N. Colangelo, S. G. Assouline, & M. U. M. Gross (Eds.), *A nation deceived: How schools hold back America's brightest students* (Vol. 1, pp. 109–119). Iowa City: The University of Iowa, The Connie Belin & Jacqueline N. Blank International Center for Gifted Education and Talent Development.

Mullet, D. R., & Rinn, A. N. (2015). Giftedness and ADHD: Identification, misdiagnosis, and dual diagnosis. *Roeper Review, 37,* 195–207.

Nelson, J. M., Rinn, A. N., & Hartnett, D. N. (2006) The possibility of misdiagnosis of giftedness and ADHD still exists: A response to Mika. *Roeper Review, 28,* 243–248.

Nielsen, M. E. (2002). Gifted students with learning disabilities: Recommendations for identification and programming. *Exceptionality, 10,* 93–111.

Olenchak, F. R., & Reis, S. M. (2002). Gifted children with learning disabilities. In M. Neihart, S. M. Reis, N. M. Robinson, & S. M. Moon (Eds.), *The social and emotional development of gifted children: What do we know?* (pp. 188–192). Waco, TX: Prufrock Press.

Olthouse, J. M., & Sauder, A. E. (2016). Purpose and process in exemplary teen writings. *Journal for the Education of the Gifted, 39,* 171–194.

Plucker, J. A., Beghetto, R. A., & Dow, G. T. (2004). Why isn't creativity more important to educational psychologists? Potentials, pitfalls, and future directions in creativity research. *Educational Psychologist, 59,* 83–96.

Proudfoot, D., Kay, A. C., & Koval, C. Z. (2015). A gender bias in the attribution of creativity: Archival and experimental evidence for the perceived association between masculinity and creative thinking. *Psychological Science, 11,* 1751–1761.

Renzulli, J. S. (1999). What is this thing called giftedness, and how do we develop it? A twenty-five-year perspective. *Journal for the Education of the Gifted, 23,* 3–54.

Russ, S. W. (1998). Play, creativity, and adaptive functioning: Implications for play interventions. *Journal of Clinical Child Psychology, 27,* 469–480.

Schultz, S. M. (2012). Twice-exceptional students enrolled in advanced placement classes. *Gifted Child Quarterly, 56,* 119–133.

Shaw, G. A., & Brown, G. (1999). Arousal, time estimation, and time use in attention-disordered children. *Developmental Neuropsychology, 16,* 227–242.

Silverman, L. K. (2002). *Upside-down brilliance: The visual-spatial learner.* Denver, CO: DeLeon.

Simonton, D. K. (2010). So you want to become a creative genius? You must be crazy! In D. H. Cropley, A. J. Cropley, J. C. Kaufman, & M. A. Runco (Eds.), *The dark side of creativity* (pp. 218–234). New York, NY: Cambridge University Press.

Southwest Educational Development Laboratory. (2008). *The professional teaching and learning cycle: Introduction* (2nd ed.). Austin, TX: Author.

Starko, A. J. (2014). *Creativity in the classroom: Schools of curious delight.* New York, NY: Routledge.

Sternberg, R. J. (1999). *Handbook of creativity.* Cambridge, England: Cambridge University Press.

Tierney, P., Farmer, S. M., & Graen, G. B. (1999). An examination of leadership and employee creativity: The relevance of traits and relationships. *Personnel Psychology, 52,* 591–620.

Torrance, E. P. (1972). Career patterns and peak creative achievements of creative high school students twelve years later. *Gifted Child Quarterly, 16,* 75–88.

Torrance, E. P. (1981). Predicting the creativity of elementary school children (1958–1980)—and the teacher who "made a difference". *Gifted Child Quarterly, 25,* 55–62.

Weisberg, R. (2010). The study of creativity: From genius to cognitive science. *International Journal of Cultural Policy, 16,* 235–253.

White, H. A., & Shah, P. (2006). Uninhibited imaginations: Creativity in adults with attention-deficit/hyperactivity disorder. *Personality and Individual Differences, 40,* 1121–1131.

White, H. A., & Shah, P. (2011). Creative style and achievement in adults with attention-deficit/hyperactivity disorder. *Personality and Individual Differences, 50,* 673–677.

White, H. A., & Shah, P. (2016). Scope of semantic activation and innovative thinking in college students with ADHD. *Creativity Research Journal, 28,* 275–282.

Zentall, S. S. (1988). Production deficiencies in elicited language but not in the spontaneous verbalizations of hyperactive children. *Journal of Abnormal Child Psychology, 16,* 657–673.

Zentall, S. S. (2006). *ADHD and education: Foundations, characteristics, methods, and collaboration.* Upper Saddle River, NJ: Pearson Education.

Zentall, S. S., Moon, S., Hall, A. M., & Grskovic, J. (2001). Learning and motivational characteristics of boys with AD/HD and/or giftedness. *Exceptional Children, 67,* 499–519.

CHAPTER 5

Professional Learning Strategies for Teachers of Underachieving Gifted Students

Jennifer Ritchotte, Chin-Wen Lee, and Amy Graefe

Introduction

Underachieving gifted students often frustrate and confuse their teachers. If the "gifted" label implies advanced aptitude and achievement, then how can a student be gifted when her academic performance is average or even poor when compared to her gifted peers? Although aptitude is certainly an important criterion in determining giftedness, gifted students' actual performance in school may fluctuate for a variety of reasons, making aptitude a less reliable indicator of giftedness. Reis and McCoach (2000) defined underachievement as the discrepancy between potential and actual performance that persists over time and is not a direct result of a learning disability. Potential is most often determined by cognitive ability tests, while actual performance, or achievement, refers to class grades. Understanding why gifted students underachieve and how to prevent this pattern of behavior requires sustained professional learning that is relevant to teachers and can be easily applied to their current classroom situations.

Factors Contributing to Underachievement

Underachieving behaviors are often noticed for the first time when students are in middle school (Peterson, 2001; Peterson & Colangelo, 1996; Ritchotte, Matthews, & Flowers, 2014). The onset of underachievement at this level may be attributed to curriculum that is perceived by gifted students as unchallenging or boring. Unfortunately, this perception has the potential to lead to academic underachievement of students who decide not to invest the time and effort into assignments they feel hold no value and serve no purpose for them. Kanevsky and Keighley (2003) referred to this as the honor of underachievement.

Conversely, gifted students may also underachieve when they are faced with new academic challenges during the secondary years of schooling. Gifted students are often not taught how to self-regulate during elementary school. This presents an issue because many gifted students progress effortlessly through elementary school and even middle school without needing to know how to selectively focus, inhibit impulsive actions, ignore distractions, study, and purposefully attend to tasks—even when they do not feel like it. They may choose the path of least resistance and disengage from learning that requires these skills. Further, having never learned how to persevere through challenge, a fear of no longer being gifted if effort is required, or a belief that they do not possess the skills necessary to successfully complete a difficult task, may also cause gifted students to underachieve (Ritchotte et al., 2014).

Siegle and McCoach (2005) developed a model that addresses why gifted students underachieve. Their Achievement-Orientation Model (AOM) suggests that gifted students who are achieving in school not only have the aptitude to perform at high academic levels, but also value what they are being asked to do by teachers (i.e., task meaningfulness), feel supported in those efforts (i.e., environmental perception), and believe that they have the capability of competently completing assignments and activities (i.e., self-efficacy; see Figure 5.1). As a result, gifted students self-regulate to perform academic tasks, engage in these tasks, and achieve at levels commensurate with their ability. However, the AOM also suggests that even when gifted students have the aptitude necessary to perform at high levels academically, if their self-perceptions of task meaningfulness, environmental perceptions, or self-efficacy are low, motivation will be negatively impacted, and they will not self-regulate, which will ultimately lead to disengagement and, often, underachievement (Ritchotte et al., 2014).

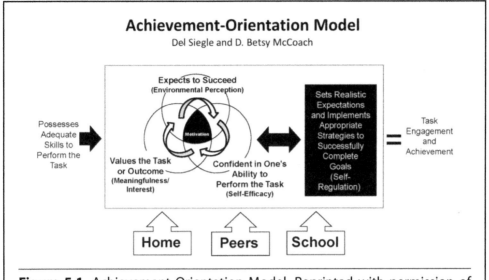

Figure 5.1. Achievement-Orientation Model. Reprinted with permission of the author.

Reversal of Underachievement

Effective interventions to help reverse the trend of underachievement in gifted students have been inconsistent and inconclusive (McCoach & Siegle, 2003). The complex nature of underachievement makes it impossible to identify one solution that will address the myriad reasons why gifted students underachieve. In fact, reversing the underachievement pattern of gifted students has often led to unsuccessful attempts because many "researchers [have] failed to understand the individual sufficiently and [have] failed to investigate systematically all aspects of the problem" (Emerick, 1992, p. 140).

Although there is no one-size-fits-all solution appropriate for every gifted student who is underachieving (Baum, Renzulli, & Hébert, 1995), there have been examples of successful interventions that have positively impacted the pattern of underachievement for some gifted students. For example, The Cupertino Program (Whitmore, 1986) was designed specifically for highly gifted students who were underachieving. This self-contained therapeutic program focused on teachers developing the social and academic skills of gifted students with high IQs who were scoring at least one grade level below expected on academic assessments. These students demonstrated apathy toward schoolwork and had not responded well to others' efforts to motivate them to achieve. However, by focusing on self-acceptance, designing meaningful learning activities, and providing opportunities for these students to experience and embrace success, educators helped the majority of the students in the Cupertino Program reverse their underachievement. Many went on to become high achievers and to participate in gifted education programs.

Most recently, the Achievement-Orientation Model has been used as a theoretical foundation for developing interventions to address gifted students' underachievement (see Figure 5.1). Rubenstein, Siegle, Reis, McCoach, and Burton (2012) reported on two separate studies that utilized interventions based on the AOM to reverse underachievement. In the first study, Rubenstein et al. implemented an intervention entitled Project ATLAS (Autonomous Thinkers Learning as Scholars) with middle school gifted underachievers. This intervention consisted of students' assessment of their short- and long-term learning goals and individualized instruction provided by the researchers on how to propose alternative class assignments to teachers that would increase student engagement in class while still meeting the learning objectives of the original assignments. In the second study, middle school gifted underachievers were identified and then given an intervention that specifically addressed the component of the Achievement-Orientation Model in which they demonstrated a deficit. Students' grades in reading and mathematics, on average, increased by a full letter grade throughout the course of the study.

Although there is growing recognition in the field of gifted education regarding the causes and implications of underachievement for gifted students, consistently reversing that pattern of underachievement has proven more difficult. It seems that, just as the reasons for underachievement vary for gifted students, the solutions also vary. Researchers have found interventions that are successful with some gifted students; however, these same interventions are often unsuccessful with other gifted students. Additionally, classroom teachers often lack knowledge about both characteristics and causes of underachievement in gifted students, as well as potential strategies for mitigating underachievement. Professional learning, therefore, must provide a comprehensive examination of gifted underachievement.

Overview/Need

The myth that *giftedness* and *high achievement* are synonymous terms is still pervasive in many schools. When gifted students perform below teachers' expectations, they risk being "ungifted" (Ritchotte, 2015). Ungifting happens when teachers decide gifted students no longer require differentiated programming options because they are underachieving. This phenomenon is most prominent in middle school, in part, because reading and mathematics achievement are often the focus of gifted programming options at this level (Callahan, Moon, & Oh, 2013a, 2013b). Gifted students who cannot keep up with their peers may be encouraged by teachers to take regular reading and math classes instead. Too often, during these critical years in gifted students' education, there is little to no focus on their psychosocial needs (Ritchotte, Suhr, Alfurayh, & Graefe, 2016). In this scenario, underachievement is seen as a justification to weed these students out of gifted classes rather than an opportunity to provide the support they need (Ritchotte & Graefe, 2017).

Professional learning on gifted underachievement can provide valuable insights into why students underachieve and help teachers reframe how they see these students, as well as gifted students in general. To be most effective, evidence-based professional learning activities must be employed. Research has consistently demonstrated that the professional learning activities with the most positive impact on educators' and students' growth have the following features in common: (a) sustained duration, (b) content focus, and (c) active learning (Darling-Hammond, Hyler, & Gardner, 2017). These components are defined here and then applied specifically to professional learning on the topic of gifted underachievement.

- **Sustained/intensive duration:** There is adequate time for teachers to "learn, practice, implement, and reflect upon new strategies that facilitate changes in their practice" (Darling-Hammond et al., 2017, p. vi). Gifted and general education teachers are constantly asked to do more with less. Ongoing professional learning sessions may represent additional work if presented in the wrong manner. Although a one-shot, one-hour-long professional development presentation on underachievement may garner more buy-in from teachers, it is less likely to result in meaningful change for teachers and students (Desimone, 2009). With that said, it may be unreasonable for teachers to commit to professional learning on underachievement throughout an entire school year. Therefore, a minimum of four to six intensive professional learning sessions (10 or more hours total; Dixon, Yssel, McConnell, & Hardin, 2014) that are clustered closely together throughout a month or two may yield more teacher buy-in and produce more meaningful outcomes in the long term.

- **Content focus:** In most cases, this type of professional learning is aligned with school and district priorities that aim to improve student achievement in literacy, science, or mathematics, and is geared toward teachers who have opportunities to try new content-specific strategies in their classrooms. With the ever-present focus of most school districts on raising student achievement, administrators and teachers are more likely to be supportive of professional learning on underachievement if the potential result is higher levels of academic achievement and growth.
- **Active learning:** Different than presentations designed for a wide variety of participants, active professional learning is highly contextualized, thereby striving to meet the individualized needs of adult learners. Teachers participating in active learning choose learning opportunities based on their classroom needs and use these authentic experiences to construct new, personal learning. Professional learning on underachievement is more likely to be successful if teachers are actively engaged and given ample opportunities to apply new learning to the realities of their classrooms. According to Darling-Hammond et al. (2017), active learning is an umbrella term for "collaboration, coaching, feedback, and reflection and the use of models and modeling" (p. 7).
    - **Collaboration:** Collaboration may take place in the form of one-on-one interaction, in small groups, or through collaborative projects with colleagues in school or professionals outside the school setting. Collaboration is a necessary component of professional learning on underachievement. Most teachers learn best when they can share ideas with one another. Given the complex nature of underachievement, providing teachers with opportunities to problem solve together is crucial (Ritchotte, Rubenstein, & Murry, 2015).
    - **Modeling:** Teachers learn new strategies and make sense of their learning from modeling, which may take the form of (a) case studies of underachieving gifted students, (b) lesson and unit plans that can be easily adapted to meet the needs of underachieving gifted students, and (c) observations of peers who have found success with specific strategies.
    - **Coaching and expert support:** Specially trained master teachers, instructional leaders, researchers, or university faculty can be wonderful sources of coaching and expert

support. They may be willing to not only share their expertise on gifted underachievement, but also coach teachers on how to address underachievement in their unique classroom situations.
- **Feedback and reflection:** Effective professional learning has built-in time for teachers to receive feedback and reflect on their practices. This is an important component of professional learning on underachievement, as this topic often leads to teacher frustration. Constructive feedback and time to openly reflect mitigates frustration by validating teachers and reinforcing the positive steps they are taking toward understanding and supporting the underachieving gifted students.

In order to obtain the most positive outcomes from professional learning for both educators and students, it is also necessary to determine what teachers already know about the various aspects of gifted underachievement and even giftedness in general. A sample needs assessment is provided in Appendix 5.1 at the end of this chapter. This will help to determine what foundational knowledge in gifted education and gifted underachievement, more specifically, is needed. Just as teachers compact gifted students' learning to ensure they are not having to relearn what they have already mastered, this type of professional learning compacting serves the same purpose. Once needs are determined, teachers are then exposed to learning strategies that incorporate the effective components of professional learning.

Professional Learning Strategies

Gifted and general education professionals are likely to have differing levels of knowledge about gifted underachievement. For many general education teachers, gifted underachievement may seem paradoxical (Hoover-Schultz, 2005). A limited understanding of what giftedness entails is likely to perpetuate misconceptions when discussing gifted underachievement during professional learning activities. Therefore, general education teach-

ers will need fundamental knowledge about gifted education before tackling the issue of underachievement. Suggested topics include:
- defining and identifying giftedness,
- giftedness beyond high achievement,
- what it means to "ungift" a gifted child and potential ramifications,
- common myths about giftedness,
- social-emotional issues and needs of gifted learners,
- defining and identifying gifted underachievement,
- characteristics of underachieving gifted learners,
- common reasons gifted students underachieve,
- strategies to prevent gifted underachievement,
- individualized strategies to reverse gifted underachievement, and
- being open to collaboration with other stakeholders in the underachieving student's life.

Gifted education teachers, depending on the amount of graduate coursework and prior professional development on giftedness they have had, may also need professional learning on this topic (National Association for Gifted Children, 2015). A needs assessment may be given to teachers prior to professional learning to ascertain their comfort level with certain requisite gifted education topics needed in order to meaningfully participate in professional learning activities on gifted underachievement. If no additional knowledge about gifted education is needed, teachers can begin their learning about underachievement with the following topics:
- defining and identifying gifted underachievement,
- characteristics of underachieving gifted learners,
- underlying factors that influence underachieving behaviors,
- underachievement theories (e.g., AOM),
- cognitive and affective needs of underachieving gifted learners,
- strategies to prevent gifted underachievement,
- individualized strategies to reverse gifted underachievement, and
- how to collaborate with other stakeholders in the underachieving students' life.

Table 5.1 has suggested activities for professional learning on underachievement that utilize many of the features of effective professional learning. These activities can be easily adapted to address the topics listed previously. Further, many of the suggested topics can also be embedded into these activities through mini-lessons and group discussion.

Table 5.1
Professional Learning Activity Examples

Teacher-Led Activities	Overview	Sustained Duration	Content Focus	Active Learning				Embedded Topics (Through Mini-Lessons, Discussion, etc.)	Activity Resources	Outcomes
				Collaboration	Models/Modeling	Coaching and Expert Support	Feedback and Reflection			
Student voices	Teachers share anecdotes from underachieving gifted students. These can be current or past students. Quotes from research and practitioner articles can also be used. Discuss the following: What are our underachieving students trying to tell us? What do they need in order to be successful? Teachers reflect on (new) strategies that can facilitate long-term changes in their professional practice. For example, they can practice developing a complete picture of a child and his or her needs (through school record review, informal observations of the child and interviews with the child, past teachers, and parents) before jumping to conclusions and assuming the child must not be gifted if he or she is underachieving in school.	x		x				Defining and identifying gifted underachievement Characteristics of underachieving gifted learners Cognitive and affective needs of underachieving gifted learners Underlying factors that influence underachieving behaviors	Achievement-Orientation Model (see p. 91). Based on this model, where are teachers seeing deficits in individual students? Kanevsky & Keighley, 2003 Reis & McCoach, 2000 Rimm, 2008 Ritchotte, 2015 Siegle, 2012	**Prevention:** To learn from our students in order to proactively mitigate the underlying causes of underachievement. **Intervention:** To meet the individualized learning needs of students who are underachieving.

Underachieving Gifted Students 97

Table 5.1, continued.

Teacher-Led Activities	Overview	Active Learning						Embedded Topics (Through Mini-Lessons, Discussion, etc.)	Activity Resources	Outcomes
		Sustained Duration	Content Focus	Collaboration	Models/Modeling	Coaching and Expert Support	Feedback and Reflection			
Lesson study	Form a lesson/unit plan study group. Teachers work together to adapt lessons to ensure they are engaging for students. They may approach this activity with specific, underachieving gifted students in mind and support each other in modifying these lessons to address those students' individualized needs. After implementing modified lessons, the study group will meet again to discuss the results of their implementation.	x	x	x			x	Strategies to prevent gifted underachievement Individualized strategies to reverse gifted underachievement	CAST (http://www.cast.org) has fantastic resources for incorporating Universal Design for Learning principles into instruction. One of these principles is Providing Multiple Means of Engagement. Guidelines are presented on the site and can easily be embedded into teachers' lesson plans to support underachieving gifted students' engagement in learning.	**Prevention:** To engage students by offering relevant learning experiences. **Intervention:** To meet the individualized learning needs of students who are underachieving.

Table 5.1, continued.

Teacher-Led Activities	Overview	Active Learning						Embedded Topics (Through Mini-Lessons, Discussion, etc.)	Activity Resources	Outcomes
		Sustained Duration	Content Focus	Collaboration	Models/Modeling	Coaching and Expert Support	Feedback and Reflection			
Student investigation	Teachers are given case studies of underachieving gifted students and artifacts that can be used to determine underlying causes of underachieving behaviors (e.g., school records, teacher observation data, parent interviews, student work samples). Individually, in pairs, or in small groups, they attempt to determine why the student is underachieving and brainstorm individualized strategies that address this issue. They identify the steps they took to accomplish this task and reflect on how they can continue to conduct student investigations in the future. To make this more sustainable, if their school already has a prevention team in place, they might consider becoming a member of this team, training members of the team on these steps, or simply become more active in referring underachieving gifted students for extra support. If a prevention team does not exist, they may decide to approach the administration about starting one for their grade level.	x	x	x	x	x	x	Underlying factors that influence underachieving behaviors Strategies to prevent gifted underachievement Individualized strategies to reverse gifted underachievement	Delisle, 2018 Ritchotte, Rubenstein, & Murry, 2015	**Prevention:** To monitor the progress of all students.

Table 5.1, continued.

| Teacher-Led Activities | Overview | Active Learning ||||| Embedded Topics (Through Mini-Lessons, Discussion, etc.) | Activity Resources | Outcomes |
		Sustained Duration	Content Focus	Collaboration	Models/Modeling	Coaching and Expert Support	Feedback and Reflection			
Action plan	Teachers bring in their own cases of underachieving students and artifacts from their own classrooms. They support each other in developing a collaborative action plan that addresses the source of their students' underachievement and involves key people in the students' lives (e.g., counselor, parent, other teachers).	x		x			x	Underlying factors that influence underachieving behaviors Individualized strategies to reverse gifted underachievement How to collaborate with other stakeholders in the underachieving student's life	Create an action plan template. This should include the following components: A primary goal for the collaboration; personal motivation for engaging in the collaboration; action steps; timeframe for completion; resources/supports needed; progress monitoring (several check-in points need to be established to ensure each team member is doing his/her part and to determine if the goal needs to be revised); evaluation (was the goal attained?); and reflection of the collaborative process. Ritchotte, Zaghlawan, & Lee, 2017	**Intervention:** To provide individualized support to students. Create an action plan, implement it, examine the results, create a new action plan, and begin a new cycle of investigation.

The majority of the activities presented in Table 5.1 are designed for small teams of educators. However, these activities may also be implemented through one-on-one interactions with a knowledgeable facilitator and an educator who is eager to engage in professional learning on the topic of gifted underachievement. In this case, the facilitator would act as more of a mentor or coach during the professional learning activities. Ideally, professional learning activities should be led by an educator who is knowledgeable not only about gifted education in general, but also gifted underachievement, specifically. Given the planning and time commitment involved in facilitating professional learning, two educators (e.g., teachers, administrators, support staff) may choose to cofacilitate professional learning activities. Cofacilitation provides an opportunity for more one-on-one support during professional learning activities, as well as the opportunity for participants to hear varied perspectives from knowledgeable facilitators.

Implications/New Insights

The most effective professional learning consists of activities that are intensive in nature or extended over time, are content-area focused, and foster active engagement. Teachers have opportunities to collaborate with other professionals, they learn from models and observations, and they grow through intensive coaching and expert support that involves continual feedback and reflection (Darling-Hammond et al., 2017). The latter is important given that gifted students who underachieve commonly report cognitive, behavioral, and affective disengagement from learning (Landis & Reschly, 2013). Professional learning facilitators, therefore, need to practice what they teach. A primary goal of professional learning on gifted underachievement needs to be meaningfully engaging teachers in the many facets of this complex topic. Specific implications focused on embedding these components into professional learning on gifted underachievement follow.

Sustained/Intensive Duration:
- **Early and Ongoing Opportunities:** As stated earlier, underachievement typically starts in middle school (although sometimes it can begin as early as elementary school; Hansen & Toso 2007; Ritchotte & Graefe, 2017). Because of this, it is important to have professional learning opportunities available for teachers prior to the onset of this student behavior. Professional learning on gifted

underachievement also needs to be recursive, in that these topics need to continue to be addressed in subsequent school years. This practice will help ensure that as new teachers join the school and new underachievement concerns arise, both teachers and students will have the support they need.

- **Support Team Approach:** Within the time constraints of the school year, providing sustained professional learning is difficult. Creating a small team that is responsible for putting professional learning systems in place can be very helpful in maintaining momentum. This structure allows for shared preparation of professional learning activities on gifted underachievement and for shared support of individual staff members as they work to implement the strategies. A team approach also makes it more feasible to implement multiple progress monitoring checkpoints throughout the year to gauge movement toward building- or district-level professional learning goals.
- **Flexible Implementation:** Different teachers have different needs when it comes to professional learning—even when that professional learning is focused on just one main topic, such as underachievement. Just as teachers are encouraged to design learning opportunities based on student needs, facilitators should design and modify goals for professional learning based on teacher needs. Professional learning goals should be developed based on the knowledge and experience of the participants, which may be identified through a needs assessment. However, adaptations may be needed due to changing circumstances, such as a teacher needing targeted support with a student she has identified as at-risk for underachievement (even though others in the professional learning group may not be at the point where they are ready to address that issue). It might also be necessary to change the length and/or duration of learning sessions based on situations that arise within the educational institution.

Content Focus:
- As teachers begin to learn about preventative and intervention strategies for gifted underachievement, they should have dedicated time and support to determine how to implement these strategies in specific content areas (e.g., math, science, language arts).
- Grouping teachers by content area and/or grade level can make professional learning activities more applicable and meaningful. In these groups, teachers would typically be working with similar con-

tent goals and objectives and could collaborate on designing relevant and appropriate student activities.
- There is also a benefit to having crosscurricular or multigrade discussions within professional learning sessions. Particularly beneficial are discussions about what other departments might have found beneficial in dealing with gifted underachievement concerns. Multiple teachers of the same student can also work collaboratively to plan preventative or intervention strategies based upon the professional learning.

Active Learning:
- Preventing and/or reversing gifted underachievement through appropriate academic challenge and social-emotional support requires a group effort (e.g., parents, teachers, counselors, administrators, community members). Discussion about individual students, including what is working, what is not working, and what else could be tried, allows teachers to benefit from the varied ideas and experiences of their colleagues. For the same reason, collaboration with other educational staff members (e.g., counselors, gifted education coordinators, administrators) can also be beneficial, as each person will bring expertise in a different area and be able to provide diverse perspectives.
- Offering to observe and coach a peer who is having difficulty supporting an underachieving gifted student is a great opportunity to extend professional learning throughout a school. First, prior to conducting an observation, an educator should informally interview the peer about the student in question and the peer's perceptions of the issue. Ensuring that feedback derived from the observation is constructive and nonjudgmental and to develop a goal for coaching support together is likely to yield the most positive outcomes for the peer and the student.
- Teachers sharing their experiences supporting underachieving gifted students with a larger audience can be empowering. With the information acquired from their professional learning experiences, teachers can have a larger impact on the educational community by disseminating this knowledge in many different ways. They may share newly acquired knowledge at local and state professional conferences. Additionally, they may publish newsletter articles or practitioner-friendly manuscripts with important tips for supporting gifted underachievers. Further, they may choose to design and implement workshops for relevant stakeholders outside of their

professional learning community on relevant gifted underachievement topics.

In general, professional learning on gifted underachievement should have a prevention focus. Too often, teachers wait to react, meaning they do not intervene on a student's behalf until they are presented with overt evidence of underachievement (Ritchotte, Zaghlawan, & Lee, 2017). Prevention, first and foremost, entails understanding why gifted students underachieve and how to make meaningful adaptations to our teaching practices in order to mitigate these factors. Although there will always be cases in which teachers have to intervene, especially if a student's underachievement started during a previous school year or comes on suddenly due to a specific school or home issue, professional learning that has a strong prevention focus is critical for proactively addressing gifted underachievement.

Summary

One of education's goals, regardless of whether a student achieves at high levels or not, is to provide all students with the opportunity to reach their full academic potential. Unfortunately, there is a general lack of understanding about gifted underachievement, leaving this population, all too often, to fend for themselves. Uninformed and misguided educators can negatively shape the educational trajectories of gifted students. In order to prevent stories of unfulfilled potential, informed and passionate teachers must be a voice for underachieving gifted students and be persistent about helping others to see why these students deserve understanding and support. Professional learning on gifted underachievement that is intensive, relevant, and actively engaging holds great promise for creating a school and classroom culture that values and supports the whole gifted child, even when he or she does not appear "gifted" on the surface.

Resources

National Association for Gifted Children. (n.d.). *Underachievement.* Retrieved from https://www.nagc.org/resources-publications/resources/achievement-keeping-your-child-challenged/underachievement

Siegle, D. (2012). *The underachieving gifted child: Recognizing, understanding, and reversing underachievement.* Waco, TX: Prufrock Press.

References

Baum, S. M., Renzulli, J. S., & Hébert, T. P. (1995). Reversing underachievement: Creative productivity as a systematic intervention. *Gifted Child Quarterly, 39,* 224–235.

Callahan, C. M., Moon, T. R., & Oh, S. (2013a). *Status of elementary gifted programs.* Charlottesville: University of Virginia, National Research Center on the Gifted and Talented.

Callahan, C. M., Moon, T. R., & Oh, S. (2013b). *Status of middle school gifted programs.* Charlottesville: University of Virginia, National Research Center on the Gifted and Talented.

Darling-Hammond, L., Hyler, M. E., & Gardner, M. (2017). *Effective teacher professional development.* Palo Alto, CA: Learning Policy Institute.

Delisle, J. (2018). *Doing poorly on purpose: Strategies to reverse underachievement and respect student dignity.* Minneapolis, MN: Free Spirit.

Desimone, L. M. (2009). Improving impact studies of teachers' professional development: Toward better conceptualizations and measures. *Educational Researcher, 38,* 181–199.

Dixon, F. A., Yssel, N., McConnell, J. M., & Hardin, R. (2014). Differentiated instruction, professional development, and teacher efficacy. *Journal for the Education of the Gifted, 37,* 111–127.

Emerick, L. J. (1992). Academic underachievement among the gifted: Students' perceptions of factors that reverse the pattern. *Gifted Child Quarterly, 36,* 140–146.

Hansen, J., & Toso, S. J. (2007). Gifted dropouts: Personality, family, social, and school factors. *Gifted Child Today, 30*(4), 31–41.

Hoover-Schultz, B. (2005). Gifted underachievement: Oxymoron or educational enigma? *Gifted Child Today, 28*(2), 46–49.

Kanevsky, L., & Keighley, T. (2003). To produce or not to produce? Understanding boredom and the honor in underachievement. *Roeper Review, 26*(1), 20–28.

Landis, R. N., & Reschly, A. L. (2013). Re-examining gifted underachievement and dropout through the lens of student engagement. *Journal for the Education of the Gifted, 36,* 220–249.

McCoach, D. B., & Siegle, D. (2003). Factors that differentiate underachieving gifted students from high-achieving gifted students. *Gifted Child Quarterly, 47,* 144–154. doi:10.1177/001698620304700205

National Association for Gifted Children. (2015). *Turning a blind eye: Neglecting the needs of the gifted and talented through limited accountability, oversight, and reporting: 2014–2015 state of the nation in gifted education.* Retrieved from http://www.nagc.org/sites/default/files/key%20reports/2014-2015%20State%20of%20the%20Nation.pdf

Peterson, J. S. (2001). Successful adults who were once adolescent underachievers. *Gifted Child Quarterly, 45,* 215–229.

Peterson, J. S., & Colangelo, N. (1996). Gifted achievers and underachievers: A comparison of patterns found in school files. *Journal of Counseling and Development, 74,* 399–406.

Reis, S. M., & McCoach, D. B. (2000). The underachievement of gifted students: What do we know and where do we go? *Gifted Child Quarterly, 44,* 152–170. doi:10.1177/00169 8620004400302

Rimm, S. (2008). *Why bright kids get poor grades and what you can do about it.* Tucson, AZ: Great Potential Press.

Ritchotte, J. A. (Winter, 2015). Ungifting the gifted underachiever. *Teaching for High Potential, 1,* 16–18.

Ritchotte, J. A., & Graefe, A. K. (2017). An alternate path: The experience of high-potential individuals who left school. *Gifted Child Quarterly, 61,* 275–289.

Ritchotte, J. A., Matthews, M. S., & Flowers, C. P. (2014). The validity of the Achievement- Orientation Model for gifted middle school students: An exploratory study. *Gifted Child Quarterly, 58,* 183–198.

Ritchotte, J. A., Rubenstein, L., & Murry, F. (2015). Reversing the underachievement of gifted middle school students: Lessons from another field. *Gifted Child Today, 38,* 103–113.

Ritchotte, J. A., Suhr, D, Alfurayh, N. F., & Graefe, A. K. (2016). An exploration of the psychosocial characteristics of high achieving students and identified gifted students: Implications for practice. *Journal of Advanced Academics, 27*(1), 23–38.

Ritchotte, J. A., Zaghlawan, H., & Lee, C. -W. (2017, March). Paving the path to engagement for high-potential children. *Parenting for High Potential,* 8–13.

Rubenstein, L. D., Siegle, D., Reis, S. M., McCoach, D. B., & Burton, M. G. (2012). A complex quest: The development and research of underachievement interventions for gifted students. *Psychology in the Schools, 49,* 678–694.

Siegle, D. (2012). *The underachieving gifted child: Recognizing, understanding, and reversing underachievement.* Waco, TX: Prufrock Press.

Siegle, D., & McCoach, D. B. (2005). Motivating gifted students. In F. A. Karnes & K. R. Stephens (Series Eds.), *The practical strategies series in gifted education.* Waco, TX: Prufrock Press.

Whitmore, J. R. (1986). Understanding a lack of motivation to excel. *Gifted Child Quarterly, 30,* 66–69. doi:10.1177/001698628603000204

Appendix 5.1
Sample Needs Assessment for Professional Learning on Gifted Underachievement

We will be engaging in professional learning together on the topic of gifted underachievement. Please complete this short survey to help me ensure I am making the best use of your time. Thank you!

Put an X in the box that best indicates your level of agreement with each statement.

	Strongly Agree	Agree	Disagree	Unsure
I have had graduate-level training or engaged in extensive professional learning on gifted education topics.				
I can comfortably explain what giftedness is when prompted.				
I can accurately describe the gifted identification process at my school.				
I understand the learning needs of gifted students.				
I understand the social-emotional needs of gifted students.				
I know how to differentiate instruction for gifted learners.				

Put an X in the box that best indicates your level of agreement with each statement.

	Strongly Agree	Agree	Disagree	Unsure
Gifted students may lack motivation and earn poor grades.				
Gifted students who do not perform well academically should be removed from gifted programming.				
I can define the term *gifted underachievement*.				
I understand and can confidently explain the reasons why gifted students underachieve in school.				
I know how to prevent gifted students from underachieving in school.				
I know how to reverse a gifted student's pattern of underachieving behavior.				

Please list any priorities you have for professional learning on gifted education and gifted underachievement more specifically:

Please rate the learning activities you'd prefer. A "1" is your top preference, while a "5" is an activity you'd least prefer.

_____ Working with case studies of underachieving gifted students

_____ Presentations/mini-lectures from experts

_____ Video clips

_____ Short readings

_____ Modifying lesson plans

_____ Creating and implementing a plan for addressing gifted students' needs

Please list any other professional learning activities you'd prefer:

Thank you for completing this needs assessment survey!

CHAPTER 6

Professional Learning for the Parent:
How Educators Can Support Parents

Tracy Ford Inman and Lynette Breedlove

This chapter differs from the others in this book and in this series: The focus is parents. Parents and families can be powerful allies when provided appropriate opportunities to learn about their gifted children's needs and ways in which educators work to meet those needs. Parents are in desperate need of basic information in order to not only better understand their children, but also advocate more effectively for them. Although there has not been a vast amount of research conducted on parenting gifted children per se (Jolly & Matthews, 2014), almost 90 years of research supports the positive impact parents can have on their children's education through effective parenting techniques and partnering with schools (Robinson, Shore, & Enerson, 2007). Parents need to understand how existing research on parenting gifted children is best put into action. Therefore, this chapter is designed to assist educators in supporting parents and families of gifted children. This chapter will provide not only research-based information on myths and advocacy (Inman & Kirchner, 2016), but also strategies and techniques for educators to use with parents, whether they are used through a parent meeting, a mini-course, or through print information.

Professional learning for educators differs from professional learning for parents in several ways. First, although content may prove similar, delivery of that content may not. For example, multiple days of professional learning experiences, including job embedment, coaching, modeling, and reflection, define best practice for educators, but these strategies are neither practical nor appropriate for parents. Timing of professional learning also differs. Daylong weekday training or afterschool training so prevalent with educators is not realistic for working parents and parents needing childcare. And although both educators and parents need similar content (e.g., myths about gifted learners, policies and procedures, best practice learning environments, etc.), the emphasis of that content varies. For example, a parent may need to understand what effective enrichment, acceleration, and differentiation look like, but an educator must focus on specific strategies with an emphasis on how best to implement and assess strategies. Additionally, although educator interest remains constant (at least through the active years of their careers), parent interest or involvement tends to wane as their children age, petering out in middle and high school.

Topics of Interest

Professionals working with families of gifted children could readily list topics pertinent to most parents (e.g., working with schools or understanding test scores); certainly, parents share some commonalities. However, certain issues pertain to gifted children only, or, if the topic applies to all learners, it may vary in nuance, degree, or approach with gifted learners. A discussion of some of these issues follow.

Myths

Not only do parents believe some of the myths plaguing gifted learners, but their teachers, administrators, and other educators do as well. Unfortunately, so does the average citizen. Some believe that gifted students will make it on their own, so educators focus attention on struggling learners (Loveless, Farkas, & Duffett, 2008). Others argue that students with learning disabilities and other exceptionalities cannot also be gifted. If a teacher truly feels that a student identified in one area of giftedness is gifted in all areas, those children gifted in one area may suffer greatly in class. Whether the myth is that children suffer socially and emotionally when grade-accelerated or that IQ tests are the only way to identify a gifted learner, myths can be very damaging. The topic of myths serves as the perfect example for this chapter when describing the need for, and topics about, professional learning experiences for parents.

Laws, Regulations, Policies, and Procedures

Parents cannot successfully advocate for their children unless they know the vital information. This does not simply include information about the child's interests and abilities; it also includes understanding of definitions, laws, regulations, policies, and procedures. Without a federal definition, each state defines the terms *giftedness, gifted and talented, talent development,* and even *high-ability* in multiple ways. Parents need to know their state's terminology and definitions. States also have very different laws, regulations, and policies regarding identification and services (National Association for Gifted Children [NAGC], n.d.a). Moreover, districts and schools themselves interpret and implement those state mandates differently. Professional learning exploring everything from legislation to teacher implementation of school policy is critical for parents.

Advocacy

In theory, parents know their children best. Their insights and opinions should be considered and valued when it comes to both identification and services. However, not all parents understand the importance of advocacy, much less the nuances and strategies that prove most effective. In fact, parents may know little about it or underestimate its importance, so advocacy may not even show up on a survey of topics that interest parents. From empowering their children to be their own advocates (Douglas, 2011), to creating and honing their advocacy toolkits, parents need to learn the who, what, where, when, how, and why of speaking up for their children at the local, state, and even national levels.

Best Practices: Identification and Services

Except for the parents who are educators of the gifted, most will need a thorough understanding of what ideal identification and services look like in a school and classroom. Many parents and even educators of general classrooms may not know that student-outcome-based gifted standards exist (NAGC, 2010), which prove to be foundational in effective schools. From multiple identification measures, to blanket assessments of all children, to equity (Borland, 2014), parents need to understand best practice. Likewise, they need to understand the services offered and the services provided for their children. Terms like *acceleration, enrichment*, and *differentiation* can even confuse education professionals. What are these terms? What do they look like? How can a parent tell if a strategy is effective? Parents need to be well-informed to generate appropriate questions.

Underrepresented Populations

Parents of children who speak a language other than English at home, qualify for free and/or reduced lunch, have another exceptionality like ADHD or a learning disability, or are Black, Hispanic, or any other minority besides Asian (specifically Japanese, Chinese, and Indian) need to know that their children are much less likely to be identified as gifted (Esquierdo & Arreguín-Anderson, 2012; Ford & Scott, 2010). These parents especially need information. Johnsen (2018) cited a synthesis of scholarly thought:

> Families need to understand the identification process, particularly those from lower income backgrounds who may not request nomination forms (Scott, Perou, Urbano, Hogan, & Gold, 1992), be reluctant to refer their children for assessment (Frasier, Garcia, & Passow, 1995), or not understand or approve behaviors associated with giftedness (Coleman & Cross, 2005). To increase the representation of special populations in the referral phase, schools need to send home information in a language that parents understand, include information about the gifted program at school orientations and special meetings, and make announcements through public and social media (Coleman, 1994; Dawson, 1997; Johnsen & Ryser, 1994; Reyes, Fletcher, & Paez, 1996; Shaklee & Viechnicki, 1995). (p. 126)

Social-Emotional Needs

Perfectionism, intensity, bullying, loneliness, Dabrowski's overexcitabilities (Piechowski, 1991), growth versus fixed mindset (Dweck, 2006), grit, asynchronous development, excessive self-criticism, multipotentiality—the list of social and emotional considerations for gifted and talented children is long. In fact, these social-emotional needs tend to trump cognitive needs for many parents. Social-emotional needs manifest in a variety of ways and can appear differently at home than they do at school. Both environments must be designed to support students socially and emotionally, not just academically. Parents are often especially interested in learning strategies to use at home to work through issues that arise as a result of these characteristics.

Professional Learning Focus

Given the varied topics, the many issues resulting from them, and the parents' individual concerns, how does the school or district decide on the focus of the professional learning for parents? Just as an effective teacher preassesses her students to determine need, interest, and readiness (Roberts & Inman, 2015), so, too, should the parents—or any recipients of professional learning—be preassessed (Evans, 2018). After all, data are included as one of Learning Forward's (2011) seven Standards for Professional Learning. Needs assessments take many forms: questionnaires, surveys, open-ended questions, etc. Professional learning providers (e.g., schools, districts, universities, and advocacy organizations) may even choose online versions, so parents may complete them at their leisure. See Figure 6.1 for a sample needs assessment. Once results of the preassessment are tallied and the topic or topics are finalized, the next step is determining the optimal format of professional learning.

Teaching Strategies

The Every Student Succeed Act (ESSA, 2015), which establishes federal educational law, defines *professional learning* as activities that "are sustained (not standalone, 1-day, or short term workshops), intensive, collaborative, job-embedded, data-driven, and classroom-focused" (S.1177, 2015, p. 295).

Parent Needs Assessment

In order to enhance our partnership with you in the education of your child, we are planning parent sessions in which we will share information and answer questions regarding specific topics in gifted education. Please answer the following questions to help us plan sessions that will best meet your needs and interests.

1. Which of the following would be of interest to you as topics?
   - _____ Myths about gifted children
   - _____ Programs and resources within our schools available for gifted children
   - _____ Resources for gifted children outside our schools
   - _____ Rights and responsibilities: laws, regulations, policies, and procedures
   - _____ Parent/school/child communication and interaction
   - _____ Social-emotional needs of gifted children
   - _____ Planning higher education for the gifted child
   - _____ Living/dealing with the gifted child within the family/community
   - _____ Advocacy: the importance of speaking up for gifted children
   - _____ Identification procedures related to gifted and talented education
   - _____ Underrepresented populations in gifted and talented education
   - _____ Others: Please list _____

2. What days and times work best for you? Circle your choice(s).

Monday	Wednesday	Friday
Tuesday	Thursday	Saturday
After School	Evening	Day

3. What type of learning session works best for you? (Choose up to three.) Childcare will be provided.
   - _____ Formal classes (meet weekly for 60 minutes for 4 to 6 weeks depending on topic)
   - _____ Book study (meet weekly or every other week for 60 minutes; length depends on book)
   - _____ Seminar (one-day session)
   - _____ Conference (one-day or half-day with a general session and breakout sessions)
   - _____ Professional development series (weekly or monthly meeting emphasizing networking)
   - _____ Articles (distribute through website or newsletter)
   - _____ Online options (any of the above offered through the Internet rather than face-to-face)
   - _____ Other: Please list _____

4. Comments and Suggestions:

Please return the form to your child's teacher by the end of the week.

Figure 6.1. Parent needs assessment.

This definition is specific to educators but, in many ways, can be applied to parents. Although experiences for parents will not be job-embedded, they may be collaborative, intensive, and data-driven. Experiences for parents may focus on the classroom or the home. Optimal professional learning for parents should take place over a period of time, such as a formal class that meets face-to-face over several weeks, rather than a one-time session like a single webinar. However, due to parents' work and familial obligations, many may not be able to commit to more sustained experiences. A variety of strategies are presented in this section. Providing a single opportunity for parents to learn more about their children is preferable to opportunities they cannot access.

School personnel must identify the combination of topics and strategies that best fit their parents' needs over time. A school will likely need to offer professional learning in several different formats in order to provide access to their diverse population of parents. After surveying parents to identify their stated preferences (see Figure 6.1 for a sample), then offering different options and seeing which are attended the most, school personnel can determine the best fit.

Although there seems to be a lack of empirical research investigating gifted parent support groups, there are several resources that anecdotally indicate their importance. NAGC (2011) published an e-book entitled *Starting and Sustaining a Parent Group to Support Gifted Children*. Supporting Emotional Needs of the Gifted (SENG, 2019), an organization focused on the emotional and mental health of gifted children, developed a model specifically for gifted parent groups called the SENG Model Parent Group (SMPG) and provides both guidelines and training for group facilitators. Even state gifted organizations encourage and support the formation of gifted parent groups, such as the Texas Association for the Gifted and Talented (TAGT), which provides resources on its website and mentoring through the process of creating a parent group.

One topic that is especially important for parents to understand is the myths regarding gifted and talented children. These myths are pervasive and affect how educators and the general population regard gifted and talented children and their learning needs. We will use this topic to illustrate the various professional learning strategies that can be used with an audience of parents. Several publications, both online and in print, describe and dispel the typical myths regarding gifted students. For the purposes of this chapter, we will be using the myths described by NAGC (n.d.b).

Formal Class

The most intensive strategy is to create a formal class structure for the professional learning, similar to a high school or university night class. The class meets weekly at a set time for 60 to 90 minutes for a specific number of weeks based on the topics to be covered. The class instructor creates a syllabus for the class that outlines the schedule and topics to be discussed each week, along with homework assignments and resources. Schools should consider if they will provide childcare during the class each week and if refreshments will be available. Offering childcare and refreshments tends to increase parent participation, as doing so removes barriers for many families. See Figure 6.2 for an example of a syllabus for a formal class dispelling the typical myths regarding gifted and talented children.

At the first meeting, the class facilitator should introduce him- or herself and describe the purpose of the class. Communicating the expectations of participants is important. For example, some expectations may include a willingness to commit to attending every week, being respectful of each other's opinions, and completing the homework that prepares them to participate in the next week's discussion. The facilitator should also establish ground rules for how questions and concerns will be handled related to specific schools and school district personnel. Parents may want to vent or seek solutions to very specific problems during the class. Provide them a way to share their concerns and to seek assistance for solving more personal problems outside of class time. The facilitator might make appointments during work hours with individual participants to hear their concerns, or he or she might plan to talk with participants privately at the conclusion of the meeting.

As a formal class, the facilitator should teach a small amount of content each week related to the week's myth. During the first week, the facilitator should introduce the myths on which the course is based, providing participants with the URL of NAGC's "Myths about Gifted Students" (n.d.b): https://www.nagc.org/myths-about-gifted-students. During the second week, focusing on the myth "All children are gifted," the facilitator might briefly introduce participants to different theories of giftedness. This would provide participants a foundational understanding of the components theorists suggest are a part of giftedness. The facilitator could have participants compare these theories to one another to identify what they have in common and in what ways they vary. Next, the facilitator could review the definition of giftedness from NAGC, the state, and the school or school district. Finally, the participants could have a discussion sharing their reflections from the reading homework previously assigned. The facilitator might provide customized reflection questions or a standard list of questions to which

Syllabus: Exploring the Myths About Gifted and Talented Children

Instructor: Jane Doe, School GT Facilitator
Meeting Schedule: Tuesdays, 6:00 p.m.–7:00 p.m.
Location: School Library
Childcare and homework support available.

Expectations: Participants will keep a journal in which they respond to the weekly readings. These readings and responses will be the basis of discussion during class. Participants can miss no more than one class meeting.

Week 1, date: Introduction, Syllabus Review, Questions and Answers. Homework: Read and reflect in your journal on Janet Kragen's 2017 article "Gifted Isn't Good" available here: https://www.nagc.org/blog/gifted-isn%E2%80%99t-good.

Week 2, date: Myth 1—All children are gifted. Homework: Read NAGC's "Why are Gifted Programs Needed?" available here: https://www.nagc.org/resources-publications/gifted-education-practices/why-are-gifted-programs-needed. Then, read "Be Your Gifted Child's Coach," available here: http://www.giftedguru.com/be-your-gifted-childs-coach. Be sure to write your reflections in your journal.

Week 3, date: Myth 2—Gifted students don't need help; they'll do fine on their own. Homework: Read and reflect in your journal on Part 2 of *High-Achieving Students in the Era of NCLB* (Loveless, Farkas, & Duffett, 2008). The publication is available here: https://edex.s3-us-west-2.amazonaws.com/publication/pdfs/20080618_high_achievers_7.pdf.

Week 4, date: Myth 3—Teachers challenge all students, so gifted kids will be fine in the regular classroom. (*Note.* The homework listed would be appropriate preparation to discuss the next myth.)

And so on. One week for each myth.

Week 13, date: Class review and graduation. A graduation ceremony will take place, during which all participants will receive certificates to recognize their hard work and completion of the course.

Figure 6.2. Syllabus for a formal class dispelling the myths regarding gifted and talented children.

participants might respond for every chapter. See Figure 6.3 for sample questions. As the class concludes, the facilitator should remind participants of the date and time of the next meeting, as well as what the homework assignment is and how to access it. Facilitators should consider the participants' access to Internet resources. Providing paper copies of the assigned homework may benefit those who do not have regular Internet access.

The final meeting is an appropriate time to assess participants' experiences in the class, as well as their learning. Unlike in a high school or university course, participants should not be tested or given a final exam. Rather, the purpose of the assessment is to determine the effectiveness of the class and to provide feedback for improvement prior to the class being offered again. Having a graduation or completion ceremony to honor participants' commitment and learning is also appropriate. Participants will likely have become close to one another, and celebrating their success in completing the class will provide closure. Some participants may wish to continue to be involved in some way with the school or school district. The facilitator should provide suggestions on how participants may positively support the gifted and talented program through volunteering, participating in a parent support group, or advocating for the gifted program.

Book Study

A professional learning strategy often used with educators is a book study. This approach also works for supporting and educating parents. Much like a formal class, the book study group meets at regular intervals, usually weekly, for 60 to 90 minutes. The book study facilitator creates a syllabus that lists the chapter or chapters to be read prior to each week's meeting, along with guiding questions or response questions to focus their reading. The number of weeks and amount of reading each week should vary based on the book selected. For example, the facilitator might select Ellen Winner's (1996) *Gifted Children: Myths and Realities* as the focus for the book study. It has 11 chapters related to myths about giftedness, with the first chapter entitled "Nine Myths About Giftedness." Depending on what works best for parents the your area, the school might provide or sell books at the first meeting and schedule 11 additional weeks, or participants might be expected to purchase the book and read the first chapter prior to the first meeting.

Just as with a formal class, the facilitator should consider offering childcare and homework assistance as well as refreshments. Again, the facilitator will need to set expectations and communicate how he or she will handle questions and concerns related to specific schools or school personnel at the first meeting. Gentle reminders may need to be provided throughout

---

Reflection Questions

What surprised you in this reading?

Describe something that you agreed or disagreed with and explain your response.

Do you see your child or yourself in this reading? If so, explain.

What questions do you have about the reading?

What might you change, if anything, after reading this?

What parts or passages might you share with someone else? Who would that be? Why?

What was most valuable in the reading? Why?

Figure 6.3. Sample reflection questions.

---

the course of the book study. Participants should be encouraged to ask questions and share their experiences that relate to the reading. However, they should not share names of specific school personnel or grievances. As with a formal class, participants are likely to become close and want to stay involved with each other and with the school or district at the conclusion of the book study. The last meeting is a good time to communicate opportunities to volunteer, support, and advocate for the gifted and talented program.

There are many books that can be used as the basis for a parent book study depending on the desired focus. *A Parent's Guide to Gifted Children* by Webb, Gore, Amend, and DeVries (2007) is a classic book that addresses many aspects of parenting gifted children in some depth. *Parenting Gifted Children 101: An Introduction to Gifted Kids and Their Needs* by Inman and Kirchner (2016) provides an overview for parents and is very accessible to parents of all backgrounds. It can also be helpful to parents to focus on one aspect of supporting their gifted children. *Emotional Intensity in Gifted Students: Helping Kids Cope with Explosive Feelings* by Fonseca (2015) would allow parents to discuss the emotional needs of their children in depth.

Professional Learning Series

Some parents who are interested in professional learning related to gifted education and supporting their gifted children cannot commit to attending weekly meetings or completing assignments such as those required of a formal course or a book study. To meet the needs of these parents, a series on related topics offers ongoing learning opportunities. Each session should be designed to be interactive and provide opportunities for participants to get to know each other. An important benefit of face-to-face professional learning is connecting with people who have something in common. Hearing how another parent approaches a challenge with her gifted children provides a parent with ideas and with a community. Parents of gifted children often feel alone and are unsure with whom they can talk about their children in a frank and open fashion. Meeting other parents of gifted children at a professional development session builds a much-needed network of support.

A series based on NAGC's "Myths about Gifted Students" (NAGC, n.d.b) could focus on one myth each session. The sessions could take place weekly, be spread across a semester, or occur throughout the year. To introduce the first myth, "gifted students don't need help; they'll do fine on their own," the facilitator could ask participants how they would go about learning a world language. After gathering ideas from the audience, the facilitator could then ask participants how they would go about improving their basketball skills. This discussion could emphasize that, to learn something fairly complex, people need some resources that provide instruction and they need feedback. The feedback not only helps people know if they are correct, but also helps them identify ways in which they can refine their understanding and skill. These are all elements provided by a teacher or coach. Although gifted and talented children seem to absorb knowledge and understanding from their environment, they need a teacher to help them refine their understanding and skill. The facilitator could next share Van Gemert's (2011) blog post "Be Your Gifted Child's Coach," which suggests a coaching approach to parenting gifted children. After a review of the blog post, participants could discuss how coaches tend to give feedback in a different way than parents and how they might use this approach in the future. Then, the facilitator could share expectations for instructional approaches used in meeting the needs of gifted and talented children in classrooms. To wrap up the session, the facilitator could offer ways that parents might support teachers in meeting their children's needs. Finally, the schedule and topics for the remainder of the series could be shared.

Conference

Another way to offer professional learning to parents that mirrors a strategy used for educators is to offer a one-day or half-day conference. This could be held in a school building. The auditorium, cafeteria, or gym could be used for a general session, and breakout sessions could take place in classrooms. The anticipated size of the audience would dictate the size of the school needed to host the event. The conference could be for one school, a specific range of students' grade levels (e.g., grades 3–5), a district, a community, or a city. Unlike the other types of professional learning strategies, a conference requires multiple facilitators offering sessions at the same time, as well as support staff to direct participants as they arrive and move between sessions.

A conference on the topic of "Myths About Gifted Students" could offer sessions on each myth from which parents could choose (NAGC, n.d.b). The general session could focus on the myth that "All children are gifted." Much like in the second week of the formal class, the facilitator could have participants discuss different theories and definitions of giftedness, then share the school, district, or state definition depending on the audience. The facilitator could draw comparisons to athletics and the common understanding that all children do not have the abilities and interests to be highly competitive athletes. The general session could wrap up by showing a video created by students in Maryland and posted on YouTube by the Gifted and Talented Association of Montgomery County (2010) called "Myths in Gifted Education." Finally, the general session should include schedule and location information for the breakout sessions.

Standalone Session

If the school has not offered professional learning for parents previously, a simple way to start is to offer a single, standalone session. This requires few resources and can be effective in providing support for parents. The school may need to experiment with the timing that draws the largest audience. In some communities, offering a "brown bag" lunch session to which participants bring their lunches to eat during the session works well. In other communities, a morning session that takes place right after student drop-off draws the best attendance. The school might also try an evening session timed to catch parents on their drives home from work. Attendance may increase if childcare with homework assistance is offered for an evening session.

A standalone session on the myths could cover all 11 of the myths described in NAGC's (n.d.b) "Myths About Gifted Students," or the facilitator could choose to address the myths most often heard in the school and community. To introduce the myths, the facilitator might offer participants a myth/reality quiz on paper or do a live poll online using a response system, such as Poll Everywhere (available at https://www.polleverywhere.

com), which allows participants to answer using their smartphones or personal devices. Using the live polling system would allow the facilitator to customize the session to the audience by selecting the myths to dispel based on the polling results.

A standalone session on myths would not allow the facilitator to address each myth to the same depth as other professional learning strategies, but it can provide a broad understanding. The facilitator could choose one to three points to dispel each myth during a 75- to 90-minute session. For example, to address the myth that "gifted students don't need help; they'll do fine on their own" (NAGC, n.d.b), the facilitator could reference *Mind the (Other) Gap!* (Plucker, Burroughs, & Song, 2010), which explains that the "minimum competency achievement gap" (p. 1) has been reduced in recent years, but significant gaps remain among the highest performing students (termed *excellence gaps*). If gifted students did fine without help, there would be no excellence gaps—all gifted children would be performing at the highest levels. The facilitator could compare intellectual giftedness with athletic giftedness. Elite athletes have elite coaches. NFL teams have quarterback coaches, even though there are only two or three quarterbacks on a team of 50 or so players. NFL quarterbacks are gifted athletes, yet NFL team owners spend money on coaches rather than expecting them to be fine on their own. This pattern could be followed to illustrate the realities of the other myths.

Articles

Some parents will be unable to attend a face-to-face session due to their work and family obligations. One way to provide professional learning for these parents is to provide short articles for school newsletters and the school or district websites. Articles that are brief can provide basic information, while including a reference or link to more in-depth information. One approach could be to summarize recent blog posts or research articles related to gifted and talented children. The summary could provide the main highlights and pathways for those who are interested to read the full post or article when they have more time. Another approach could be to describe a resource or reference that would be helpful to gifted children and their families, such as Khan Academy (available at https://www.khanacademy.org) for enrichment learning. A series of articles could be provided for newsletters on the myths about gifted students. Each article would briefly address the myth and provide resources for finding out more. Figure 6.4 is an example of an article for the myth, "That student can't be gifted; he is receiving poor grades" (NAGC, n.d.b).

> ## Myth: Gifted and Talented Students Always Make Good Grades
>
> Many people expect gifted and talented students to make very high grades in every class. But giftedness and grades do not automatically go together. First, most gifted students are not gifted in every content area. A student may have exceptional abilities in language arts but more average abilities in mathematics, or the reverse. Other students may have exceptional abilities in the visual or performing arts, but more average abilities in core content areas. Second, some gifted and talented students underachieve. In order to help students improve their performance, parents and teachers must understand the underlying factors. The student may have a disability or other serious issue, there may be a poor fit between the student and the learning environment, the student may not believe he or she is as capable or that school is as important as others believe, or the student may not have the study skills or habits necessary to be successful (Siegle & McCoach, 2005). Once the underlying factor is identified, parents and teachers can work together to implement strategies to support the student.
>
> To learn more, read a teacher's story about helping a seventh-grade student in her classroom: "Reversing Gifted Underachievement: The Intervention That Set One Student on the Path to Success" by Jennifer Ritchotte (http://www.nagc.org/sites/default/files/Reversing_Underacheivement_PHP_June_2010.pdf) You might also enjoy reading the article that helped Ms. Ritchotte support her student: "Making a Difference: Motivated Gifted Students Who Are Not Achieving" by Del Siegle and Betsy McCoach (https://www.researchgate.net/publication/237377718_Making_a_Difference_Motivating_Gifted_Students_Who_Are_Not_Achieving).

Figure 6.4. Sample newsletter article.

Online Options

All of the strategies for professional learning for parents in this chapter could be offered in a format that utilizes today's technology. A formal online course complete with recorded content, interactive polls, and discussion boards is one option. A book study could be offered online through a blog or website with the comment section used for discussion on each chapter. A professional learning series could be offered as a succession of webinars or Facebook Live events. The same could be done with a standalone session. The specific technology tool and format will depend on the facilitator's and parents' access to web-based content.

Carefully considering how a selected online professional learning session will provide opportunities for parents to connect is important. An online community could provide a sustaining element to professional learning that began as a standalone event. Increasing parents' knowledge and understanding of their gifted children's needs and how to meet them is a primary goal of professional learning. An important secondary goal is to create a sense of community. Parents of gifted children benefit from simply knowing they are not alone. Having the opportunity to interact with another parent with similar challenges and successes is invaluable. Therefore, ensuring parents have the opportunity to comment, ask questions, and respond to one another in online professional learning is key.

Summary

Parents are essential partners in the education of their children. Professional learning for parents provides them with an increased understanding of their children and gifted education as a whole, as well as an understanding of the importance of advocacy and the skills to act upon it. With a common vocabulary, parents and educators can develop a robust, healthy relationship that enhances children's educational experiences. District and school personnel also build important relationships with parents through designing and delivering learning opportunities that address the specific interests and needs of the parents in their community. By informing parents and preparing them with appropriate advocacy skills, parents become better advocates not only for their own children, but also for all children and youth who are gifted and talented. Parents can be powerful. Their voices are heard on the district, state, and national levels—many times with more volume than educators' voices.

References

Borland, J. H. (2014). Identification of gifted students. In J. A. Plucker & C. M. Callahan (Eds.), *Critical issues and practices in gifted education: What the research says* (2nd ed., pp. 323–342). Waco, TX: Prufrock Press.

Douglas, D. (2011). Four simple steps to self-advocacy. In J. Jolly, D. Treffinger, T. F. Inman, & J. F. Smutny (Eds.), *Parenting gifted children: The authoritative guide from the National Association for Gifted Children* (pp. 360–368). Waco, TX: Prufrock Press.

Dweck, C. S. (2006). *Mindset: The new psychology of success.* New York, NY: Ballantine Books.

Esquierdo, J. J., & Arreguín-Anderson, M. (2012). The "invisible" gifted and talented bilingual students: A current report on enrollment in GT programs. *Journal for the Education of the Gifted, 35,* 35–47. doi:10.1177/0162353211432041

Evans, M. (2018). Professional development. In J. L. Roberts, T. F. Inman, & J. H. Robins (Eds.), *Introduction to gifted education* (pp. 415–433). Waco, TX: Prufrock Academic Press.

Every Student Succeeds Act, Pub. L. No. 114–95. (2015).

Fonseca, C. (2015). *Emotional intensity in gifted students: Helping kids cope with explosive feelings* (2nd ed.). Waco, TX: Prufrock Press.

Ford, D. Y., & Scott, M. T. (2010). Under-representation of African American students in gifted education: Nine theories and framework for information, understanding, and change. *Gifted Education Press Quarterly, 24*(3), 2–6.

Gifted and Talented Association of Montgomery County. (2010). *Top 10 myths in gifted education* [Video file]. Retrieved from https://www.youtube.com/watch?v=MDJst-y_ptI

Inman, T. F., & Kirchner, J. (2016). *Parenting gifted children 101: An introduction to gifted kids and their needs.* Waco, TX: Prufrock Press.

Johnsen, S. K. (2018). Identification. In J. L. Roberts, T. F. Inman, & J. H. Robins (Eds.), *Introduction to gifted education* (pp. 121–144). Waco, TX: Prufrock Academic Press.

Jolly, J. L., & Matthews, M. S. (2014). Parenting. In J. A. Plucker & C. M. Callahan (Eds.), *Critical issues and practices in gifted education: What the research says* (2nd ed., pp. 481–492). Waco, TX: Prufrock Press.

Learning Forward. (2011). *Standards for professional learning.* Oxford, OH: Author.

Loveless, T., Farkas, S., & Duffett, A. (2008). *High-achieving students in the era of NCLB.* Washington, DC: Thomas B. Fordham Institute.

National Association for Gifted Children. (n.d.a). *Gifted by state.* Retrieved from https://www.nagc.org/resources-publications/gifted-state

National Association for Gifted Children. (n.d.b). *Myths about gifted students.* Retrieved from http://www.nagc.org/myths-about-gifted-students

National Association for Gifted Children. (2010). *Pre-k-grade 12 gifted programming standards.* Retrieved from http://www.nagc.org/

resources-publications/resources/national-standards-gifted-and-talented-education/pre-k-grade-12

National Association for Gifted Children. (2011). *Starting and sustaining a parent group to support gifted children.* Waco, TX: Prufrock Press.

Piechowski, M. M. (1991). Emotional development and emotional giftedness. In N. Colangelo & G. A. Davis (Eds.), *Handbook of gifted education* (pp. 285–306). Boston, MA: Allyn & Bacon.

Plucker, J., Burroughs, N., & Song, R. (2010). *Mind the (other) gap! The growing excellence gap in K–12 education.* Center for Evaluation and Education Policy, Indiana University: Bloomington, IN.

Ritchotte, J. (2010, June). Reversing gifted underachievement: The intervention that set one student on the path to success. *Parenting for High Potential*, 21–26.

Roberts, J. L., & Inman, T. F. (2015). *Strategies for differentiating instruction: Best practices in the classroom* (3rd ed.). Waco, TX: Prufrock Press.

Robinson, A., Shore, B. M., & Enerson, D. L. (2007). *Best practices in gifted education: An evidence-based guide.* Waco, TX: Prufrock Press.

Siegle, D., & McCoach, D. B. (2005). Making a difference: Motivating gifted students who are not achieving. *Teaching Exceptional Children, 38*(1), 22–27.

Supporting Emotional Needs of the Gifted. (2019). *SMPG facilitator training.* Retrieved from http://sengifted.org/smpg-facilitator-training

Van Gemert, L. (2011). *Be your gifted child's coach* [Web log post]. Retrieved from http://www.giftedguru.com/be-your-gifted-childs-coach

Webb, J. T., Gore, J. L., Amend, E. R., & DeVries, A. R. (2007). *A parent's guide to gifted children.* Scottsdale, AZ: Great Potential Press.

Winner, E. (1996). *Gifted children: Myths and realities.* New York, NY: Basic Books.

Section 2

Programmatic Topics

CHAPTER 7

Identifying and Supporting Culturally, Linguistically, and Economically Diverse Gifted Learners:
Guiding Teachers Through the Four Zones of Professional Learning

Katie D. Lewis and Angela M. Novak

Introduction

Culturally, linguistically, and economically diverse (CLED) students are underrepresented in gifted programs. District administration and educational researchers are looking to reverse this inequitable trend through a variety of means—identification protocol, service models, and staff development, just to name a few. This chapter describes a combination of these approaches and provides K–12 administrators and gifted coordinators with a four-zone approach for delivering to teachers high-quality and sustainable professional learning focused on increasing knowledge of and meeting the needs of CLED student populations. This chapter details the Four Zone Professional Learning Approach, a well-rounded program that addresses problems associated with underrepresentation of gifted CLED students from four different angles: (1) increasing understanding of culture, (2) bolstering teacher recognition of the unique gifted characteristics of CLED students, (3) providing support in the classroom for CLED students, and (4) developing partnerships with CLED parents and the community. The chapter is divided into sections that describe each of these components, or zones; following each of these sections is a list of practical ways to implement the particular professional learning zone strategies.

Throughout this chapter, its authors use the acronym CLED (culturally, linguistically, and economically diverse) as an umbrella term, encompassing other terms such as CLD (culturally, linguistically diverse), as well as Hispanic, Indigenous, African American, or Black populations. Note that, depending on a researcher's use of the acronym, the "e" can represent *ethnically* rather than *economically* (see, for example, Briggs, Reis, & Sullivan, 2008; Hines, Anderson, & Grantham, 2016; Olszewski-Kubilius & Steenbergen-Hu, 2017). Additionally, Ford (2010a) argued that a better term might be *culturally different* rather than *diverse*, "because every individual and group has a culture" (p. 50). The authors of this chapter respectfully acknowledge that each of these terms and cultural groups is distinct in many ways, and it can be a disservice to lump them together as if they are coindicated at all times. A student living in poverty is not of one ethnic group, and students of a given ethnic group are not relegated to one economic stratum. Moreover, among the cultural groups and ethnicities, there exists a broad range of cultural identities and social mores. However, a common thread exists that is the impetus of this chapter and of the term's frequent use: stark underrepresentation in gifted programs and the need for professional learning as one (of several) essential tools to combat this prevalent discrepancy.

Overview/Need

Underrepresentation

Gifted potential exists across race, culture, ethnicity, socioeconomic status, and gender. The U.S. Department of Education's (1993) definition stated:

Children and youth with outstanding talent perform or show the potential for performing at remarkably high levels of accomplishment when compared with others of their age, experience, or environment. These children and youth exhibit high performance capacity in intellectual, creative, and/or artistic areas, and unusual leadership capacity, or excel in specific academic fields. *They require services or activities not ordinarily provided by the schools. Outstanding talents are present in children and youth from all cultural groups, across all economic strata, and in all areas of human endeavor.* (emphasis added, p. 26)

In a survey of teacher beliefs about CLED students in gifted programs, de Wet and Gubbins (2011) found, via a multistate survey instrument, that "teachers believed that CLED students should be included in gifted programs and that it would benefit gifted programs and gifted students already in gifted programs if CLED students were included" (p. 104). Further, surveyed teachers indicated that gifted abilities are found in all ethnic groups and socioeconomic strata, and that IQ tests were not representative of CLED student potential. Despite the national definition and widely held beliefs, CLED students are drastically underrepresented in gifted programs. The 2015 Digest of Education Statistics report (Snyder, de Brey, & Dillow, 2016) indicated that the total gifted and talented student population in the United States was 6.4% (see Table 7.1). According to the 1972 Marland Report to Congress, 5%–7% of the total student population should be represented within gifted programs. Therefore, as a nation, gifted programming identification was doing well in 2015. Collectively, the national data on gifted race/ethnicity data are within the 5%–7% targeted range, with the exception of Black and Hispanic students. But, when examining the data at the state level, the underrepresentation of racial/ethnic groups varies dramatically, and in many states, the underrepresentation is glaringly apparent. For example, in Florida, 4.5% of the student population is enrolled in gifted programming (Snyder et al., 2016). The racial/ethnic breakdowns reveal the varying degrees of underrepresentation of students in the state's gifted programming: 7.1% are White, 2.2% are Black, 5.1% are Hispanic, 12.1% are Asian, 3.6% are Pacific Islander, 4.3% are American Indian/Alaska Native, and 5.8% are two or more races (Snyder et al., 2016).

Hodges, Tay, Maeda, and Gentry (2018) conducted a meta-analysis of identification practices, finding that in all examples of studied identification procedures, disproportionality exists. CLED students, grouped as historically underrepresented in this study, were two-thirds less likely to be identified as gifted compared to White and Asian students. However, on a positive note, certain locations had a better, although not ideal, repre-

Table 7.1
2011–2012 Public School Gifted and Talented
Programs Student Enrollment

	Total U.S. Gifted Population	White	Black	Hispanic	Asian	Pacific Islander	American Indian/ Alaska Native	Two or More Races
Identified Gifted Students	3,189,757 (6.4%)	1,939,266 (7.6%)	281,135 (3.6%)	538,529 (4.6%)	301,633 (13%)	11,053 (5%)	30,103 (5.2%)	88,038 (6.8%)

Note. Data are from Synder, de Brey, & Dillow, 2016.

sentation—specifically some areas of the South and Southwest. However, although the study lists Asian as a comparison group, Asian Americans from Southeast Asia and the Pacific Islands (AAPI) are more likely to be English language learners (ELLs), of high poverty, and underrepresented in gifted programs (Siegle et al., 2016).

Linguistically diverse underrepresentation is also seen in the national data; linguistically diverse refers to ELLs and bilingual students of any language or culture. The Office for Civil Rights's (OCR) 2013–2014 gifted and talented enrollment estimations indicated that, nationwide, gifted ELLs represent 2.8% of the national gifted student population (OCR, 2014). This is significantly below 5%–7% of the total student population, which is recommended by the 1972 Marland Report to Congress.

Underrepresentation within gifted programming based on economic status is also seen in the national data. Yaluma and Tyner (2018) examined how different groups of students in high-poverty schools gained access and experienced gifted programming. Their findings showed that gifted programming was present in more than two-thirds of elementary and middle schools. Low-poverty students are "more than twice as likely to participate in such programs" (Yaluma & Tyner, 2018, p. 5), even though both low-poverty and high-poverty schools are equally likely to have gifted programming. Black and Hispanic students are less likely to participate in gifted programming within the low- and high-poverty schools (Yaluma & Tyner, 2018).

Identification and Retention

Teachers are considered gatekeepers in many gifted programs. Although the impetus of identification of CLED students by no means lies solely at the feet of teachers, they are often a first step in the process—and a significant one at that (Betts, 2016; Ford, Grantham, & Whiting, 2008; Milner & Ford, 2007). Betts (2016) stated that ensuring that highly able learners are recognized through systematic programming is of the highest importance. All teachers must be able to recognize a high-ability student who needs more depth and complexity in instruction or a referral for further assessment and services. (para 1)

However, identification protocols, instruments, and services are all designed with the traditionally gifted student in mind. Therefore, some CLED students are not identified, as the classroom teacher neither recognizes nor values the students' ways of communicating understanding. This is particularly true of the ELLs who are often conversing in multiple languages, which could be an indicator of giftedness. Yet, being bilingual is not always valued by mainstream culture, and, therefore, the student is recommended for remediation services, rather than the gifted services (Abellán-Pagnani & Hébert, 2013; Allen, 2017; Olthouse, 2013).

Retention is the second hurdle for school districts to surpass with regard to gifted CLED students. The struggle to retain CLED students can be caused by culturally insensitive curriculum, lack of support for cultural differences within the program, and lack of parental engagement and support (Briggs et al., 2008; Grantham, Frasier, Roberts, & Bridges, 2005; National Association for Gifted Children [NAGC], 2011). Deficit thinking—from teachers and their view of CLED gifted students and families, and from students' own perceptions of gifted education—can cause some of these issues. Student perceptions of gifted programming can lead to deliberate underachievement that results in a student not qualifying for gifted services, refusing to go through the identification process, or refusing services (Ford & Grantham, 2003).

Professional Learning

Teacher quality is one of the most important factors in increasing student achievement. Effective professional learning enables teachers to target the knowledge and skills that will increase student engagement and learning, and, in turn, will have a direct impact on student achievement (Mizell, 2010). The field of education is fluid and dynamic, a complexity that requires educators to be constantly learning and engaging in best practices. Effective professional development is systematic and provides opportunities for practice and implementation of new ideas, as well as constructive feedback (Mizell, 2010).

The Every Student Succeeds Act (ESSA, 2015) updated the definition of professional development: "section 8101(42) defines 'professional development,' specifically noting that the professional development activities are sustained (not standalone, 1-day, or short term workshops), intensive, collaborative, job-embedded, data-driven, and classroom-focused." With the updated definition and an updated mindset, districts are moving away from one-day workshops. This pedagogical shift in adult learning has transitioned the field of professional development to professional learning, which embodies these research-based best practices.

Across the country, the level of gifted and talented training that classroom teachers are required to have varies greatly. Only three states mandate the regular education classroom teacher to have any training on the nature and needs of gifted students (NAGC, 2014b). Classroom teachers are often the first responders in the identification process for gifted students. NAGC Past-President George Betts (2016) issued a call that certain skills are necessary not just for gifted education teachers, but for all educators:

All teachers should be able to:
- recognize the learning differences, developmental milestones, and cognitive/affective characteristics of gifted and talented students, including those from diverse cultural and linguistic backgrounds, and identify their related academic and social-emotional needs;
- design appropriate learning and performance modifications for individuals with gifts and talents that enhance creativity, acceleration, depth and complexity in academic subject matter and specialized domains; and
- select, adapt, and use a repertoire of evidence-based instructional strategies to advance the learning of gifted and talented students. (para. 7)

Benefits of targeted professional learning acting as a catalyst for change in teachers is evident in ESSA (2015) and the NAGC-CEC Teacher Preparation Standards in Gifted and Talented Education (NAGC & the Council for Exceptional Children, The Association for the Gifted [CEC-TAG], 2013), as well as state and local district policies. Research documenting these benefits for increasing identification and retention of minority students and those from poverty is well-established in the field of gifted education. A growing awareness of the underrepresentation of CLED students in gifted programming has helped increase diversity. Research from the fields of multiculturalism, bilingualism, and gifted education all explore the impact professional development has on changing teacher perceptions and increasing cultural awareness. The Four Zone Professional Learning Approach is grounded in best practices and proposes a comprehensive strategic plan for increasing identification and retention of CLED gifted students. The authors developed the Four Zone Professional Learning Approach after: (1) reviewing literature on best practices for professional development, gifted student identification, and retention, and the impact of teacher perception on student achievement, and (2) conducting research on the influence of teacher perceptions on identification of gifted students.

Guiding Teachers Through the Four Zones of Professional Learning to Increase Representation and Retention of CLED Gifted Students

One professional development session on one topic will not beget change. Research-based best practices in education indicate that professional learning should be ongoing, sustained, and substantive (Learning Forward, 2011). This professional learning cannot center around gifted education alone, but should include cultural, linguistic, and economic diversity (Ford et al., 2008), and be conducted through a culturally responsive lens. The Four Zone Professional Learning Approach strives to meet the needs of diversifying and attaining representation of gifted CLED students by providing ongoing professional learning that is tailored to the unique needs of each school's CLED population. The four zones are equally weighted, and delivery of the professional learning should be sequential. However, because professional learning is an ongoing process, previous zones may need to be revisited. Shifts in cultural mindsets take time and are influenced by many factors, including the individual and school climate. Therefore, ongoing professional learning is key to realizing true changes. The Four Zone Professional Learning Approach is most effective when all zones are implemented. Although the zones each approach a different component of the CLED gifted child, together the four zones are united, forming a comprehensive approach to professional learning. Look closer at the four zones in Figure 7.1.

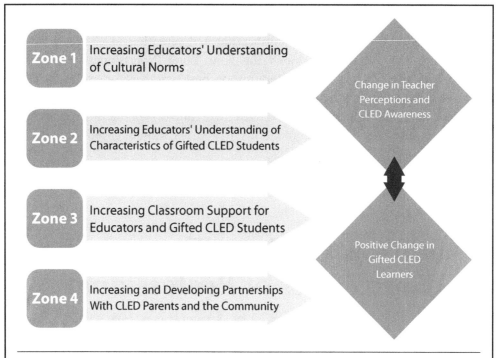

Figure 7.1. Four zones of professional learning to increase identification of gifted CLED learners.

Zone 1: Increasing Educators' Understanding of Culture

Zone 1 focuses on increasing educators' understanding of the cultural norms of various CLED groups. Culturally responsive teaching integrates crosscultural competence through the use of cultural characteristics, experiences, and perspectives of CLED students (Gay, 2010; McKoy, MacLeod, Walter, & Nolker, 2017). The culturally responsive pedagogy affirms the values of various CLED groups and applies these varying perspectives to enrich and diversify the curriculum and experiences of students. In order for culturally responsive teaching to be effective, the teacher must first be aware of his or her own cultural background.

Zone 1 is a critical stage in the professional learning process, as one's personal beliefs and perceptions of a cultural group may impact one's treatment of/attitude toward that group. In order to change one's perceptions, one must first self-reflect. Culturally responsive teachers are "mindful of the role culture plays in the knowledge that educators bring to their practices, as well as how educators learn and make sense of their own daily practice" (King, Artiles, & Kozleski, 2009). Zone 1 emphasizes how a person's history and professional identity influences his or her perceptions about culture. This zone also considers the influence of culture on shaping how students engage in learning, and how circumstances shape a cultural identity and understanding of social justice.

Professional learning during this zone should address the characteristics that culturally responsive teachers possess. The first characteristic is sociocultural consciousness. Teachers need sessions in which they are able to self-reflect, critically think about their own cultural identity, and recognize any personal bias they have toward cultural groups. Recognizing one's own cultural identity opens the door for reflection about how these beliefs may consciously or subconsciously influence one's perceptions about gifted CLED learners. Briggs et al. (2008) indicated that diverse gifted programs feature an "increased staff awareness of the impact of student culture on learning and achievement . . . [and] a strength-based model for working with CLED students with gifted potential" (p. 142).

The second characteristic teachers need is an affirming attitude toward CLED students. Formally recognizing and respecting cultural differences is essential to a student's learning, self-efficacy, and academic achievement. Committing to an affirming attitude positively influences school climate, making it inclusive to all CLED groups. The third characteristic is tightly aligned with the second, as school personnel must also commit to becoming agents of change (King et al., 2009). As agents of change, teachers take on a growth mindset, recognizing personal bias and cultural differences, and addressing any cultural bias within the school.

After reflecting on personal cultural identity and committing to being agents of change, professional learning sessions should focus on the unique student body. This allows schools to narrow their focus in order to address the specific culturally diverse student population. With ever-changing student demographics, the student body makeup should be closely monitored and adjusted to include new cultural groups. During this professional learning experience, educators need to learn about the students' "past experiences, home and community culture, and the world both in and outside of school," (Kea, Campbell-Whatley, & Richards, 2006). Additionally, teachers need to be provided with professional learning focused on how to build parent and community relationships.

Throughout the first zone of professional development, creating and maintaining a safe learning environment is critical. Teachers must feel comfortable asking hard questions and sharing personal beliefs and experiences, as well honestly reflecting on their own cultural identity. Teachers must also have a support system in place in which they can follow up workshops with discussions and extensions of the learning sessions. Beliefs about culture will not change in a one-stop professional development session; rather, change occurs over time when there is an opportunity for critical thinking and reflection found in professional learning. Most K–12 schools reflect a culturally diverse student body mirrored in society, while the cultural diversity of teachers has remained stagnant over the years. These differences in culture lead to conflict within the schools, but Ford (2010a) reflected that

> the good news is that teachers can decrease cultural misunderstandings and miscommunication with culturally different students when they become more self-reflective, recognize cultural differences between themselves and students, work to become more culturally competent professionals, and create classrooms that are culturally responsive rather than assaultive. (p. 53)

Figure 7.2 describes several professional learning activities in each of the three areas the authors have detailed: sociocultural consciousness, affirming attitudes and becoming a change agent, and narrowing to a building-level focus.

Zone 2: Increasing Educator's Recognition of Gifted Characteristics in CLED Students

The second zone focuses on teacher recognition of how gifted characteristics are manifested in different cultural groups. Teachers are often the first step in the identification process; therefore, they must be open-minded and aware of possible cultural bias. Pierce et al. (2007) found that without training, teachers tend to rely on their own understandings of giftedness, which may limit their ability to recognize giftedness in gifted CLED students. Teachers may fail to identify students who do not exhibit characteristics that align with their view of giftedness (Moon & Brighton, 2008). Teacher referral is an ideal way to identify students if the classroom teachers are prepared and trained to identify the characteristics of giftedness. Research suggests positive effects of training on teachers' abilities to recognize gifted characteristics in both social and academic realms (Moon & Brighton, 2008; Rizza & Morrison, 2003; Szymanski & Shaff, 2013). However, teachers may overlook a CLED student for identification if the student does not fit the traditional characteristics of giftedness, or if the teacher's personal bias toward or lack of understanding about a cultural group limits his or her perceptions of giftedness (Lewis, Novak, & Coronado, 2015). As part of a Texas equity initiative, Slocumb and Olenchak (2006) looked at how gifted students from poverty exhibit different characteristics of giftedness from

Professional Learning Activities: Sociocultural Consciousness

- Create individual cultural identity pie charts: Each person creates a pie chart displaying the percentage of influence each of the areas of diversity shapes who he or she is (including socioeconomic status, race, ethnicity, gender, religion, sexual orientation, age, and language).
- Participate in 2-minute talks: Teachers pair up. Partner One speaks for 2 minutes about an area of diversity and the influence on his or her life. After 2 minutes, partners switch, and Partner Two shares his or her story.
- Watch a "What Would You Do?" TV segment, and discuss the scenario in small groups.

Professional Learning Activities: Affirming Attitudes and Becoming a Change Agent

- Establish a forum for idea exchanges and a safe place for inquiring about different cultures.
- Provide collaboration opportunities to build content knowledge and skills.
- Create visual signage representative of diverse cultural groups and display it within the school, as well as include it on school flyers.

Professional Learning Activities: Narrowing the Focus to Your Building

- Invite a panel of parent representatives to come in and share about their culture and experiences with schools.
- Use high-quality literature in a book study to provide teachers with an opportunity to learn about a culture.
- Provide workshops focused on learning about a specific culture represented in the school/district, diving deeply into the heart of the culture, exploring cultural norms, stereotypes, educational experiences, and expectations.

Figure 7.2. Zone 1 professional learning activities.

their peers; they further explored the intersectionality that exists between poverty, ELLs, students with special needs, and twice-exceptional students, recommending that attributes of these students be included in identification instruments. To address this, multicultural education and gifted education should be combined through professional learning, creating a culturally responsive gifted training that incorporates academic, affective, cognitive, cultural, psychological, and social domains mirrored by the students (Ford et al., 2008).

Research shows that teacher awareness of gifted CLED students directly impacts their perceptions of these students. Allen (2017) conducted a qualitative study focused on teacher perceptions of gifted CLED learners. With increased professional development focused on the characteristics of gifted CLED students, the teacher awareness levels increased, resulting in a more favorable outcome for gifted CLED students. Milner and Ford (2007) stated that, "Teachers must rethink how they define and evaluate students' academic potential as they see students and themselves through cultural lenses and pursue cultural competence" (p. 170).

The second zone of the professional development plan is critical for increasing the percentage of identified gifted CLED students. Here, the teachers receive targeted professional learning experiences, individualized based on the student body population. Teachers may only recognize traditional traits of gifted children and not recommend a CLED student for the identification process. Some CLED students fall into multiple diverse groups, which further masks the presentation of their giftedness, according to typical gifted characteristics. See Table 7.2 for examples of atypical gifted characteristics and how these are seen in culturally, linguistically, and economically diverse students.

Research-based best practice in identification includes multiple measures toward identification: assessment instruments that are both valid and reliable for the population, student interviews and portfolios, parent rating scales, and "the use of checklists, incorporating multiple criteria, to be completed by teachers trained to recognize how giftedness is manifested in CLD learners" (NAGC, 2011, p. 1). This second indicator is addressed by Zone 2, providing focused professional learning experiences on the manifestations of giftedness that are particular to different CLED facets, specifically those found in the school district. Figure 7.3 provides examples of such activities.

Zone 3: Increasing Classroom Support for Educators and CLED Gifted Students

The third zone focuses on ways to increase support in the classroom for the identified gifted CLED student. Districts that have changed their identification procedures to include students from culturally diverse backgrounds may struggle with the retention of these gifted students. Often the gifted CLED students' experience does not align with that of their gifted peers.

Table 7.2
Selected Atypical Gifted Characteristics

		Atypical Gifted Characteristics				
Culturally Diverse	African American	Prefer hands-on learning (Stambaugh & Ford, 2015)	Prefer concrete methods of learning (Stambaugh & Ford, 2015)	Creative storytellers (Stambaugh & Ford, 2015)	Leadership qualities, more likely to question authority (Stambaugh & Ford, 2015)	Underachievers due to peer pressure to fit cultural norms (Stambaugh & Ford, 2015)	Variations in academic performance (Stambaugh & Ford, 2015)
	Hispanic	High academic achievement, ability to transfer knowledge; methodical problem solvers who take time to process information (Lara-Alecio & Irby, 2000)	Prefer to work in groups; females tend to defer to males in leadership roles (Esquierdo & Arreguin-Anderson, 2012)	Methodical problem solvers who take time to process information (Lara-Alecio & Irby, 2000)	Creative thinking abilities (Brulles, Castellano, & Laing, 2011)	Collective society, prefer to work in groups (Esquierdo & Arreguin-Anderson, 2012)	Strong familial connections: interpersonal relationships (Lara-Alecio & Irby, 2000)
	Native American	Delayed, thoughtful responses (Siegle et al., 2016)	May struggle with English, as many are bilingual; speak Native American languages and dialects (Gentry, 2015)	Observe, watch, and listen (Gentry, 2015)	Aspire to positively contribute to their tribal culture (Fisher, 2008)	Oral storytelling (Christensen, 1991; Lewis, 2017)	Value cooperation, not competition (Siegle et al., 2016)
Linguistically Diverse	English Language Learners	Quickly learn second language: both academic and social (Lara-Alecio & Irby, 2000)	May have limited vocabulary and vivid language, but language is rich with imagination (Blackburn, Cornish, & Smith, 2016)	Advanced problem-solving skills (Blackburn et al., 2016)	Ability to code-switch at an advanced level compared to peers (Lara-Alecio & Irby, 2000)	Exit English language programs at a quicker rate than their peers (Blackburn et al., 2016)	Diverse cultural backgrounds, circumstances for entering K–12 schools, all factors that influence the expressions of giftedness (Blackburn et al., 2016)
Economically Diverse	Poverty	Exceptional memory or knowledge (VanTassel-Baska & Stambaugh, 2007)	Creative (VanTassel-Baska & Stambaugh, 2007)	Highly imaginative-storytellers (VanTassel-Baska & Stambaugh, 2007)	High energy (VanTassel-Baska & Stambaugh, 2007)	Academic performance varies based on pressures to fit into peer group (VanTassel-Baska & Stambaugh, 2007)	Diverse cultural backgrounds, circumstances for entering K–12 schools, all factors that influence the expressions of giftedness (Blackburn et al., 2016)

> **Professional Learning Activities: CLED Gifted Characteristics**
>
> - Case studies provide an excellent way of synthesizing and analyzing different ways giftedness is portrayed in CLED.
> - Provide sessions in which CLED gifted characteristics are contrasted with typical gifted characteristics.
> - Provide sessions focused on recognizing gifted potential and gifted ability.
> - Provide sessions focused on ways to foster gifted behaviors.
> - Lunch and learn: Teachers share sample student work and discuss potential gifted characteristics.
> - Provide sessions to review the referral process within the district and the difference between identification and referrals.

Figure 7.3. Zone 2 professional learning activities.

They may also struggle with the traditional gifted programming because the program is trying to serve a unique student population using traditional methods, without accommodating for cultural differences (Ford & Grantham, 2003; Hines et al., 2016). For example, a gifted English language learner may struggle in a gifted class in which language barriers impede his or her understanding of the material. If this student was provided the same gifted content in his or her native language, the student would be given the opportunity to soar. Schools, however, tend to operate in a deficit model focused on remediation instead of exploring opportunities for developing potential (Allen, 2017; Baldwin, 2002; Ford & Grantham, 2003). Zone 3 has two topical considerations for professional learning: curricular shifts and implementing support structures.

Swanson (2016) conducted a review of five Javits projects examining how effective innovative practices were. One of the major findings was that powerful curriculum and instruction have the potential to change teacher mindsets and practices, and that "the degree of teacher impact was tied to the level of supports found in the school/district in terms of coaching, demonstration, development opportunities, access to materials, and consistency of leadership involvement" (p. 179). With continuous professional development and support for teachers, the teachers experienced a shift in their perceptions from a deficit mindset toward CLED to a strength view, seeking out potential within CLED students (Swanson, 2016).

Within Zone 3, professional learning should aim to reflect, examine, and modify the gifted curriculum currently used by teachers. Even prior to identification, a curricular shift can occur that benefits gifted CLED students. Advanced exposure to critical and creative thinking and entry-level exposure to gifted curriculum is recommended prior to the formal identification process, thereby exposing students to the kind of thinking and understandings that they are being screened for and will be learning when they have access to the gifted program (Briggs et al., 2008; NAGC, 2011; Olszewski-Kubilius & Steenbergen-Hu, 2017). This process is often referred to as frontloading; it "bridges the gap in the readiness of some CLED students, nurtures their abilities, and prepares them for success in advanced content programs," (Briggs et al., 2008, p. 137).

Milner and Ford (2007) suggested incorporating open learning environments in which the goal of learning is knowledge acquisition, seeking answers to questions, and making meaning out of content. When teachers encourage students to share their own voices, unique perspectives, and personal experiences, gifted programs are more likely to retain CLED students who feel empowered by their roles in the learning process. Both content and context matter in culturally responsive gifted curriculum (Milner & Ford, 2007; Swanson, 2016). As seen earlier, the first zones are deeply rooted in cultural competence; the same holds true for Zone 3. Curriculum for CLED students must be responsive to their readiness and interests because:

> when curriculum is rigorous and multicultural—culturally responsive—then more Black and Hispanic students will be engaged and motivated. With engagement and motivation comes performance; with higher performance or achievement comes greater representation in gifted education. (Ford, 2010b, p. 35)

NAGC (2011) recommended creating curriculum for CLED students using best practices found across the fields of gifted education, multicultural education, and bilingual education:

> High-quality, advanced curriculum designed for CLED students needs to continue to be created, providing students, who might otherwise be overlooked, an opportunity to demonstrate that they can respond to advanced curriculum. . . . Such options can be provided only in environments free from single-criteria admissions, discriminatory counseling, and narrow recruitment. (p. 1)

Figure 7.4 presents different activities that can be useful in working with teachers in creating curricular shifts that support CLED gifted students.

NAGC (2011) created a research-driven position statement with regard to identifying and serving CLED students. This stated the importance of not just identification, but also retention of CLED students:

> **Professional Learning Activities: Curricular Shifts**
>
> - Develop a student-centered curriculum that incorporates cultural themes.
> - Provide sessions focused on ways to develop talent and potential during gifted programming.
> - Provide sessions focused on early intervention in the years prior to gifted screening.
> - Create hands-on units that provide scaffolding for CLED students.
> - Partner with the English as a second languge (ESL) teachers to develop materials, including bilingual materials.
> - Partner with the ESL teachers to explore strategies for teaching English language learners.
> - Provide sessions linking how cultural groups express their giftedness and explicit ways to modify the gifted curriculum to include these variations.
> - Provide sessions that offer the time, guidance, and support to create differentiated curriculum.
>
> **Figure 7.4.** Zone 3 professional learning activities.

Attending to social and emotional development is also critical to the success of CLD populations. These students are often less likely to remain in gifted programs without psychological support and appropriate programming. Program supports may come in various forms. The establishment of cohort groups of students with shared cultural background has been found to have positive impact on retention, promoting a sense of belonging and support. Instituting gender- and culture-specific mentoring programs potentially enhances self-esteem and provides strong role models. School counselors may also facilitate small-group sessions to address concerns of CLD students. (p. 2)

During professional learning experiences in Zone 3, providing teachers with strategies to support gifted CLED students in the classroom is essential. One strategy utilizes Response to Intervention (RtI) with gifted ELLs. RtI is frequently used in schools to intervene with behavior and academic concerns. RtI is a three-level intervention process. Tier I interventions meet the needs of 70% of the classroom, Tier II interventions meet the needs of 20% of the classroom, and Tier I interventions address the needs of 10% of the classroom. At each Tier, the instruction and instructor become more specialized and tailored to the student's learning profile. Strength-Based RtI supports talent developed through the tier system of support (Bianco, 2010;

Bianco & Harris, 2014). This model utilizes culturally responsive curriculum and pedagogy, along with tiered levels, which support talent development, while engaging with the cultural norms, values, and beliefs. Strength-Based RtI encourages student inquiry, exploration and development of talent, and interests and strengths opposed to most deficit types of models (Bianco & Harris, 2014; Ford & Trotman Scott, 2013). One downside to this model is that it relies on the teachers having a knowledge and skill base to work with this set of students.

Yet, if one follows the Four Zone Professional Learning Approach, Strength-Based RtI has the potential to have a great impact on student talent development and retention in gifted programming. Tier I intervention hinges on a core curriculum that is culturally responsive and instructional strategies that provide opportunities for talent development of ELLs. Students are provided opportunities to demonstrate understanding through multiple measures, highlighting their CLED strengths, while minimizing those measures that inhibit their demonstration of understanding. For example, an English language learner would focus on oral products while minimizing the use of written assessments. A multicultural curriculum that challenges and promotes higher order thinking skills along with universal screening of students fosters growth within the CLED student. The universal screening provides educators with data to use in identifying those students who would benefit from Tier II intervention (Bianco & Harris, 2014). Tier II intervention occurs in the regular education classroom but provides the acceleration or depth exploration of content. Collaboration between the classroom, gifted, and English as a second language (ESL) teachers is important in Tier II to ensure quality enrichment. The goal of this tier is to challenge the student and increase expectations (Bianco & Harris, 2014). Tier III interventions occur when students' needs are not fulfilled at the Tier II level. According to Langley (2016):

> Rather than simply looking for manifest ability, preparation programs are designed to support young students in developing latent abilities through a variety of talent development methods. Similarly, adaptations to the Response to Intervention (RTI) model employ a strength-based approach with increasing levels of gifted interventions in response to student potential to foster identification of underrepresented populations including GT EL or specifically for GT EL. Both preparation and RTI programs benefit from key stakeholders understanding GT EL characteristics and working collaboratively to meet their needs. (para. 7)

Coteaching is an example of professional learning experience that is critical to the retention of gifted CLED students with the potential to address both curricular shifts and classroom supports. Coteaching requires collaboration between teachers to discuss, plan, and foster student growth, and can be used as a method of professional learning, on the part of either teacher, depending on their strengths and roles in the school (Fogarty & Tschida, 2018). Successful coteachers rely on each other's strengths to guide the instruction. For example, the classroom teacher partnering with both the gifted and ESL teacher to provide high-quality, challenging gifted curriculum for CLED students may not only result in academic gains, but also an increased awareness of student language and culture on the part of the gifted teacher and an increased knowledge of gifted pedagogy on the part of the ESL teacher.

Professional learning sessions that model coteaching strategies, partner teachers, and provide examples of the various ways coteaching can be implemented are critical to the successful implementation of coteaching. Additionally, follow-up sessions—virtual chat rooms, informal meetings, or formal sessions—are essential to the successful implementation of the coteaching model (Hughes & Murawski, 2001). Educators are working cooperatively to enhance each other's skill sets while fostering student achievement. Coteaching has the potential to increase gifted CLED student retention rates as educators learn best practices from their peers. For example, the gifted cluster teacher who is partnered with a bilingual teacher would benefit by learning strategies and techniques for modifying the curriculum for language needs, while the bilingual teacher increases her skill set related to gifted characteristics. It is important for participating teachers to recognize coteaching as a symbiotic relationship rather than a predatory one. The goal of coteaching is to provide opportunities for "dialogue, planning, shared and creative decision making, and follow-up between at least coequal professionals with diverse expertise" (Hughes & Murawski, 2001, p. 196). NAGC (2014a) supported the coteaching model:

> NAGC believes that high quality collaboration does not obviate the need for gifted education services or for gifted education specialists, but rather redefines the roles of educators in the plan for serving gifted and talented students. Collaboration calls for shared responsibility for recognizing indicators of giftedness and responding to those unique characteristics through more comprehensive and individualized programming options. Collaboration builds a community of insightful educators who create learning environments that are more challenging and engaging for all students, that better meet the needs of those who have been identified for gifted services, and that enable teach-

ers to recognize potential giftedness in diverse populations. (para. 4)

Differentiation is part curriculum, part support structure, and wholly needed to engage and retain CLED students in gifted programs (Baldwin, 2002; Ford, 2010b). This differentiation must be "inclusive of the histories and significant events of the cultures of students selected for the program . . . it is not being suggested that there be a separate curriculum . . . but one that students of all cultures will explore in a differentiated manner" (Baldwin, 2002, p. 143). Baldwin recommended differentiated curriculum that includes creating belief statements and goals with regard to the inclusive and responsive nature of the curriculum. Figure 7.5 lists activities that can be used in professional learning to support teachers pedagogically.

Zone 4: Increasing and Developing Partnerships With CLED Parents and Community

Parental and community outreach is a significant factor in the success of gifted CLED students. Ford and Grantham (2003) indicated that although schools identify this factor as important, few schools take steps to build partnerships. The reason could be due to a deficit view, causing teachers not to reach out to their culturally diverse families to share information about gifted programming. Also, parents may "view schools with suspicion and doubt the school's commitment to their children. Such parents are unlikely to involve themselves in school settings because of the belief that they are not valued as a resource and member of the school community" (Ford & Grantham, 2003, p. 223).

Briggs et al. (2008) studied gifted programs that were successful at identifying and serving CLED students. They found that successful programs incorporated some form of parental involvement and/or community support, including distributing newsletters and holding information sessions for parents, and seeking mentorship programs, university partnerships, field trips, and donation support from the community. A 2011 NAGC position paper summarized this need:

> Research linking the success of CLD gifted learners to positive family relationships and home environment provides examples of students excelling in school despite economic and social barriers. Building relationships among home,

> **Professional Learning Activities: Supporting the Classroom Teachers and CLED Students**
>
> - Provide sessions focused on Strength-Based RtI.
> - Provide sessions focused on coteaching.
> - Build professional learning communities.
> - Provide sessions focused on ways to differentiate the curriculum for CLED students
> - Provide sessions focused on how to support CLED students' social-emotional needs, including academic identity and coping strategies for peer pressure and discrimination.

Figure 7.5. Zone 3 professional learning activities.

school, and communities of CLD students requires active support for, and involvement of, families in gifted education programs. A positive view of home contexts can also help to improve home-school relationships. Advocacy training led by CLD parents, teachers, and other school personnel with dual expertise in diversity education and gifted education can lead to family-school-community support groups. (p. 2)

Educators and administrators are responsible for building a bridge to parents and community, helping shift the culture of deficit thinking to strength-based, or dynamic, thinking, and providing learning experiences around identification and serving CLED students with gifted potential (Ford & Grantham, 2003; Hines et al., 2016). Grantham et al. (2005) recommended that families of gifted CLED students gain knowledge in three areas: underachievement, barriers to identification, and gifted attributes.

Schools and programs reap the benefit of parental outreach, not just the students (Grantham et. al, 2005). Parents can help teachers infuse cultural perspectives into the program, while helping to provide consistency in the home-school connection. When parents are involved in identification and placement, cultural manifestations of student giftedness, such as those discussed in Zone 2, become a natural part of the procedures. Baldwin (2002) recommended that parents be a part of the process, from identification to development and evaluation of the program. Finally, "as non-partisan advocates, parents' role in school initiatives to address the needs of culturally diverse gifted students . . . can provide the support to make grassroots, as well as large scale school improvements" (Grantham et al., 2005, p. 146). Figure 7.6 offers suggestions of professional learning sessions to utilize with parents and communities of gifted CLED students.

> ### Professional Learning Activities: Increasing and Developing Partnerships With CLED Parents and Community
>
> - Host sessions in which community partners are invited to share about their organizations and involvement with the CLED youth.
> - Host sessions in which parents are invited to share about their cultural group and experiences with giftedness, as well as bond with each other, forming relationships and informal support groups.
> - Provide a session in which community partners participate in a Gifted 101 workshop and are given the opportunity to share their thoughts.
> - Provide sessions targeting the parents of CLED students prior to identification to explore:
>   - what it means to be gifted,
>   - the benefits of being in the gifted program,
>   - how to develop and foster talent in their children, and
>   - how giftedness is expressed differently amongst different groups.
> - Provide sessions targeting the parents of CLED students after identification to explore:
>   - "my child has been identified for gifted services, now what?";
>   - how to provide support for the gifted student at home;
>   - how to connect your child with other gifted students from the same CLED groups;
>   - parental support groups within the same CLED groups; and
>   - how to develop and foster talent in your child.

Figure 7.6. Zone 4 professional learning activities.

Professional learning for parents and the community is twofold. District administrators can provide the learning experiences for the parents and community themselves, which is a form of professional learning, or they can train teachers via districtwide professional learning sessions, so that teachers can conduct the family and community outreach efforts.

Summary

The underrepresentation of CLED students in gifted programs is a national problem. As a field, time, research, and attention must be paid to address this disturbing deficiency. Recommendations vary for identification practices, from testing suggestions to identification procedures. One such recommendation is to eliminate teachers as the gatekeepers to the testing process for identification (Peters, n.d.); however, many districts across the United States still use teacher recommendation as part of the identification process. Acting as the change agent, this Four Zone Professional Learning Approach provides teachers with high-quality professional learning that is ongoing, multifaceted, tailored to their specific student demographics, and supportive. Throughout this chapter, the authors have given specific suggestions for professional learning activities that schools and districts can put into play. When fully implemented, this approach has the potential to significantly impact teacher perception and understandings, which, in turn, impact student referrals, opportunities for gifted identification, and retention within gifted programming.

References

Abellán-Pagnani, L., & Hébert, T. P. (2013). Using picture books to guide and inspire young gifted Hispanic students. *Gifted Child Today, 36*(1), 47–56.

Allen, J. K. (2017). Exploring the role teacher perceptions play in the underrepresentation of culturally and linguistically diverse students in gifted programming. *Gifted Child Today, 40,* 77–86.

Baldwin, A. Y. (2002). Culturally diverse students who are gifted. *Exceptionality, 10,* 139–147.

Betts, G. (2016). *Gifted education standards to guide teaching and deepen student learning* [Web log post]. Retrieved from http://www.nagc.org/blog/gifted-education-standards-guide-teaching-and-deepen-student-learning

Bianco, M. (2010). Strength-based RTI: Conceptualizing a multi-tiered system for developing gifted potential. *Theory Into Practice, 49,* 323–330.

Bianco, M., & Harris, B. (2014). Strength-based RTI: Developing gifted potential in Spanish-speaking English language learners. *Gifted Child Today, 37,* 169–176.

Blackburn, A. M., Cornish, L., & Smith, S. (2016). Gifted English language learners: Global understandings and Australian perspectives. *Journal for the Education of the Gifted, 39,* 338–360.

Briggs, C. J., Reis, S. M., & Sullivan, E. E. (2008). A national view of promising programs and practices for culturally, linguistically, and ethnically diverse gifted and talented students. *Gifted Child Quarterly, 52,* 131–145.

Brulles, D., Castellano, J. A., & Laing, P. C. (2011). Identifying and enfranchising gifted English language learners. In J. A. Castellano & A. D. Frazier (Eds.), *Special populations in gifted education: Understanding our most able students from diverse backgrounds* (pp. 249–269). Waco, TX: Prufrock Press.

Christensen, R. A. (1991). A personal perspective on tribal-Alaska Native gifted and talented education. *Journal of American Indian Education, 31,* 10–14.

de Wet, C. F., & Gubbins, E. J. (2011). Teachers' beliefs about culturally, linguistically, and economically diverse gifted students: A quantitative study. *Roeper Review, 33,* 97–108.

Esquierdo, J. J., & Arreguín-Anderson, M. (2012). The "invisible" gifted and talented programs. *Journal for the Education of the Gifted, 35,* 35–47.

Every Student Succeeds Act, Pub. L. No. 114–95. (2015).

Fisher, T. (2008). *Identifying and teaching gifted Native American students* [Web log post]. Retrieved from http://blogs.edweek.org/teachers/unwrapping_the_gifted/2008/01/identifying_and_teaching_gifte.html

Fogarty, E. A., & Tschida, C. M. (2018). Using coteaching as a model of professional learning. In A. M. Novak & C. L. Weber (Eds.), *Best practices in professional learning and teacher preparation: Methods and strategies for gifted professional development* (Vol 1., pp. 151–171). Waco, TX: Prufrock Press.

Ford, D. Y. (2010a). Culturally responsive classrooms: Affirming culturally different gifted students. *Gifted Child Today, 33*(1), 50–53.

Ford, D. Y. (2010b). Underrepresentation of culturally different student in gifted education: Reflections about current problems and recommendations for the future. *Gifted Child Today, 33*(3), 31–35.

Ford, D. Y., & Grantham, T. C. (2003). Providing access for culturally diverse gifted students: From deficit to dynamic thinking. *Theory Into Practice, 42,* 217–225.

Ford, D. Y., Grantham, T. C., & Whiting, G. W. (2008). Culturally and linguistically diverse students in gifted education: Recruitment and retention issues. *Exceptional Children, 74,* 289–306.

Ford, D. Y., & Trotman Scott, M. (2013). Culturally responsive response to intervention: Meeting the needs of students who are gifted and culturally different. In M. R. Coleman & S. K. Johnsen (Eds.), *Implementing RtI with gifted students: Service models, trends, and issues* (pp. 209–228). Waco, TX: Prufrock Press.

Gay, G. (2010). Culturally responsive teaching: Theory, research, and practice (2nd ed.). In J. A. Banks (Series Ed.), *Multicultural education series*. New York, NY: Teachers College Press.

Gentry, M. (2015, November). *Identifying and serving gifted and talented Native American students: Future directions for research, partnerships, and practices*. Breakout session presented at the annual conference of the National Association for Gifted Children, Phoenix, AZ.

Grantham, T. C., Frasier, M. M., Roberts, A. C., & Bridges, E. M. (2005). Parent advocacy for culturally diverse gifted students. *Theory Into Practice, 44,* 138–147.

Hines, M. E., Anderson, B. N., & Grantham, T. C. (2016). Promoting opportunity, rigor, and achievement for underrepresented students. In R. D. Eckert & J. H. Robins (Eds.), *Designing services and programs for high-ability learners: A guidebook for gifted education* (2nd ed., pp. 151–168). Thousand Oaks, CA: Corwin.

Hodges, J., Tay, J., Maeda, Y., & Gentry, M. (2018). A meta-analysis of gifted and talented identification practices. *Gifted Child Quarterly, 62,* 147–174.

Hughes, C. E., & Murawski, W. A. (2001). Lessons from another field: Applying coteaching strategies to gifted education. *Gifted Child Quarterly, 45,* 195–204.

Kea, C., Campbell-Whatley, G. D., & Richards, H. V. (2006). *Becoming culturally responsive educators: Rethinking teacher education pedagogy*. Tempe, AZ: National Center for Culturally Responsive Educational Systems.

King, K. A., Artiles, A. J., & Kozleski, E. B. (2009). *Exemplar brief series: Professional learning for culturally responsive teaching*. Tempe, AZ: National Center for Culturally Responsive Educational Systems.

Langley, S. D. (2016). *Fostering equitable access to gifted services for English learners through a balance of measures and program options*. Retrieved from https://www.nagc.org/blog/fostering-equitable-access-gifted-services-english-learners-through-balance-measures-and

Lara-Alecio, R., & Irby, B. (2000). The culturally and linguistically diverse in gifted. In C. Reynolds (Ed.), *Encyclopedia of special education* (pp. 506–510). New York: NY: John Wiley.

Learning Forward. (2011). *Standards for professional learning*. Oxford, OH: Author.

Lewis, K. D. (2017). Culturally responsive gifted educators: Reaching every child, every day. *TEMPO, 38*(1), 14–19.

Lewis, K. D., Novak, A. M., & Coronado, J. (2015). Teachers' perceptions of characteristics of gifted Hispanic bilingual students: Perspectives from the border. *Texas Forum of Teacher Education, 5*(1), 71–91.

Marland, S. P., Jr. (1972). *Education of the gifted and talented: Report to the Congress of the United States by the U.S. Commissioner of Education and background papers submitted to the U.S. Office of Education*, 2 vols. Washington, DC: U.S. Government Printing Office. (Government Documents, Y4.L 11/2: G36)

McKoy, C. L., MacLeod, R. B., Walter, J. S., & Nolker, D. B. (2017). The impact of an in-service workshop on cooperating teachers' perceptions of culturally responsive teaching. *Journal of Music Teacher Education, 26,* 50–63.

Milner, H. R., & Ford, D. Y. (2007). Cultural considerations in the underrepresentation of culturally diverse elementary students in gifted education. *Roeper Review, 29,* 166–173.

Mizell, H. (2010). *Why professional development matters.* Oxford, OH: Learning Forward.

Moon, T. R., & Brighton, C. M. (2008). Primary teachers' conceptions of giftedness. *Journal for the Education of the Gifted, 31,* 447–480.

National Association for Gifted Children. (2011). *Identifying and serving culturally and linguistically diverse gifted students* [Position statement]. Washington, DC: Author.

National Association for Gifted Children. (2014a). *Collaboration among all educators to meet the needs of gifted learners* [Position statement]. Washington, DC: Author.

National Association for Gifted Children. (2014b). *State of the nation in gifted education: Work yet to be done.* Washington, DC: Author.

National Association for Gifted Children, & The Association for the Gifted, Council for Exceptional Children. (2013). *NAGC-CEC teacher preparation standards in gifted education.* Retrieved from http://www.nagc.org/sites/default/files/standards/NAGC-%20CEC%20CAEP%20standards%20%282013%20final%29.pdf

Office for Civil Rights. (2014). *2013-14 state and national estimation* [Data file]. Retrieved from https://ocrdata.ed.gov/StateNationalEstimations/Estimations_2013_14

Olszewski-Kubilius, P., & Steenbergen-Hu, S. (2017). Blending research-based practices and practice-embedded research: Project Excite closes achievement and excellence gaps for underrepresented gifted minority students. *Gifted Child Quarterly, 61,* 202–209.

Olthouse, J. (2013). Multiliteracies theory and gifted education: Creating "smart spaces" in the language arts classroom. *Gifted Child Today, 36,* 247–253.

Peters, S. J. (n.d.). *Identifying under-served student populations for gifted programs: Some methods and frequently asked questions.* Roseville, MN: Minnesota Department of Education.

Pierce, R. L., Adams, C. M., Neumeister, K. L. S., Cassady, J. C., Dixon, F. A., & Cross, T. L. (2007). Development of an identification procedure for a large urban school corporation: Identifying culturally diverse and academically gifted elementary students. *Roeper Review, 29*, 113–118.

Rizza, M. G., & Morrison, W. F. (2003). Uncovering stereotypes and identifying characteristics of gifted students and students with emotional/behavioral disabilities. *Roeper Review, 25*, 73–77.

Siegle, D., Gubbins, E. J., O'Rourke, P., Langley, S. D., Mun, R. U., Luria, S. R., . . . Plucker, J. A. (2016). Barriers to underserved students' participation in gifted programs and possible solutions. *Journal for the Education of the Gifted, 39*, 103–131.

Slocumb, P. D., & Olenchak, F. R. (2006). *Equity in gifted/talented education: A state initiative.* Austin, TX: Texas Education Agency.

Snyder, T. D., de Brey, C., & Dillow, S. A. (2016). *Digest of education statistics 2015* (NCES 2016-014). Washington, DC: National Center for Education Statistics, Institute of Education Services, U.S. Department of Education.

Stambaugh, T., & Ford, D. Y. (2015). Microaggressions, multiculturalism, and gifted individuals who are Black, Hispanic, or low income. *Journal of Counseling & Development, 93*, 192–201.

Swanson, J. D. (2016). Drawing upon lessons learned: Effective curriculum and instruction for culturally and linguistically diverse gifted learners. *Gifted Child Quarterly, 60*, 172–191.

Szymanski, T., & Shaff, T. (2013). Teacher perspectives regarding gifted diverse students. *Gifted Children, 6*(1). Retrieved from: http://docs.lib.purdue.edu/giftedchildren/vol6/iss1/1

U.S. Department of Education. (2016). *Non-regulatory guidance for Title II, Part A: Building systems of support for excellent teaching and leading.* Washington, DC: Author.

VanTassel-Baska, J., & Stambaugh, T. (2007). *Overlooked gems: A national perspective on low-income promising learners.* Washington, DC: National Association for Gifted Children.

Yaluma, C. B., & Tyner, A. (2018). Is there a gifted gap?: Gifted education in high-poverty schools. *Thomas B. Fordham Institute.* Retrieved from http://edex.s3-us-west-2.amazonaws.com/publication/pdfs/%2801.31%29%20Is%20There%20a%20Gifted%20Gap%20-%20Gifted%20Education%20in%20High-Poverty%20Schools.pdf

CHAPTER 8

Empowering Educators to Implement Acceleration:
Professional Learning Is Essential

Laurie J. Croft and Ann Lupkowski-Shoplik

Introduction

The act of teaching requires deliberate interventions to ensure that there is cognitive change in the student; thus the key ingredients are being aware of the learning intentions, knowing when a student is successful in attaining those intentions, having sufficient understanding of the student's prior understanding as he or she comes to the task, and knowing enough about the content to provide meaningful and challenging experiences so that there is some sort of progressive development. (Hattie, 2012, p. 19)

Most contemporary educational researchers have acknowledged that teachers can be important catalysts for student learning (Fisher, Frey, & Hattie, 2016; Hattie, 2009; Jimerson & Haddock, 2015), noting that "teachers matter more to student achievement than any other aspect of schooling" (RAND Corporation, 2012, p. 1). Hattie (2012) suggested that teachers can be effective only if they consciously see themselves as change agents, focusing on their students' cognitive engagement with content, knowing "where to go next in light of the gap between students' current knowledge and understanding" (p. 22). Hattie also emphasized that teachers must be aware of how they are impacting the "progress and proficiency of all of their students" (p. 23). According to Fisher et al. (2016), "great teachers know that different approaches work for some students better than for other students" (p. 3).

In order to serve as effective catalysts for the transformation of student abilities into exceptional talent—that is, to engage gifted learners' needs, interests, and motivation (Gagné, 2010)—teachers of the gifted require professional learning experiences that will facilitate their understandings of and ability to implement educational and instructional strategies that address unique academic needs of gifted students. A wide variety of such strategies is included within the broad concept of academic acceleration, which allows talented students to move through the curriculum at a pace that matches their abilities or "at ages younger than conventional" (as cited in Southern & Jones, 2015, p. 9). Just as professional development enhances the quality of educators in general education, from their pedagogical practice to their impact on student learning (Borko, 2004; Desimone, Porter, Garet, Yoon, & Birman, 2002; Guskey, 2002; Penuel, Fishman, Yamaguchi, & Gallagher, 2007; Yoon, Duncan, Lee, Scarloss, & Shapley, 2007), professional development focused on best practices in gifted education is essential (Dettmer & Landrum, 1998; Dettmer, Landrum, & Miller, 2006; Karnes, Stephens, & Whorton, 2000; Reis & Westberg, 1994).

Professional Development and Gifted Education

> There is no guarantee that either teachers or school counselors in a given school have been exposed to the concept and practice of acceleration, its research underpinnings, or school district or state policies regarding acceleration. (Croft & Wood, 2015, p. 88)

Although scholars recognize the importance of professional development in gifted education, and the 2014–2015 State of the States in Gifted

Education (National Association for Gifted Children [NAGC] & Council of State Directors of Programs for the Gifted [CSDPG], 2015) affirmed that "the availability of qualified teachers and other personnel is a critical factor to the success of programs for gifted and talented students" (p. 10), the State of the States reported that just 19 states require professionals working in gifted programs to have credentials/endorsements, with seven of those states requiring annual professional development for these educators. Only five states require any professional development about gifted education for general education teachers, and preservice teachers have a guarantee of substantive information about gifted education in only one state. Professional development about gifted education, ensuring qualified professionals, is limited.

Professional understanding about acceleration is even more limited. "Acceleration" is included in the Glossary of the NAGC-CEC Teacher Preparation Standards in Gifted and Talented Education (NAGC & the Council for Exceptional Children, The Association for the Gifted [CEC-TAG], 2013, p. 6), and the Pre-K–Grade 12 Gifted Programming Standards (NAGC, 2010) explicitly referred to acceleration in Standard 5, Programming. However, the State of the States (NAGC & CSDPG, 2015) reported that only eight of the responding states required schools to allow content-based acceleration. Subject acceleration was mentioned by 12 states as a frequent strategy for upper elementary gifted learners, by 11 states for middle school students, and by six states for high school students. "Honors/advanced coursework" was used by 15 states at the middle school level (pp. 35–36) and by 17 states at the high school level (p. 36). Advanced Placement programs were utilized by 23 states to provide an acceleration option for high school students. No state prohibited "acceleration" (p. 41), although 13 states prohibited early entrance to kindergarten, and two did not permit dual/concurrent enrollment at the middle school level. Although only 13 states had policies that specifically permitted acceleration, 12 explicitly directed local education agencies (LEAs) to determine policy, and 15 had no state-level policies, leaving decisions to LEAs. The NAGC and CSDPG (2015) State of the States survey of local practices included references to additional specific accelerative options, including grade-level advancement, continuous progress, self-paced learning, telescoped learning, mentoring, curriculum compacting, pre-Advanced Placement programming, and the International Baccalaureate—some cited for just one state.

Professional Development and Acceleration

> Acceleration is the best-researched, yet most under-utilized educational option available for gifted students. (Lupkowski-Shoplik, 2015)

On a webpage dedicated to gifted education practices, NAGC (n.d.) reminded readers that:

> educational acceleration is one of the cornerstones of exemplary gifted education practices, with more research supporting this intervention than any other in the literature on gifted individuals. The practice of educational acceleration has long been used to match high-level students' general abilities and specific talents with optimal learning opportunities. (para. 3)

Hattie (2012), in syntheses of research about strategies that have an impact on student learning, supported acceleration for gifted learners. Hattie ranked acceleration as 15th on a list of 150 influences on achievement, acknowledging its large and positive effect size averaged from 75 meta-analyses of 4,340 studies. Nevertheless, the term *acceleration* is not conceptualized as a broad concept encompassing multiple strategies, because it is often thought to be synonymous with grade-skipping. Even educators of the gifted may be ill-prepared to implement one of the accelerative strategies that would benefit a student because they simply have not had the opportunity to learn about acceleration. A review of the archives of the Gifted Teachers Listserv (Gifted-Teachers Homepage, 2013–2017), a list supported by the University of Iowa Belin-Blank Center with more than 1,200 subscribers, found that, over 5 years (January 2013–December 2017), only 3% of messages included the word "acceleration" in the subject line. Some 10% included a reference specifically to acceleration in the body of the message. Even among practitioners, this topic, with its extensive research base, seldom comes up in online exchanges. As reflected in the State of the States (NAGC & CSDPG, 2015), additional considerations are given to specific accelerative options (e.g., Advanced Placement), but notably, most of the discussions on the Gifted-Teachers Homepage (2013–2017) Listserv come from teachers requesting recommendations for research that will help convince colleagues and administrators to consider the academic acceleration of a student.

A Model of Professional Development for Acceleration

> Accelerated students are more successful, have higher productivity rates, more prestigious occupations and they earn more and increase their income faster compared to older, similar-ability, non-accelerated peers. Therefore, acceleration provides both short-term (within educational settings) and long-term (workplace settings) benefits. (McClarty, 2015, p. 171).

Croft and Wood (2015) proposed a model of professional development relevant specifically to acceleration that emphasizes professional reflection and the willingness to question both attitudes and practice (see Figure 8.1). Without a candid exploration of preexisting attitudes and beliefs about the efficacy of academic acceleration for gifted learners, professional learning experiences about acceleration strategies may have no impact on practice. These beliefs were internalized years before, when educators spent thousands of hours as students themselves. Without encouragement, these educators might not recognize as implicit their attitudes about student behaviors, characteristics, ability, and responsibility for learning and behaving in certain ways, impacting their own professional efforts to ensure student success (Miller, 2009; Nespor, 1987; Pajares, 1992).

Figure 8.1 builds on Guskey's (1986) Model of the Process of Teacher Change, as well as on Clarke and Hollingworth's (2002) Interconnected Model of Teacher Growth, with elements of the informal conceptualization of "Characteristics of Effective Special Educators" (Benedict, Brownell, Park, Bettini, & Lauterbach, 2014). Professional learning about acceleration can be envisioned as a dependable recipe, with supplementary directions added as appropriate for each individual educator. Each recipe blends the ingredients differently, as teachers perceive unanticipated student needs and begin a quest to meet those needs. As Lynn (2002) suggested, "teachers have different attitudes, knowledge, skills, and behaviors at various points during their career [sic]" (p. 179), and successful professional learning occurs within the context of individual career stages, as well as the organizational environment and personal willingness to reflect and grow, adopting new practices. When accelerative interventions result in greater student and parent satisfaction, as well as in academic growth, the positive feedback from students and parents alike affirm the adoption of acceleration practices and policies.

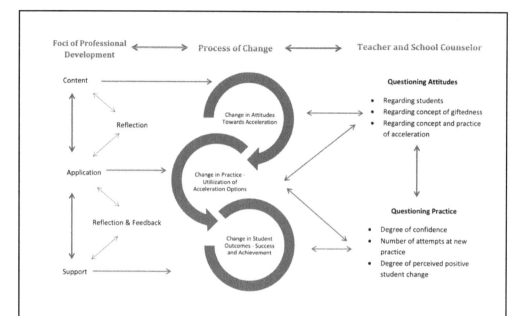

Figure 8.1. A proposed model of professional development around acceleration. From "Professional Development for Teachers and School Counselors: Empowering a Change in Perception and Practice of Acceleration," by L. Croft and S. M. Wood, in *A Nation Empowered: Evidence Trumps the Excuses Holding Back America's Brightest Students* (Vol. 2, p. 94), by S. G. Assouline, N. Colangelo, J. VanTassel-Baska, and A. Lupkowski-Shoplik (Eds.), 2015, Iowa City: University of Iowa, The Connie Belin & Jacqueline N. Blank International Center for Gifted Education and Talent Development. Copyright 2015 The Connie Belin & Jacqueline N. Blank International Center for Gifted Education and Talent Development. Reprinted with permission.

What Educators Need to Know About Acceleration

Acceleration is one of the most curious phenomena in the field of education. I can think of no other issue in which there is such a gulf between what research has revealed and what most practitioners believe. The research on acceleration is so uniformly positive, the benefits of appropriate acceleration so unequivocal, that it is difficult to see how an educator could oppose it. (Borland, 1989, p. 185)

Because educators do not receive much training in their preservice education about academic acceleration, it is important to consider what specific information educators need to learn about acceleration. Table 8.1 provides an overview of main points that teachers, administrators, school counselors, and school psychologists need to know about this topic. As a starting point in professional learning, professionals may need to be encouraged to recognize that their districts are already providing some forms of acceleration (e.g., Advanced Placement classes). Awareness that their schools already do at least some type of acceleration may be helpful in putting aside negative assumptions or reluctant feelings when considering specific forms of acceleration (e.g., whole-grade acceleration or dual enrollment for middle school students). The goal of professional development about acceleration is to help educators reflect on their attitudes and practices, as illustrated in the Proposed Model of Professional Development Around Acceleration (see Figure 8.1), as well as to understand the research and to believe that one or more of the 20 types of acceleration can provide the best possible opportunity for success for some gifted students. To alter existing beliefs, teachers, administrators, school counselors, and school psychologists need to know where to find the research that can better inform reflections on Borland's curious phenomenon stated at the start of this section.

At Least 20 Types of Acceleration Appropriate for Specific Student Needs

> Acceleration is a central consideration in gifted education, with close linkages to most definitions and conceptions of giftedness in childhood and adolescence. (Little, 2018, p. 374)

Acceleration can be divided into two main categories: grade-skipping and subject acceleration (also called content acceleration). In the grade-skipping category, the student completes school in a shorter overall amount of time (e.g., a student who skips 10th grade would finish high school in 3 years instead of 4). Subject acceleration does not necessarily result in the student graduating at a younger age than typical, but it does mean that the student is placed in a more advanced class for at least part of the day. Although grade-skipping typically means that the student is moved into a higher grade and, therefore, has little impact on the "system" of the school, subject acceleration might engender issues, such as transportation questions (e.g., if a student needs to move from one building to another

Table 8.1
What Do Teachers, Administrators, School Counselors, and School Psychologists Need to Know About Acceleration?

1. At least 20 different types of acceleration can be tailored to the specific needs of a gifted student. These include content acceleration (in which a student moves ahead in a specific subject), curriculum compacting, dual enrollment in high school and college, and whole-grade acceleration.
2. Acceleration is an effective option for gifted students. Research demonstrates that acceleration works for gifted students, both in the short term and long term (e.g., Assouline, Colangelo, VanTassel-Baska, & Lupkowski-Shoplik, 2015).
3. Research-based tools can help in making informed decisions about acceleration:
    - Decisions for whole-grade acceleration: Iowa Acceleration Scale (e.g., Assouline, Colangelo, Lupkowski-Shoplik, Lipscomb, & Forstadt, 2009)
    - Decisions for subject acceleration: Above-level testing, talent search model
4. Acceleration supports students' social and emotional development by placing them with like-minded peers—students who demonstrate similar academic abilities and interests.
5. Acceleration provides students with academic challenges and intellectual stimulation. These are required for the continuous development of students' abilities.
6. Acceleration is inexpensive; it does not require pricey training on the part of teachers, and it does not require special equipment. The additional costs of acceleration might include transportation (if the student is subject accelerated and must move from one building to another during the school day) or the cost of online courses (if advanced courses are unavailable in the student's school).

during the school day) and scheduling conflicts (e.g., if a student is moving to a higher math class, but that higher math class is scheduled at the same time as the student's history class).

The 20 different types of acceleration are highlighted in Figure 8.2, allowing educators to quickly recognize strategies implemented in their districts. Southern and Jones (2015) provided clear explanations of each and included examples, allowing educators to fully understand the breadth of accelerative options, from the familiar and more widely accepted, to alternatives that generate more opposition. These 20 different types of acceleration allow educators to tailor programs to the needs of the student.

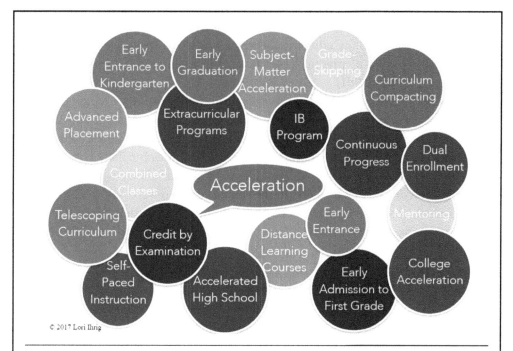

Figure 8.2. Types of acceleration (Southern & Jones, 2015). From "Gifted Education Awareness Month: Academic Acceleration" [Web log post], by Ann Lupkowski-Shoplik, 2018, retrieved from https://belinblank.wordpress.com/2018/10/16/gifted-education-awareness-month-academic-acceleration. Copyright 2017 by Lori Ihrig. Reprinted with permission of The Connie Belin & Jacqueline N. Blank International Center for Gifted Education and Talent Development.

Acceleration Is Effective

> Acceleration options appear to be the most cost effective and the best researched of all educational policy options available for consideration, even though they receive less public acclaim than other options. (VanTassel-Baska, 2015, p. 43)

Research demonstrates that acceleration works for gifted students, both in the short term and long term. Much of the current research on acceleration is summarized in the publication *A Nation Empowered* (Assouline, Colangelo, VanTassel-Baska, & Lupkowski-Shoplik, 2015). The chapter by Rogers (2015) includes an analysis similar to Hattie's (2012) work, grouping many studies together into a much larger study, culminating in the metric known as effect size. Essentially, larger effect sizes equate to more significant impacts. Many educational researchers consider an effect size of at least 0.30 to be of practical significance in a classroom setting (Glass, McGaw, & Smith, 1981).

Table 8.2 lists selected effect sizes from Rogers's (2015) chapter. All of the academic effects were of practical significance (greater than 0.30). Every one of these effects was positive, indicating that accelerated students performed better than the comparison group. Studies typically compared accelerated students to same-age students of similar ability who were not accelerated *or* to older students in the same class who were not accelerated. In general, accelerated students performed quite well academically relative to the comparison group; the effect sizes were all positive and greater than 0.30.

Longitudinal research with several different groups of academically talented students also endorses the use of acceleration as an educational option for gifted students. For example, longitudinal studies conducted by the Study of Mathematically Precocious Youth (SMPY) offer a positive long-term outlook. Adults who were accelerated in middle and high school recalled their experiences before college more positively than nonaccelerated intellectual peers; furthermore, these accelerated students did not regret their acceleration, and some even wished they had accelerated more (Lubinski, 2004). Additional SMPY studies indicated positive outcomes for accelerated students: These students attained advanced degrees, produced scholarly works, and contributed professionally at high rates (Lubinski, Benbow, Webb, & Bleske-Rechek, 2006; Wai, 2015). In a separate study using the 1988 National Education Longitudinal Study data, McClarty (2015) controlled for changing economic cycles by comparing accelerated students to older students of similar ability who began their careers at the same time. The accelerated students demonstrated advantages over the older peers of similar ability. They worked in more prestigious occupations, were more successful, showed higher rates of productivity, earned more money, and increased incomes faster than older, similar-ability, nonaccelerated peers. These many longitudinal and short-term studies indicate that academic acceleration is an educational success story. Indeed, we consider ignoring the evidence from these decades of research studies to be educational malpractice.

Table 8.2
Selected Effect Sizes From Rogers (2015)

Type of Acceleration	Type of Effect	Average Effect Size
Accelerated/honors high school classes	Academic	+0.69
	Social	+0.11
	Psychological	+0.60
Advanced Placement courses	Academic	+0.60
	Social	+0.01
	Psychological	+0.19
Computer online courses	Academic	+0.72
	Psychological	+0.24
Concurrent/dual enrollment	Academic	+0.41
	Psychological	-0.04
Early entrance to kindergarten or first grade	Academic	+0.30
	Social	+0.20
	Psychological	-0.20
Grade-skipping	Academic	+0.67
	Social	+0.34
	Psychological	+0.42
Radical acceleration (students skipped two or more grades)	Academic	+0.61
	Social	+0.18
	Psychological	+0.42
Single-subject acceleration	Academic	+0.42
	Social	+0.07
	Psychological	+0.35

Tools to Make Objective, Informed Decisions About Acceleration

Thousands of students are told to lower their expectations, and put their dreams on hold. Whatever they want to do, their teachers say, it can wait. (Colangelo, Assouline, & Gross, 2004, p. 3)

Gone are the days of one person (perhaps the principal) calling on his or her "gut feelings" to make a decision about a grade skip for a student.

As Vescio, Ross, and Adams (2008) reported, professional learning provides opportunities for educators to acquire new knowledge and skills and to reflect on and improve teaching practice. Educators have easy access to objective tools that focus on the many different aspects of a student's development, facilitating informed, balanced, research-driven decisions about acceleration. Two effective tools are the Iowa Acceleration Scale (Assouline, Colangelo, Lupkowski-Shoplik, Lipscomb, & Forstadt, 2009) and the Talent Search Model (Assouline & Lupkowski-Shoplik, 2012). Teachers can independently review how to utilize these tools, or they can participate in professional learning communities to understand how to gather information essential for making objective decisions, changing the professional cultures of their schools (Vescio et al., 2008).

Iowa Acceleration Scale

The Iowa Acceleration Scale (IAS) is designed to help educators and parents make decisions about a grade skip for students in kindergarten through eighth grade; it is also useful in making decisions about early entrance to kindergarten or first grade. Additionally, for students who might not be good candidates for a grade skip, the data collected as part of the process of completing the IAS can be useful in thinking about subject acceleration. The IAS is a guidance tool, not a test. It guides a child study team (including parents, teachers, administrators, school counselors, and other professionals) through a discussion of the academic and social characteristics of the student. The goal is to look at the student more objectively, document the student's strengths and concerns, weigh the major factors in the decision, and compare the student to others who have successfully accelerated.

Talent Search Model

Educators need to understand and explain to administrators, colleagues, and parents that making objective decisions about subject acceleration requires collecting relevant information about the students' achievements and aptitudes in the specific subject area. Above-level testing, as used in the Talent Search Model, provides the necessary information for making informed decisions about moving students ahead in a particular subject. Since the 1970s, above-level testing has been used with hundreds of thousands of students as a way of identifying exceptional talent (Assouline & Lupkowski-Shoplik, 2012; VanTassel-Baska, 1984). As the first step in the Talent Search Model, students have already performed very well on grade-level tests (such as the Iowa Assessments or Terra Nova). Typically, experts recommend that students scoring at the 95th percentile or above on one or more sections of their grade-level test participate in above-level testing, although the recommended cutoff can vary.

In the second step of the Talent Search Model, the students take a test designed for older students. The idea is that these young, bright students have "hit the ceiling" of the grade-level test, demonstrated by their perfect, or near perfect scores. When they take the above-level test, the test ceiling is raised and students have the opportunity to showcase the extent of their talents. Some of the tests currently used in this process include the SAT and ACT (for students in grades 7–9) and I-Excel (for students in grades 4–6). Students often participate in above-level testing opportunities through a university-based talent search, such as the Belin-Blank Exceptional Student Talent Search at the University of Iowa, the Center for Talent Development at Northwestern University, the Center for Talented Youth at Johns Hopkins University, or the Talent Identification Program at Duke University. These university-based talent searches have developed extensive interpretations of the above-level tests and have demonstrated that students scoring at varying levels on these tests benefit from differentiated educational programming. VanTassel-Baska (1984) noted that the utilization of the Talent Search Model "has clearly shown and demonstrated, on a case study basis, that students have profited enormously from exposure to accelerated programs and coursework," leading to a "'change of attitude' about acceleration," as well as "the implementation of acceleration policies and practices at both the local and state levels" (p. 175).

Additional Resources

Additional resources useful in learning about academic acceleration and making informed decisions are listed in Table 8.3. Any of these can be explored by sole practitioners who learn about and disseminate information related to gifted learners in their districts or by professional learning communities that commit to better understanding how to implement academic acceleration. All of the resources are accessible to interested individuals who want their districts to provide best practices to their advanced learners. One of the most comprehensive resources is *A Nation Empowered* (Assouline, Colangelo, & VanTassel-Baska, 2015; Assouline, Colangelo, VanTassel-Baska, & Lupkowski-Shoplik, 2015), a two-volume publication that synthesizes research from the last 70 years demonstrating the efficacy of acceleration for gifted students, as well as various websites and online groups or organizations.

Table 8.3
Resources About Acceleration

Resource	Website	More Information
Acceleration Institute	https://www.accelerationinstitute.org	• Website devoted to providing resources about academic acceleration • Special sections for educators, parents, researchers, and policymakers • Provided by the University of Iowa Belin-Blank Center
Belin-Blank Center, College of Education, University of Iowa	https://belinblank.education.uiowa.edu	• Online graduate courses and webinars on acceleration • Summer programs for teachers • Talent Search • Online Advanced Placement courses for students and professional development in Advanced Placement programs for teachers
Davidson Institute for Talent Development	https://www.davidsongifted.org	• A national nonprofit organization supporting profoundly gifted students • Includes an Educators' Guild, a free online community
Hoagies' Gifted Education Page	https://www.hoagiesgifted.org	• Extensive information on gifted education • Educators and parents can find many resources related to accelerative options, including differentiation and grouping
IDEAL Solutions for STEM Acceleration	https://www.idealsolutionsmath.com	• An online system for informing decisions about academic acceleration in STEM subjects based on above-level test scores • Individualized recommendations aligned with national standards

Table 8.3, continued.

Resource	Website	More Information
Iowa Acceleration Scale	https://www.accelerationinstitute.org/Resources/IAS.aspx	• A guidance tool for educators and families to make informed decisions about whole-grade acceleration • Available from Great Potential Press
National Association for Gifted Children	https://www.nagc.org	• Annual conference provides sessions on acceleration and recent research on its effectiveness • NAGC also provides publications on acceleration (e.g., parent TIP sheets, including one on acceleration available at https://www.nagc.org/resources-publications/resources-parents/parent-tip-sheets)
A Nation Empowered	https://www.accelerationinstitute.org/nation_empowered	• A significant update to the 2004 watershed publication, A Nation Deceived (https://www.accelerationinstitute.org/nation_deceived)

Note. Adapted from Croft & Wood (2015).

Talking Points on Acceleration

Educators can facilitate straightforward professional discussions related to acceleration by familiarizing themselves with research related to traditional concerns. These talking points can be helpful in such a discussion.

1. Acceleration Supports Students' Social and Emotional Development

People often mention concerns about a student's social and psychological well-being when beginning a conversation about acceleration. As can be seen in the effect sizes listed in Table 8.2, the findings from many studies conducted over many years do not support these concerns. In many of the studies included in Rogers's (2015) research syntheses, there were very small or no differences between the accelerated students and the comparison groups. In other syntheses reported by Rogers, the accelerated students performed notably better than comparison groups. This means that there were no major negative effects on students' socialization correlated with acceleration. Although it is critical to look at each student individually and to consider all aspects of their development when discussing acceleration, educators need to feel confident that stopping the discussion about acceleration because of concerns about social development simply is not supported by the research.

Gifted students tend to gravitate toward older students for their friendships; this makes sense because gifted students, as a group, demonstrate more psychosocial maturity (e.g., Robinson, 2004). In other words, they tend to seek out older students because they are ready to play more sophisticated games, to study more advanced concepts, and to engage in more nuanced conversations than their age-mates. Academic acceleration can provide like-minded peers for gifted students and, therefore, provide a more suitable socialization setting for them.

2. Acceleration Provides Academic Challenges and Intellectual Stimulation

In order for students to develop their abilities, they need continuous academic challenges. Not only does the appropriate development of academic talent benefit the wider community, but also it benefits the individual student. Students who experience appropriate educational challenges are more engaged in school, have a reason to work hard, and avoid learning bad educational habits of mind. Engaging in challenging experiences may help students avoid underachievement. Students who are challenged and engaged in school are more likely to have positive social interactions; therefore, appropriate levels of challenge, which can be found by allowing students to move ahead to more advanced academic material, enhance students' social development. Advanced curriculum is essential to challenge bright students (Assouline, Colangelo, & VanTassel-Baska, 2015).

3. Acceleration Is Inexpensive

Utilizing acceleration does not require investment in expensive professional development, and it does not require special equipment. Very little additional cost is involved if a student is simply moved from one classroom to another. Additional costs of acceleration might include transportation (if the student is subject accelerated and must move from one building to another during the school day) or the cost of online courses (if advanced courses are unavailable in the student's school). Educators and families must inform themselves about—and access—the tools and information helpful in making decisions about acceleration and to participate in careful planning that weighs the important factors in making those decisions.

Professional Learning About Academic Acceleration

> In spite of evidence supporting the efficacy of acceleration for gifted students, widespread resistance to the concept and practice exists. . . . Many teachers and administrators are reluctant to allow or create variances for individual students. (Schiever & Maker, 2003, p. 166)

Although much has been published about academic acceleration, many of the strategies are still not practiced widely. Typically, acceleration practices are not discussed in professional preparation programs for either teachers or school counselors (Croft & Wood, 2015). Sometimes, parents who have done their homework about acceleration are better informed than the administrators and teachers with whom they are discussing their child's placement. Regular classroom teachers, gifted education specialists, school counselors, school psychologists, and administrators would all benefit from learning about the research and tools supporting decisions about acceleration. Table 8.4 lists many different ways for educators to connect with peers interested in acceleration, facilitating just-in-time professional learning about acceleration. This type of information serves as the content essential to launching the process of change in attitudes toward acceleration (review the Proposed Model of Professional Development Around Acceleration).

Because acceleration includes so many options, introducing acceleration into a school or district might seem overwhelming. As an initial step in their reflection about existing attitudes and beliefs about acceleration, educators should list the accelerative options that the school is already utilizing (such as honors classes, Advanced Placement classes, or ability grouping for mathematics). They should explore the positive results from these options. Once individuals realize that their school is already "doing" acceleration successfully and recognize positive impacts on student achievement, as suggested in the Proposed Model of Professional Development Around Acceleration, their professional reflections can make it easier to utilize additional types of acceleration, such as grade-skipping or curriculum compacting.

Questioning attitudes sometimes arise in one educator in a district who is motivated to learn about academic acceleration because of a need presented by a single student. What that first educator learns underpins the process of change, providing positive feedback that bolsters the degree of confidence expressed in the district, so that additional students might benefit. Some resources and important points for reflection that need to be included in professional learning opportunities about academic acceleration include the following:

1. Misunderstandings and a lack of knowledge regarding the concept and practice of acceleration result in reluctance to try new strategies. These misunderstandings suggest that acceleration means "rushing" a student, that acceleration will somehow damage a student's social development, and that age is the best determiner for grade placement. A frank discussion among colleagues and administrators about some of these misunderstandings and assumptions, when examined in light of extensive research findings, will be helpful in shining a light on the issues (see Colangelo et al., 2004, for a helpful discussion).

2. The PowerPoint presentation developed by the Acceleration Institute (https://www.accelerationinstitute.org) at the University of Iowa Belin-Blank Center is appropriate to share with colleagues, administrators, and even child-study teams: https://www.accelerationinstitute.org/Resources/PowerPoint/Default.aspx. This PowerPoint presentation explores educators' reluctance to accelerate students because they haven't had previous opportunities to learn about the practice. The presentation offers examples of successful applications of whole-grade and subject acceleration and summarizes the research that focuses on successful student outcomes that result from accelerative options.

3. Resources for parents are important. Educators in the district who are beginning their quests to understand acceleration can download

Table 8.4
Connecting With Other Educators Interested in Academic Acceleration

1. Follow the Twitter hashtag #nationempowered.

2. Investigate the "Blog Hops" provided by the Hoagies' Gifted Education Page, available at https://www.hoagiesgifted.org/blog_hops.htm. Hoagies has offered at least two blog hops focused on acceleration (https://www.hoagiesgifted.org/blog_hop_acceleration.htm and https://www.hoagiesgifted.org/blog_hop_acceleration_2.htm).

3. Live educational chats are offered on Twitter. These help to highlight current issues and information in education. For example, see the weekly chats offered by the Texas Association for Gifted and Talented (https://www.txgifted.org/gtchat) and the Ohio Association for Gifted Children (https://ohiogtchat.weebly.com). These chats sometimes focus on academic acceleration.

4. The Belin-Blank Center at the University of Iowa offers a Gifted Education and Talent Development Ning (https://giftededucationandtalentdevelopm.ning.com). It is a free resource for those interested in gifted and talented education. In the top righthand corner, notice the link to sign up and create a new account. You must log in to access the content.

5. The Belin-Blank Center also provides a listserv for gifted teachers and coordinators as another way to connect. To subscribe to the Gifted Teachers e-mail list, send an e-mail to listserv@list.uiowa.edu and, in the text of your message (not the subject line), write: SUBSCRIBE GIFTED-TEACHERS First-Name Last-Name.

6. Connect with other educators through your local educational agency, and establish a book study for *A Nation Empowered* (Assouline, Colangelo, & VanTassel-Baska, 2015; Assouline, Colangelo, VanTassel-Baska, & Lupkowski-Shoplik, 2015) or articles about academic acceleration.

7. Explore coaching and follow up. As you continue learning about acceleration, make a note of experts you might connect with to help you as you consider questions about acceleration.

8. Sign up for online professional learning through live and recorded webinars offered by the Belin-Blank Center (https://belinblank.education.uiowa.edu/Educators/Webinar) or through the National Association for Gifted Children (https://www.nagc.org/professional-learning/e-learning-demand).

9. Consider university courses about academic acceleration. For example, the Belin-Blank Center offers a 3-semester-hour course on acceleration each year. See https://belinblank.education.uiowa.edu/Educators/Courses.

10. Subscribe to the Belin-Blank Center electronic newsletter, which often includes articles about acceleration, available at https://mailchi.mp/uiowa/whats-new-at-the-belin-blank-center-980265.

and share the NAGC Tips for Parents about acceleration (Guilbault & Lupkowski-Shoplik, 2017). This TIP Sheet provides a general overview, resources about acceleration, and questions to ask about implementing acceleration. Although written for parents, it is also useful as an introduction to reflect on unexplored professional attitudes about acceleration for gifted learners.

4. One section of the Acceleration Institute website is specifically tailored to educators. It includes general questions and answers about the educational practice of acceleration (https://accelerationinstitute.org/Resources/QA), and an extensive list of resources freely available from *A Nation Empowered* (https://accelerationinstitute.org/Nation_Empowered/NE_Vol2_AppendixE.pdf). As delineated in the Proposed Model of Professional Development Around Acceleration, the easy accessibility of research-based resources allows professionals to reflect on the origins of their attitudes about acceleration. Reflection facilitates changes in attitudes toward acceleration, encouraging school personnel to utilize a greater variety of acceleration options; positive outcomes for students reinforce growing support for the practice.

Conclusions

> Studies . . . have investigated what specific qualities gifted students expect in their teachers. All parties involved believe that in the case of gifted students, teachers play a very significant role. (Khalil & Accariya, 2016, p. 409)

For educators to be effective catalysts for the development of talent among their most capable learners, as envisioned in the Proposed Model of Professional Development Around Acceleration, they must reflect on the most successful ways to impact student achievement for their gifted learners. "Great teachers know that different approaches work for some students better than for other students" (Fisher et al., 2016, p. 3), and acceleration is key to both short-term and long-term success for many high-ability students. Most educators were not introduced to acceleration strategies in their teacher education programs, and very few states mandate annual professional development for teachers of the gifted, or professional learning about gifted education for general education teachers (NAGC, 2015). Individual student need often inspires professional interest in, questioning attitudes regarding, and personal professional learning about the concept and practice of acceleration. This individual student need may be the initial motivation for teachers, counselors, school psychologists, and administrators to reflect on their existing concerns about acceleration and to learn more about the extensively researched best practices for accelerative options; this disposition toward reflection is integral to the Proposed Model of Professional Development Around Acceleration. Interested professionals have easy access to the research that unequivocally reports positive short-term academic and social-emotional outcomes for students, as well as positive long-term professional outcomes, associated with acceleration strategies. Professionals have access to the Iowa Acceleration Scale, a tool that guides educators to review the factors that must be taken into account for each individual child for whom whole-grade acceleration is considered. As part of their professional learning, these educators need to reflect on personal attitudes and beliefs that might contrast with decades of research, recognizing that "acceleration does not mean pushing a child . . . or forcing a child to learn advanced material or socialize with older children before he or she is ready" (Colangelo et al., 2004, p. 5). When armed with the research, educators will have much greater confidence that "all highly gifted children should be at least considered for academic acceleration because it is the best chance for them to find true peers and receive an appropriate level of challenge in the learning environment" (Neihart & Yeo, 2018, p. 505).

References

Assouline, S., Colangelo, N., Lupkowski-Shoplik, A., Lipscomb, J., & Forstadt, L. (2009). *Iowa Acceleration Scale manual: A guide for whole-grade acceleration K–8* (3rd ed.). Scottsdale, AZ: Great Potential Press.

Assouline, S. G., Colangelo, N., & VanTassel-Baska, J. (Eds.). (2015). *A nation empowered: Evidence trumps the excuses holding back America's brightest students* (Vol. 1). Iowa City: University of Iowa, The Connie Belin & Jacqueline N. Blank International Center for Gifted Education and Talent Development.

Assouline, S., Colangelo, N., VanTassel-Baska, J., & Lupkowski-Shoplik, A. (Eds.). (2015). *A nation empowered: Evidence trumps the excuses that hold back America's brightest students* (Vol. 2). Iowa City: University of Iowa, The Connie Belin & Jacqueline N. Blank International Center for Gifted Education and Talent Development.

Assouline, S. G., & Lupkowski-Shoplik, A. (2012). The talent search model of gifted identification. *Journal of Psychoeducational Assessment, 30,* 45–59.

Benedict, A. E., Brownell, M. T., Park, Y., Bettini, E. A., & Lauterbach, A. A. (2014). Taking charge of your professional learning: Tips for cultivating special educator expertise. *Teaching Exceptional Children, 46,* 147–157.

Borko, H. (2004). Professional development and teacher learning: Mapping the terrain. *Educational Researcher, 33*(8), 3–15.

Borland, J. H. (1989). *Planning and implementing programs for the gifted.* New York, NY: Teachers College Press.

Clarke, D., & Hollingsworth, H. (2002). Elaborating a model of teacher professional growth. *Teaching and Teacher Education, 18,* 947–967.

Colangelo, N., Assouline, S. G., & Gross, M. U. M. (2004). *A nation deceived: How schools hold back America's brightest students* (Vol. 1). Iowa City: The University of Iowa, The Connie Belin & Jacqueline N. Blank International Center for Gifted Education and Talent Development.

Croft, L., & Wood, S. M. (2015). Professional development for teachers and school counselors: Empowering a change in perception and practice of acceleration. In S. G. Assouline, N. Colangelo, J. VanTassel-Baska, & A. Lupkowski-Shoplik (Eds.), *A nation empowered: Evidence trumps the excuses holding back America's brightest students* (Vol. 2, pp. 87–98). Iowa City: University of Iowa, The Connie Belin & Jacqueline N. Blank International Center for Gifted Education and Talent Development.

Desimone, L. M., Porter, A. C., Garet, M. S., Yoon, R. S., & Birman, B. F. (2002). Effects of professional development on teachers' instruction: Results from a three-year longitudinal study. *Educational Evaluation and Policy Analysis, 24,* 81–112.

Dettmer, P., & Landrum, M. (Eds.). (1998). *Staff development: The key to effective gifted education programs.* Waco, TX: Prufrock Press.

Dettmer, P. A., Landrum, M. S., & Miller, T. N. (2006). Professional development for the education of secondary gifted students. In F. A. Dixon & S. M. Moon (Eds.), *The handbook of secondary gifted education* (pp. 611–648). Waco, TX: Prufrock Press.

Fisher, D., Frey, N., & Hattie, J. (2016). *Visible learning for literacy, grades K–12: Implementing the practices that work best to accelerate student learning.* Thousand Oaks, CA: SAGE.

Gagné, F. (2010). Motivation within the DMGT 2.0 framework. *High Ability Studies, 21,* 81–99.

Gifted-Teachers Homepage. (2013–2017). *Gifted-teachers list.* Retrieved from LISTSERV Archives at https://list.uiowa.edu/scripts/wa.exe?A0= gifted-teachers

Glass, G. V., McGaw, B., & Smith, M. L. (1981). *Meta-analysis in social research.* Beverly Hills, CA: SAGE.

Guilbault, K., & Lupkowski-Shoplik, A. (2017). *Acceleration* [TIP sheet]. Retrieved from http://www.nagc.org/sites/default/files/Publication%20 PHP/NAGC%20TIP%20Sheet-Acceleration-FINAL.pdf

Guskey, T. R. (1986). Staff development and the process of teacher change. *Educational Researcher, 15*(5), 5–12.

Guskey, T. (2002). Professional development and teacher change. *Teachers and Teaching, 8,* 381–391. doi:10.1080/135406002100000512

Hattie, J. (2009). *Visible learning: A synthesis of over 800 meta-analyses relating to achievement.* New York, NY: Routledge.

Hattie, J. (2012). *Visible learning for teachers: Maximizing impact on learning.* New York, NY: Routledge.

Jimerson, S. R., & Haddock, A. D. (2015). Understanding the importance of teachers in facilitating student success: Contemporary science, practice, and policy. *School Psychology Quarterly, 30,* 488–493.

Karnes, F. A., Stephens, K. R., & Whorton, J. E. (2000). Certification and specialized competencies for teachers in gifted education program. *Roeper Review, 22,* 201–202.

Khalil, M., & Accariya, Z. (2016). Identifying "good" teachers for gifted students. *Creative Education, 7,* 407–418.

Little, C. A. (2018). Teaching strategies to support the education of gifted learners. In S. I. Pfeiffer, E. Shaunessy-Dedrick, & M. Foley-Nicpon (Eds.), *APA Handbook of Giftedness and Talent* (pp. 371–385). Washington, DC: American Psychological Association.

Lubinski, D. (2004). Long-term effects of educational acceleration. In N. Colangelo, S. Assouline, & M. U. M. Gross (Eds.), *A nation deceived: How schools hold back America's brightest students* (Vol. 2, pp. 23–38). Iowa City: The University of Iowa, The Connie Belin & Jacqueline N. Blank International Center for Gifted Education and Talent Development.

Lubinski, D., Benbow, C. P., Webb, R. M., & Bleske-Rechek, A. (2006). Tracking exceptional human capital over two decades. *Psychological Science, 17,* 194–199.

Lupkowski-Shoplik, A. (2015). *Acceleration: Making informed decisions* [PowerPoint slides]. Retrieved from http://www.nagc.org/sites/default/ files/WebinarPowerPoints/Acceleration%20Making%20Informed%20 Decisions.pdf

Lupkowski-Shoplik, A. (2018). *Gifted education awareness month: Academic acceleration* [Web log post]. Retrieved from https://belinblank.wordpress.com/2018/10/16/gifted-education-awareness-month-academic-acceleration

Lynn, S. K. (2002). The winding path: Understanding the career cycle of teachers. *The Clearing House, 75*, 179–182.

McClarty, K. (2015). Early to rise: The effects of acceleration on occupational prestige, earnings, and satisfaction. In S. G. Assouline, N. Colangelo, J. VanTassel-Baska, & A. Lupkowski-Shoplik (Eds.), *A nation empowered: Evidence trumps the excuses holding back America's brightest students* (Vol. 2, pp. 171–180). Iowa City: University of Iowa, The Connie Belin & Jacqueline N. Blank International Center for Gifted Education and Talent Development.

Miller, E. M. (2009). The effect of training in gifted education on elementary classroom teachers' theory-based reasoning about the concept of giftedness. *Journal for the Education of the Gifted, 33*(1), 65–105.

National Association for Gifted Children. (n.d.). *Gifted education practices*. Retrieved from https://www.nagc.org/resources-publications/gifted-education-practices

National Association for Gifted Children. (2010). *NAGC Pre-K–Grade 12 Gifted Programming Standards: A blueprint for quality gifted education programs*. Washington, DC: Author.

National Association for Gifted Children, & The Association for the Gifted, Council for Exceptional Children. (2013). *NAGC-CEC teacher preparation standards in gifted education*. Retrieved from http://www.nagc.org/sites/default/files/standards/NAGC-%20CEC%20CAEP%20standards%20%282013%20final%29.pdf

National Association for Gifted Children, & the Council of State Directors of Programs for the Gifted. (2015). *State of the states in gifted education: National policy and practice data 2014–2015*. Washington, DC: Authors.

Neihart, M., & Yeo, L. S. (2018). Psychological issues unique to the gifted student. In S. I. Pfeiffer, E. Shaunessy-Dedrick, & M. Foley-Nicpon (Eds.), *APA Handbook of Giftedness and Talent* (pp. 497–510). Washington, DC: American Psychological Association.

Nespor, J. (1987). The role of beliefs in the practice of teaching. *Journal of Curriculum Studies, 19*, 317–328.

Pajares, M. F. (1992). Teachers' beliefs and educational research: Cleaning up a messy construct. *Review of Educational Research, 62*, 307–332.

Penuel, W. R., Fishman, B., Yamaguchi, R., & Gallagher, L. P. (2007). What makes professional development effective? Strategies that foster curricular implementation. *American Educational Research Journal, 44*, 921–958.

RAND Corporation. (2012). *Teachers matter: Understanding teachers' impact on student achievement.* Santa Monica, CA: Author.

Reis, S. M., & Westberg, K. L. (1994). The impact of staff development on teachers' ability to modify curriculum for gifted and talented students. *Gifted Child Quarterly, 38,* 127–135.

Robinson, N. M. (2004). Effects of academic acceleration on the social-emotional status of gifted students. In N. Colangelo, S. H. Assouline, & M. U. M. Gross (Eds.), *A nation deceived: How schools hold back America's brightest students* (Vol. 2, pp. 59–68). Iowa City: The University of Iowa, The Connie Belin & Jacqueline N. Blank International Center for Gifted Education and Talent Development.

Rogers, K. B. (2015). The academic, socialization, and psychological effects of acceleration: Research synthesis. In. S. G. Assouline, N. Colangelo, J. VanTassel-Baska, & A. Lupkowski-Shoplik (Eds.), *A nation empowered: Evidence trumps the excuses holding back America's brightest students* (Vol. 2, pp. 19–29). Iowa City: The University of Iowa, The Connie Belin & Jacqueline N. Blank International Center for Gifted Education and Talent Development.

Schiever, S. W., & Maker, C. J. (2003). New directions in enrichment and acceleration. In N. Colangelo & G. A. Davis (Eds.), *Handbook of gifted education* (3rd ed., pp. 163–173). Boston, MA: Pearson.

Southern, W. T., & Jones, E. D. (2015). Types of acceleration: Dimensions and Issues. In S. G. Assouline, N. Colangelo, J. VanTassel-Baska, & A. Lupkowski-Shoplik (Eds.), *A nation empowered: Evidence trumps the excuses holding back America's brightest students* (Vol. 2, pp. 9–18). Iowa City: The University of Iowa, The Connie Belin & Jacqueline N. Blank International Center for Gifted Education and Talent Development.

VanTassel-Baska, J. (1984). The talent search as an identification model. *Gifted Child Quarterly, 28,* 172–176.

VanTassel-Baska, J. (2015). The role of acceleration in policy development. In S. G. Assouline, N. Colangelo, J. VanTassel-Baska, & A. Lupkowski-Shoplik (Eds.), *A nation empowered: Evidence trumps the excuses holding back America's brightest students* (Vol. 2, pp. 43–51). Iowa City: The University of Iowa, The Connie Belin & Jacqueline N. Blank International Center for Gifted Education and Talent Development.

Vescio, V., Ross, D., & Adams, A. (2008). A review of research on the impact of professional learning communities on teaching practice and student learning. *Teaching and Teacher Education, 24*(1), 80–91.

Wai, J. (2015). Long-term effects of educational acceleration. In S. G. Assouline, N. Colangelo, J. VanTassel-Baska, & A. Lupkowski-Shoplik (Eds.), *A nation empowered: Evidence trumps the excuses holding back America's brightest students* (Vol. 2, pp. 73–83). Iowa City: The University of Iowa, The Connie Belin & Jacqueline N. Blank International Center for Gifted Education and Talent Development.

Yoon, K. S., Duncan, T., Lee, S. W.-Y., Scarloss, B., & Shapley, K. (2007). *Reviewing the evidence on how teacher professional development affects student achievement* (Issues & Answers Report, REL 2007–No. 033). Washington, DC: U.S. Department of Education, Institute of Education Sciences, National Center for Education Evaluation and Regional Assistance, Regional Educational Laboratory Southwest.

CHAPTER 9

Designing Professional Learning Centered on Social and Emotional Issues for the Gifted

Elizabeth Shaunessy-Dedrick and Shannon M. Suldo

Introduction

Although there has been a growing interest in the social-emotional needs of the gifted, there has been some question about the classroom teacher's role in addressing social-emotional needs in the classroom because educators' domains have historically been instructional and curricular in nature, and social-emotional needs were considered to be in the realm of guidance counselors and school psychologists (Seligman, Ernst, Gillham, Reivich, & Linkins, 2009). Indeed, schools have historically focused on the business of accomplishment—but absent consideration of students' well-being (Seligman et al., 2009). Given the role that social-emotional development plays in students' lives, the current field of gifted education standards, and the proliferation of works that address these needs, professional learning must include aspects of social-emotional development of gifted students.

The field of gifted education, throughout the last 100 years, has been marked by the study of social-emotional needs of the gifted, beginning with the early work of Terman (1925)—who provided the foundation for understanding the social-emotional needs for the gifted through his longitudinal studies of gifted youth—to Hollingworth (1942), whose work echoed the major findings of Terman, but who also shed light on the social-emotional issues faced by profoundly gifted learners. More recently, other researchers have discussed racial identity issues (Cross & Vandiver, 2001), learners' psychological well-being (Jin & Moon; 2006), academic stress (Suldo & Shaunessy-Dedrick, 2013), and perfectionism (Speirs Neumeister, Williams, & Cross, 2009). One of the most notable recommendations to have emerged in recent literature is the call to nurture the emotional development of high-ability students through addressing motivation, mindset, task commitment, and coping (Subotnik, Olszewski-Kubilius, & Worrell, 2011). Furthermore, educators are asked to integrate psychological strength training in the process of supporting talented individuals in their trajectories toward eminence. Subotnik and colleagues lamented the fact that, although there is a need for these affective supports for students, few—if any—teachers receive training in this realm.

Although only a few researchers have examined social-emotional issues in intervention studies specifically targeting students who are gifted (Jen, 2017), the field has benefitted from a variety of studies that document the range of affective issues experienced among gifted learners, which can serve as a catalyst for greater attention to the nature of social-emotional issues in professional learning. As the studies mention and a multitude of others suggest, students who are identified as gifted vary both in learning and social-emotional needs.

Need for Professional Learning Targeting Social-Emotional Needs of the Gifted

Three important developments point to the need for an increased focus on social-emotional needs in professional learning. The first is a growing research base that reflects associations between social-emotional issues and academic outcomes among all students, including advanced learners (Lubinski & Benbow, 2000; Suldo, Gormley, DuPaul, & Anderson-Butcher, 2014; Suldo, Thalji-Raitano, Kiefer, & Ferron, 2016; Winner, 2000). The second development is the growing interest in a modern framework of mental health, known as positive psychology, which situates the development of individual strengths—including the improvement of the lives of all individuals and the cultivation of exceptional talent—as a core feature of its mission (see Seligman & Csikszentmihalyi, 2000). The third development is the recognition by the field of gifted education that the growing research and aims of positive psychology are indeed associated, and are evidenced in the standards for gifted education (National Association for Gifted Children [NAGC], 2010) as a central consideration in the education of students who are gifted.

Growing Research Base

The first development is a growing research base that reflects associations between social-emotional issues and academic outcomes among all students (Lubinski & Benbow, 2000; Winner, 2000). The critical importance of social-emotional development among the gifted was broached as early as the 20th century with the work of Hollingworth (1942), whose groundbreaking studies of highly and profoundly gifted learners provided great insights as to the social dynamics and needs of gifted learners and their peers. Since that foundational work, other researchers have likewise asserted the importance of supporting gifted students in managing social situations (Swiatek, 2001), academic stress (Suldo & Shaunessy-Dedrick, 2013), and perfectionism (Speirs Neumeister, 2018), among other social-emotional issues experienced by gifted children. In recent years, researchers have established connections between affective needs and social-emotional outcomes, which has elevated the conversation regarding the need to address social-emotional development in schools. Indeed, Subotnik et al. (2011) made a compelling case for such action by positing that talented individuals cannot reach eminence in adulthood without the necessary social and emotional support during the developmental years of youth. Likewise, Rinn (2012) asserted that "the academic needs of gifted individuals cannot be met without simultaneously addressing their psychosocial needs" (p. 207).

For quite some time, researchers have known of associations between challenges with social-emotional issues and poor academic performance (Chen & Kaplan, 2003; Hilsman & Garber, 1995), but during the last several years, there has been an increased interest in understanding how positive social-emotional outcomes are associated with strong academic performance. One aspect of positive psychological functioning that has gained attention is subjective well-being, which captures how individuals feel and think about their lives (Diener, 1984). Individuals who report having high subjective well-being often have lower levels of social and psychological problems, as well as higher levels of physical health, fewer school discipline problems (McKnight, Huebner, & Suldo, 2002), higher self-esteem, and greater intrinsic motivation (Huebner, 1991a) than individuals with low subjective well-being. As there has been a growing interest in the associations between subjective well-being and academic achievement, Bücker, Nuraydin, Simonsmeier, Schneider, and Luhmann (2018) analyzed more than 45 studies of subjective well-being (also known as happiness) and achievement, and found that the relationship between these two constructs is robust. In a related line of research, Suldo et al. (2014) established the interrelation of students' mental health and academic outcomes.

The Influence of Positive Psychology on Gifted Education

Positive psychology aims to cultivate individuals' "personal competencies and environmental resources that facilitate well-being" (Suldo, Hearon, & Shaunessy-Dedrick, 2018, p. 433). Three central themes undergird positive psychology, including positive emotions and experiences, such as well-being, hope, and flow; positive individual traits, such as perseverance, originality, and talent; and virtues and institutions that nurture society, such as responsibility, tolerance, and work ethic (Seligman & Csikszentmihalyi, 2000). These themes and selected examples reflect an alignment between positive psychology and gifted education in that both focus on the promotion of strengths and attainment of optimal well-being, rather than focusing on deficits, remediation, or shortcomings. Although gifted education focuses on the promotion of an individual's unique talents and/or gifts along with the learner's social-emotional development, the field of positive psychology emphasizes fostering an individual's well-being via social-emotional considerations. Thus, there is an argument to be made for professional learning around social-emotional issues, which should be geared toward three audiences: educators of the gifted, teachers of general education—with whom students who are gifted spend the majority of their academic time (Jolly & Robins, 2016), and teachers of children who are twice-exceptional.

Social-Emotional Needs Should Be a Central Consideration for the Education of the Gifted

The field of gifted education has laid a strong foundation for professional learning that focuses on gifted students' social-emotional development through the development of field standards for the education of the gifted (NAGC, 2010), which include aspects of social-emotional development that educators are encouraged to address in their practice (see Table 9.1). The NAGC Standards include standards, student outcomes, and associated evidence-based practices for educators. With respect to the standards, social-emotional issues such as self-understanding and self-awareness, coping skills, resilience, risk-taking, social skills, and relationships are among those recommended.

Ideally, professional learning would be organized to include examination of each of the above three developments (social-emotional and well-being research, gifted education standards, and tenets of positive psychology) in a context that promotes educators' knowledge and skills in addressing social-emotional needs of the gifted. Professional learning would address what has been termed *noncognitive factors*—or social-emotional aspects of an individual—which include a host of considerations, such as mental health (subjective well-being, depression, stress), self-concept, and identity, as well behavioral responses to these issues (e.g., academic coping, social coping, promotion of optimal mental health). A focus, then, of professional learning about the social-emotional needs of the gifted should be an examination of the literature and interventions that have been found to promote optimal outcomes for the gifted. Throughout the remainder of this chapter, recommendations and examples of professional learning are offered that feature an examination of selected field standards addressing social-emotional needs, extant research in the social-emotional needs of the gifted, and interventions that reflect the tenets of positive psychology.

Table 9.1
Selected NAGC (2010) Gifted Education Programming Standards and Associated Educator Standards Addressing Social-Emotional Needs of the Gifted

Standard	Student Outcome	Associated Evidence-Based (Educator) Practices	
1: Learning and Development Educators, recognizing the learning and developmental differences of students with gifts and talents, promote ongoing self-understanding, awareness of their needs, and cognitive and affective growth of these students in school, home, and community settings to ensure specific student outcomes.	**1.1. Self-Understanding.** Students with gifts and talents demonstrate self-knowledge with respect to their interests, strengths, identities, and needs in socio-emotional development and in intellectual, academic, creative, leadership, and artistic domains.	1.1.1. Educators engage students with gifts and talents in identifying interests, strengths, and gifts.	1.1.2. Educators assist students with gifts and talents in developing identities supportive of achievement.
	1.6. Cognitive and Affective Growth. Students with gifts and talents benefit from meaningful and challenging learning activities addressing their unique characteristics and needs.	1.6.1. Educators design interventions for students to develop cognitive and affective growth that is based on research of effective practices.	1.6.2. Educators develop specialized intervention services for students with gifts and talents who are underachieving and are now learning and developing their talents.

Table 9.1, continued.

Standard	Student Outcome	Associated Evidence-Based (Educator) Practices	
4: Learning Environments Learning environments foster personal and social responsibility, multicultural competence, and interpersonal and technical communication skills for leadership in the 21st century to ensure specific student outcomes.	4.1. Personal Competence. Students with gifts and talents demonstrate growth in personal competence and dispositions for exceptional academic and creative productivity. These include self-awareness, self-advocacy, self-efficacy, confidence, motivation, resilience, independence, curiosity, and risk taking.	4.1.2. Educators provide opportunities for self-exploration, development and pursuit of interests, and development of identities supportive of achievement, e.g., through mentors and role models.	4.1.5. Educators provide examples of positive coping skills and opportunities to apply them.
	4.2. Social Competence. Students with gifts and talents develop social competence manifested in positive peer relationships and social interactions.	4.2.1. Educators understand the needs of students with gifts and talents for both solitude and social interaction.	4.2.3. Educators assess and provide instruction on social skills needed for school, community, and the world of work.

Professional Learning Strategies: Strengths

One way educators can pinpoint potential areas for professional learning is to self-assess the degree to which they currently address one or more of the NAGC (2010) standards in their practice. In looking, for example, at Standard 1 (Learning and Development), educators will see that one of the affective standards within this overarching standard is considering gifted learners' self-understanding. Educators may begin professional learning with a self-assessment of how and when they engage students who are gifted and talented in identifying interests, strengths, and gifts (for self-assessments, see Cotabish, Shaunessy-Dedrick, Dailey, Kielty, & Pratt, 2015). Within a district-, school-, or even program-wide meeting of educators for a given grade band (e.g., grades 3–5, grades 6–8), teachers may begin this exercise independently. Following these self-ratings, groups of educators can then share findings with grade-band colleagues, perhaps focusing exclusively on how they embed the promotion of social-emotional strengths into the curriculum. As educators discuss these self-assessments, recorders might note when, how, and to what degree such experiences are embedded in the learning for gifted students. Using this information, the collaborative group may then design an action plan for continued learning in this area that targets specific goals. Such goals may include getting a deeper understanding of social-emotional strengths, ways of assessing Pre-K–grade 12 students' strengths, and ways of addressing these strengths within the curriculum. Depending on the within-district resources, the professional learning group may seek to learn more from a specialist on social-emotional strengths. Alternately, the group may wish to focus on developing a list of readings for discussion, which may then lead the group to identify a specific area within the literature that it would like to explore in greater depth.

In addition to looking to the literature for guidance, educators may also wish to discuss their current knowledge of Pre-K–grade 12 students' social-emotional strengths and the ways these are observed in the classroom. Through a book study, educators may identify chapters of interest to guide such discussions. One such text that may be helpful for this process is a text authored by Neihart, Pfeiffer, and Cross (2016), which provides a comprehensive overview of several dimensions of social-emotional needs, including social-emotional characteristics, areas of social or emotional risk, psychosocial aspects of talent development, and interventions. Following a reading of the selected chapter or chapters, teachers can report on the most notable aspects offered in the chapter, their reflections on these points, and make connections to classroom observations of current or former students. In such discussions, a teacher may recall one or more students who have utilized their strengths to manage learning opportunities (i.e., persevering in task commitment, using adaptive perfectionism, or drawing upon optimism) or who have been less successful in utilizing strengths for optimal social-emotional or academic outcomes. Such anecdotes can serve as a basis for the initial rationale for greater attention to supporting students or may serve as a catalyst for ongoing work with a given student.

Aligning these interests in social-emotional strengths with the aims of positive psychology, educators may wish to examine constructs that have previously been studied among gifted learners, such as life satisfaction (or happiness) and optimism. Additionally, professional learning opportunities addressing social-emotional needs of the gifted may also explore other aspects of affective development that are beyond the scope of positive psychology, such as perfectionism (Speirs Neumeister, 2018) or asynchronous development (Alsop, 2003). To illustrate how educators may organize professional learning content, three issues related to social-emotional needs—life satisfaction, optimism, and perfectionism—are presented in the following sections as individual learning strands. These strands provide examples of thematic learning experiences, such as professional readings, measures, and suggestions for ongoing professional learning. Each of the strands offers educators learning experiences that are sustained, intensive, collaborative, job-embedded, data-driven, and classroom-focused, thus aligning with the professional learning recommendations outlined by Combs and Silverman (2016) and described in the Every Student Succeeds Act (2015). A list of texts that may be useful in professional learning focused on the topics described in this chapter is provided in Table 9.2, and a list of complementary videos is listed in Table 9.3.

Life Satisfaction Strand

To better understand the links between strengths development and student outcomes, Quinlan, Swain, Cameron, and Vella-Brodrick (2015) offered educators an overview of the research that has established positive outcomes associated with promoting strengths and students' outcomes, including interventions with school-aged students. Although this work does not focus exclusively on gifted students, it incorporates a tool that will later be discussed for use with gifted students—the Values in Action Inventory of Character Strengths (VIA; Peterson & Seligman, 2004). The first author of this chapter has utilized the VIA in professional learning with teachers of the gifted, who, in turn, used the same framework for discussing character strengths with K–12 students—including students identified as gifted—in

Table 9.2
Recommended Readings for Professional Learning

Focus	Publications
Flow and optimal experiences	Csikszentmihalyi, M. (2014). *Flow and the foundations of positive psychology: The collected works of Mihaly Csikszentmihalyi.* New York, NY: Springer.
Optimism	Seligman, M. E. P. (2006). *Learned optimism: How to change your mind and your life* (Reprint ed.). New York, NY: Pocket Books. Seligman, M. E. P., Reivich, K., Jaycox, L., & Gillham, J. (2007). *The optimistic child: A proven program to safeguard children against depression and build lifelong resilience* (Reprint ed.). Boston, MA: Houghton Mifflin Harcourt.
Well-being	Seligman, M. E. P. (2002). *Authentic happiness: Using the new psychology to realize your potential for lasting fulfillment.* New York, NY: Atria. Seligman, M. E. P. (2012). *Flourish: A visionary new understanding of happiness and well-being.* New York, NY: Free Press.

graduate coursework leading to a gifted endorsement. Quinlan et al. (2015) noted that the character strengths interventions have typically focused on the development of "individual resources built by an individual for their own benefit" (p. 78). However, the authors question why little attention has been given to the development of character strengths to enhance relationships with others. Quinlan et al. pointed out the useful findings of a study by Govindji and Linley (2007) that involved individuals looking for character strengths in others (termed "strengths spotting") as a way to enhance relationships with teachers and classmates, and as a means of enhancing school climate.

For professional learning, educators would learn about the Awesome Us strengths program—the intervention detailed by Quinlan et al. (2015)—and become familiar with a measure that assesses global life satisfaction in students, called the Students' Life Satisfaction Scale (SLSS; Huebner, 1991b, 1991c). The SLSS is a self-report survey that is available in the public domain and located online; it may be used with children as young as 8 years of age. Table 9.4 directs the reader to the study that describes the initial development of the SLSS, and lists information for other social-emotional measures referenced in this chapter. In Awesome Us, educators are provided an overview of the strengths development and spotting program, which consists of six 90-minute sessions delivered over a period of 6 weeks, and evidence that the program can affect both desirable individual and classroom outcomes. Additional programs that provide classroom lessons for use by educators who aim to promote K–12 students' life satisfaction by developing students'

Table 9.3
Videos for Professional Learning

Focus	Videos
Perfectionism	Bowers, J. (2017). *We should aim for perfectionism—and stop fearing failure* [Video file]. Retrieved from https://www.ted.com/talks/jon_bowers_we_should_aim_for_perfection_and_stop_fearing_failure Haversat, C. (2015). *Perfectionism holds us back. Here's why* [Video file]. Retrieved from https://www.ted.com/watch/ted-institute/ted-state-street/charley-haversat-perfectionism-holds-us-back
Flow and well-being	Csikszentmihalyi, M. (2004). *Flow, the secret to happiness* [Video file]. Retrieved from https://www.ted.com/talks/mihaly_csikszentmihalyi_on_flow
Well-being	Etcoff, N. (2004) *Happiness and its surprises* [Video file]. Retrieved from https://www.ted.com/talks/nancy_etcoff_on_happiness_and_why_we_want_it Gilbert, D. (2004). *The surprising science of happiness* [Video file]. Retrieved from https://www.ted.com/talks/dan_gilbert_asks_why_are_we_happy#t-13000
Resilience	Gilbert, E. (2014). *Success, failure, and the drive to keep creating* [Video file]. Retrieved from https://www.ted.com/talks/elizabeth_gilbert_success_failure_and_the_drive_to_keep_creating
Mindfulness and well-being	Killingsworth, M. (2011). *Want to be happier? Stay in the moment* [Video file]. Retrieved from https://www.ted.com/talks/matt_killingsworth_want_to_be_happier_stay_in_the_moment
Positive psychology	Seligman, M. E. D. (2004). *The new era of positive psychology* [Video file]. Retrieved from https://www.ted.com/talks/martin_seligman_on_the_state_of_psychology
Gratitude and well-being	Steindl-Rast, D. (2013). *Want to be happy? Be grateful* [Video file]. Retrieved from https://www.ted.com/talks/david_steindl_rast_want_to_be_happy_be_grateful

character strengths and/or through other positive psychology activities are listed in Table 9.5.

Increasing identification and use of signature character strengths is a method to promote happiness that is frequently discussed in the positive psychology literature. There are also other interventions and strategies that fall under the umbrella of positive psychology interventions, with the intention of fostering life satisfaction through targeting the factors associated with subjective well-being. Suldo (2016) provided a useful table and brief

Table 9.4
Measures Associated With Social-Emotional Considerations

Scale	Reference
Almost Perfect Scale–Revised	Slaney, R. B., Rice, K. G., Mobley, M., Trippi, J., & Ashby, J. S. (2001). The revised Almost Perfect Scale. *Measurement and Evaluation in Counseling and Development, 34,* 130–145.
Goals Scale	Pedrotti, J. T., Edwards, L. M., & Lopez, S. J. (2008). Promoting hope: Suggestions for school counselors. *Professional School Counseling, 12,* 100–107. doi:10.5330/PSC.n.2010-12.100
Students' Life Satisfaction Scale	Huebner, E. S. (1991). Further validation of the students' life satisfaction scale: The independence of satisfaction and affect ratings. *Journal of Psychoeducational Assessment, 9,* 363–368. doi:10.1177/073428299100900408 Huebner, E. S. (1991). Initial development of the student's life satisfaction scale. *School Psychology International, 12,* 231–240. doi:10.1177/0143034391123010
Values in Action Inventory of Character Strengths	Peterson, C., & Seligman, M. (2004). *Character strengths and virtues: A handbook and classification.* New York, NY: Oxford University Press.
Youth Life Orientation Test	Ey, S., Hadley, W., Allen, D. N., Palmer, S., Klosky, J., Deptula, D., . . . Cohen, R. (2005). A new measure of children's optimism and pessimism: The youth life orientation test. *Journal of Child Psychology and Psychiatry, 46,* 548–558. doi:10.1111/j.1469-7610.2004.00372.x

descriptions of positive psychology interventions for youth that address a range of targets, including gratitude, character strengths, prolonging positive emotions via savoring, and those designed to address multiple positive psychology targets. Additionally, Seligman et al. (2009) described other interventions designed to enhance individuals' well-being. Although these interventions and strategies have not been formally examined in studies of gifted learners exclusively, the opportunities for addressing strengths with these resources are valuable for all learners, including the gifted.

Educators may collectively select an intervention for use among the grade bands and implement strategies for a selected duration, report back to the professional learning group during a regularly scheduled time, and detail the experiences of facilitating the intervention, the responsiveness of the students, observations noted, and reflections about the process. Noting the effect of the intervention with students anecdotally or through the measures suggested in this chapter for educators, teachers can collect classroom-level data to inform their understanding of students' social-

Table 9.5
Lessons/Interventions for K–12 Students

Lesson	Reference
Numerous lessons to develop character strengths aligned with the VIA	Proctor, C., & Eades, J. F. (2016). *Strengths gym*. Guernsey, England: Positive Psychology Research Center.
Numerous lessons to promote student life satisfaction	Suldo, S. M. (2016). *Promoting student happiness: Positive psychology interventions in schools.* New York, NY: Guilford.
Three-lesson intervention for perfectionism	Vekas, E. J., & Wade, T. D. (2017). The impact of a universal intervention targeting perfectionism in children: An exploratory controlled trial. *British Journal of Clinical Psychology, 56,* 458–473. doi:10.1111/bjc.12152
Celebrating Strengths	VIA Institute. (2014). *Celebrating strengths.* Retrieved from https://www.viacharacter.org/resources/celebrating-strengths

emotional development at the outset of the intervention, at the end of a given positive psychology intervention, and at the end of the school year.

Optimism Strand

With the increased attention given to positive psychology, there has been a growing interest and increased research in the roles of hope and optimism as these pertain to students. There is a growing body of research that shows the importance of hope in achieving goals, be these academic or other types. Snyder (1994) developed a theory of hope wherein individuals set goals and develop plans for achieving these goals. Pedrotti, Edwards, and Lopez (2008) discussed an introduction to the study of hope, its relationship to positive outcomes (including self-esteem, life satisfaction, managing life difficulties, academic performance, and career-building skills), and ways that hope can be promoted in the classroom. Additionally, this article included a goals scale that is described as a measure to be used with school-aged children, and the scoring information is listed in the article to assist educators in interpreting scores. Educators may also wish to read Miller, Gilman, and Martens's (2008) article on the promotion of wellness in schools for additional information about the benefits of hope and optimism for children and youth, the role of participation in structured extracurricular activities as vehicles for wellness promotion among students, and the promotion of wellness through sports and exercise.

Other works are also available that address optimism and hope. For example, Pajares (2001) found that high-achieving middle school students had higher optimism, which was linked with their academic performance. Hoekman, McCormick, and Barnett (2005) reported that middle school gifted students' positive feelings were associated with task commitment, and Seligman (2002) found that optimistic learners manage failure differently than those who are not optimistic. Fredrickson (2001) found that optimism co-occurs with positive emotions, which leads to optimal outcomes. Following an examination of the literature, teachers may want to get more specific information about their students' current levels of optimism, which may be accomplished through teacher-administered measures of optimism (see Ey et al., 2005). In this vein, teachers select topics collaboratively, discuss to inform understanding, collect classroom data to inform themselves and their students about levels of optimism, and can then make informed decisions about the type of additional avenues to pursue in their classes. Ultimately, such a process would reflect the standards for professional learning, including learning communities, resources, learning designs, outcomes, data, and implementation (Learning Forward, 2011).

Perfectionism Strand

A review of research related to the social-emotional needs of gifted learners will likely include reference to research about perfectionism, which has interested scholars for decades (Margot & Rinn, 2016; Roberts & Lovett, 1994; Schuler, 2000). Recognized as a multidimensional construct, perfectionism can be viewed as having positive aspects (often termed adaptive perfectionism) and negative aspects (termed maladaptive perfectionism; see Speirs Neumeister, 2018). Given the frequent discussion of perfectionism in the gifted education literature, educators may also seek to understand this construct through a group study. Rule and Montgomery (2013) have engaged teachers in the process of understanding adaptive and maladaptive perfectionism through the creation and analysis of cartoons reflecting aspects of each type of perfectionism following an introductory reading or discussion of the differences between each. In one illustration, Rule and Montgomery showed a set of bowling pins being knocked over by a bowling ball, with a caption alluding to the disorganization of the pins, while another pin stands by proclaiming that the pins should get reset and in order. Below the illustration, the authors provided a statement that describes a common characteristic of perfectionists: They tend to be orderly. The authors labeled the image to show the type of perfectionist illustrated—"An affinity for order and organization is a perfectionistic trait" (Rule & Montgomery, 2013, p. 256).

Additional professional learning opportunities may follow this initial examination of the literature through an exercise designed to increase educators' understanding of their own perfectionism and as a prelude to assessing students' perfectionism. One such approach is to engage teachers in completing the Almost Perfect Scale–Revised (APS-R; Slaney, Rice, Mobley, Trippi, & Ashby, 2001), a brief measure of perfectionism that has been used with an array of individuals. Then, based on the results of the scale, teachers may be encouraged to write about times they recall experiencing perfectionism and the effects of these experiences on their life. A discussion in small groups or pairs would also provide educators an opportunity to hear from others the different ways perfectionism may manifest itself. Educators would then be encouraged to note whether they have high scores in adaptive perfectionism (high standards), maladaptive perfectionism (discrepancy), both, or neither, and to discuss how students exhibiting each type (or both) may manifest these traits as learners.

To reduce students' maladaptive perfectionism and perceived stress, teachers can draw upon the findings of one study focusing on mindfulness with adults who self-report maladaptive perfectionism (Wimberly, Mintz, & Suh, 2016). The intervention focuses on the participants independently reading a book on mindfulness, titled *Present Perfect: A Mindfulness Approach to Letting Go of Perfectionism and the Need for Control* (Somov, 2010). The text includes an overview of perfectionism; questions asking readers to examine the impact of perfectionism on their life; and introductions to acceptance, nonjudgement, impermanence, and mindfulness-based concepts, including living consciously and in the moment, deepening self-acceptance, dealing with uncertainty, and compassion. Somov (2010) also included more than 150 exercises in meditation throughout focusing on breathing, visualizations, awareness, and concepts such as impermanence. This book is a useful tool in the exploration of perfectionism among educators and may serve as a prelude to discussions about addressing perfectionism through universal interventions with students. Toward this goal, teachers may hold ongoing conversations about sections of the book, particularly because the book focuses on mindfulness, which has gained considerable interest among educators (Schonert-Reichl et al., 2015; Vickery & Dorjee, 2016).

Educators may also wish to read a few works that explore classroom-based approaches to addressing perfectionism with K–12 students. For example, Nugent (2000) provided suggested learning experiences, including bibliotherapy (Rozalski, Stewart, & Miller, 2010) as a basis for such examination. Therapists have utilized the strategy of guiding clients through managing problems via directed reading, a process known as clinical bibliotherapy (Catalano, 2008). Educators, however, employ developmental bibliotherapy in order to educate "students about attitudes, feelings, and behaviors" (Catalano, 2008, p. 17) through classwide reading and discussion. Developmental bibliotherapy within the class provides students the opportunity to empathize with individuals who experience childhood trauma (such as a family member leaving for military duty, bullying, and anxiety with school). Educators may also use developmental bibliotherapy as a preventative strategy to support students in developing awareness and problem solving to provide students the opportunity to think about how to handle potential challenges that have not yet arisen, such as conflicts among friends, bullying, divorce, or loneliness. Advocates of developmental bibliotherapy identify three stages: identification, catharsis, and insight (Catalano, 2008). Identification occurs when a student is able to identify him- or herself with a fictional or real character through recalling a time when the student experienced a relevant incident so that he or she recognizes that he or she is like others in experiencing this incident. Catharsis is the release of tension, which students often recognize when reading about how others have made progress in dealing with a struggle. Insight occurs when the student recognizes how he or she has developed an understanding about him- or herself via discussion and reflection. Educators who wish to use developmental bibliotherapy are encouraged to prepare by reading the book ahead of students and anticipating what students will ask; educators can also direct discussion to solutions to a given problem, perhaps via role-play or brainstorming.

Mofield and Chakraborti-Ghosh (2010) discussed their research on the effects of an affective curriculum, *Searching for Perfect Balance*, a nine-lesson unit designed to promote healthy (adaptive) perfectionism and reduce unhealthy (maladaptive) perfectionism. The middle school gifted learners who received the curriculum had significantly lower scores in a type of unhealthy perfectionism, "Concern over Mistakes," than students who didn't receive the curriculum. Additionally, those who received the curriculum also experienced decreases in "Doubts about Actions," another indicator of unhealthy perfectionism. An overview of the nine lessons, which may be useful to educators seeking to incorporate experiences that target the reduction of unhealthy perfection, is described in the article.

Educators may wish to talk with a district school psychologist more about perfectionism in general and the ways that teachers can encourage students to appreciate high standards and the effect these may have on performance. Students also need guidance in becoming aware of the negative effects of maladaptive perfectionism well before these surface in the middle-grades years.

Summary

The field of gifted education has long been concerned with the social-emotional development of students identified as gifted. The field has also included social-emotional needs within its standards for the education of students who are gifted. In order to meet these field standards, professional learning opportunities are needed to provide educators with long-term, in-depth, data-based, classroom-focused understandings. These understandings are necessarily situated within the field of gifted education, as well as psychology, particularly positive psychology, which has aims that align well with the field of gifted education's focus on enhancing a child's strengths in order to promote optimal levels of performance and wellness among youth.

Given these goals, educators are encouraged to explore the aims of positive psychology, identify linkages with gifted education, and identify areas for continued exploration, such as life satisfaction and optimism. Furthermore, educators may deepen their understandings of commonly discussed areas of social-emotional issues—such as perfectionism—to consider how the research literature has evolved, the emergence of new understandings of these issues, and the implications for teaching students who are gifted. With this chapter's suggestions for professional learning in mind, suggested resources are provided (see Tables 9.2–9.5) to assist educators in furthering their understanding and learning about potential areas of interest.

References

Alsop, G. (2003). Asynchrony: Intuitively valid and theoretically reliable. *Roeper Review, 25,* 118–127. doi:10.1080/02783190309554213

Bücker, S., Nuraydin, S., Simonsmeier, B. A., Schneider, M., & Luhmann, M. (2018). Subjective well-being and academic achievement: A meta-analysis. *Journal of Research in Personality, 74,* 83–94. doi:10.1016/j.jrp.2018.02.007

Catalano, A. (2008). Making a place for bibliotherapy on the shelves of a curriculum materials center: The case for helping pre-service teachers to use developmental bibliotherapy in the classroom. *Education Libraries: Childrens' Resources, 31,* 17–22.

Chen, Z., & Kaplan, H. B. (2003). School failure in early adolescence and status attainment in middle adulthood: A longitudinal study. *Sociology of Education, 76,* 110–127. doi:10.2307/3090272

Combs, E., & Silverman, S. (2016). *Bridging the gap: Paving the way from current practice to exemplary professional learning.* Retrieved from https://www.frontlineeducation.com/uploads/2018/01/ESSA_Bridging_the_Gap.pdf

Cotabish, A., Shaunessy-Dedrick, E., Dailey, D., Kielty, W., & Pratt, D. (2015). *Self-assess your P–12 practice or program using the NAGC gifted programming.* Washington, DC: National Association for Gifted Children.

Cross, W. E., Jr., & Vandiver, B. J. (2001). Nigrescence theory and measurement: Introducing the Cross Racial Identity Scale (CRIS). In J. G. Ponterotto, J. M. Casas, L. A. Suzuki, & C. M. Alexander (Eds.), *Handbook of multicultural counseling* (2nd ed., pp. 371–393). Thousand Oaks, CA: SAGE.

Diener, E. (1984). Subjective well-being. *Psychological Bulletin, 95,* 542–575. doi:10.1037/0033-2909.95.3.542

Every Student Succeeds Act, Pub. L. No. 114–95. (2015).

Ey, S., Hadley, W., Allen, D. N., Palmer, S., Klosky, J., Deptula, D., . . . Cohen, R. (2005). A new measure of children's optimism and pessimism: The youth life orientation test. *Journal of Child Psychology and Psychiatry, 46,* 548–558. doi:10.1111/j.1469-7610.2004.00372.x

Fredrickson, B. L. (2001). The role of positive emotions in positive psychology: The broaden-and-build theory of positive emotions. *American Psychologist, 56,* 218–226. doi:10.1037/0003-066X.56.3.218

Govindji, R., & Linley, A. (2007). Strengths use, self-concordance and well-being: Implications for strengths coaching and coaching psychologists. *International Coaching Psychology Review, 2,* 143–153.

Hilsman, R., & Garber, J. (1995). A test of the cognitive diathesis-stress model of depression in children: Academic stressors, attributional style, perceived competence, and control. *Journal of Personality and Social Psychology, 69,* 370–380. doi:10.1037/0022-3514.69.2.370

Hoekman, K., McCormick, J., & Barnett, K. (2005). The important role of optimism in a motivational investigation of the education of gifted adolescents. *Gifted Child Quarterly, 49,* 99–110. doi:10.1177/001698620504900202

Hollingworth, L. S. (1942). *Children above 180 IQ Stanford-Binet: Origin and development.* Yonkers-on-Hudson, NY: World Book.

Huebner, E. S. (1991a). Correlates of life satisfaction in children. *School Psychology Quarterly, 6,* 103–111. doi:10.1037/h0088805

Huebner, E. S. (1991b). Further validation of the students' life satisfaction scale: The independence of satisfaction and affect ratings. *Journal of Psychoeducational Assessment, 9,* 363–368. doi:10.1177/073428299100900408

Huebner, E. S. (1991c). Initial development of the student's life satisfaction scale. *School Psychology International, 12,* 231–240. doi:10.1177/0143034391123010

Jen, E. (2017). Affective interventions for high-ability students from 1984–2015: A review of published studies. *Journal of Advanced Academics, 28,* 225. doi:10.1177/1932202X17715305

Jin, S., & Moon, S. M. (2006). A study of well-being and school satisfaction among academically talented students attending a science high school in Korea. *Gifted Child Quarterly, 50,* 169–184. doi:10.1177/001698620605000207

Jolly, J. L., & Robins, J. H. (2016). After the Marland Report: Four decades of progress? *Journal for the Education of the Gifted, 2,* 132–150. doi:10.1177/0162353216640937

Learning Forward. (2011). *Standards for professional learning.* Oxford, OH: Author.

Lubinski, D., & Benbow, C. P. (2000). States of excellence. *American Psychologist, 55,* 137–150. doi:10.1037/0003-066X.55.1.137

Margot, K. C., & Rinn, A. N. (2016). Perfectionism in gifted adolescents: A replication and extension. *Journal of Advanced Academics, 27,* 190–209. doi:10.1177/1932202X16656452

McKnight, C. G., Huebner, E. S., & Suldo, S. (2002). Relationships among stressful life events, temperament, problem behavior, and global life satisfaction in adolescents. *Psychology in the Schools, 39,* 677–687. doi:10.1002/pits.10062

Miller, D. N., Gilman, R., & Martens, M. P. (2008). Wellness promotion in the schools: Enhancing students' mental and physical health. *Psychology in the Schools, 45,* 5–15. doi:10.1002/pits.20274

Mofield, E. L., & Chakraborti-Ghosh, S. (2010). Addressing multidimensional perfectionism in gifted adolescents with affective curriculum. *Journal for the Education of the Gifted, 33,* 479–513. doi:10.1177/016235321003300403

National Association for Gifted Children. (2010). *NAGC Pre-K–Grade 12 Gifted Programming Standards: A blueprint for quality gifted education programs.* Washington, DC: Author.

Neihart, M., Pfeiffer, S., & Cross, T. L. (2016). *The social and emotional development of gifted children: What do we know?* (2nd ed.) Waco, TX: Prufrock Press.

Nugent, S. A. (2000). Perfectionism: Its manifestations and classroom-based interventions. *Journal of Secondary Gifted Education, 4*, 215. doi:10.4219/jsge-2000-630

Pajares, F. (2001). Toward a positive psychology of academic motivation. *Journal of Educational Research, 95*, 27–35. doi:10.1080/00220670109598780

Pedrotti, J. T., Edwards, L. M., & Lopez, S. J. (2008). Promoting hope: Suggestions for school counselors. *Professional School Counseling, 12*, 100–107. doi:10.5330/PSC.n.2010-12.100

Peterson, C., & Seligman, M. E. P. (2004). *Character strengths and virtues: A handbook and classification.* New York, NY: Oxford University Press.

Quinlan, D. M., Swain, N., Cameron, C., & Vella-Brodrick, D. A. (2015). How 'other people matter' in a classroom-based strengths intervention: Exploring interpersonal strategies and classroom outcomes. *Journal of Positive Psychology, 10*, 77–89, doi:10.1080/17439760.2014.920407

Rinn, A. N. (2012). Implications for addressing the psychosocial needs of gifted individuals: A response to Subotnik, Olszewski-Kubilius, & Worrell (2011). *Gifted Child Quarterly, 56*, 206–209. doi:10.1177/0016986212456076

Roberts, S. M., & Lovett, S. B. (1994). Examining the 'F' in gifted: Academically gifted adolescents' physiological and affective responses to scholastic failure. *Journal for the Education of the Gifted, 17*, 241–259. doi:10.1177/016235329401700304

Rozalski, M., Stewart, A., & Miller, J. (2010). Bibliotherapy: Helping children cope with life's challenges. *Kappa Delta Pi Record, 47*(1), 33–37. doi:10.1080/00228958.2010.10516558

Rule, A. C., & Montgomery, S.E. (2013). Using cartoons to teach about perfectionism: Supporting gifted students' social-emotional development. *Gifted Child Today, 36*, 254–262. doi:10.1177/1076217513497574

Schonert-Reichl, K. A., Oberle, E., Lawlor, M. S., Abbott, D., Thomson, K., Oberlander, T. F., & Diamond, A. (2015). Enhancing cognitive and social-emotional development through a simple-to-administer mindfulness-based school program for elementary school children: A randomized controlled trial. *Developmental Psychology, 1*, 52–66. doi:10.1037/a0038454

Schuler, P. A. (2000). Perfectionism and gifted adolescents. *Journal of Secondary Gifted Education, 11*, 183. doi:10.4219/jsge-2000-629

Seligman, M. E. P. (2002). *Authentic happiness: Using the new psychology to realize your potential for lasting fulfillment.* New York, NY: Atria.

Seligman, M. E. P., & Csikszentmihalyi, M. (2000). Positive psychology: An introduction. *American Psychologist, 55*(1), 5–14. doi:10.1037/0003-066X.55.1.5

Seligman, M. E. P., Ernst, R. M., Gillham, J., Reivich, K. & Linkins, M. (2009). Positive education: Positive psychology and classroom interventions. *Oxford Review of Education, 35*, 293–311. doi:10.1080/03054980902934563

Slaney, R. B., Rice, K. G., Mobley, M., Trippi, J., & Ashby, J. S. (2001). The revised Almost Perfect Scale. *Measurement and Evaluation in Counseling and Development, 34*, 130–145.

Snyder, C. R. (1994). *The psychology of hope: You can get there from here.* New York, NY: Free Press.

Somov, P. (2010). *Present perfect: A mindfulness approach to letting go of perfectionism and the need for control.* Oakland, CA: New Harbinger Publications.

Speirs Neumeister, K. L. (2018). Perfectionism in gifted students. In J. Stoeber, & J. Stoeber (Eds.), *The psychology of perfectionism: Theory, research, applications* (pp. 134–154). New York, NY: Routledge/Taylor & Francis Group.

Speirs Neumeister, K., Williams, K. K., & Cross, T. L. (2009). Gifted high-school students' perspectives on the development of perfectionism. *Roeper Review, 31*, 198–206. doi:10.1080/02783190903177564

Subotnik, R. F., Olszewski-Kubilius, P., & Worrell, F. C. (2011). Rethinking giftedness and gifted education: A proposed direction forward based on psychological science. *Psychological Science in the Public Interest, 12*, 3–54. doi:10.1177/1529100611418056

Suldo, S. M. (2016). *Promoting student happiness: Positive psychology interventions in schools.* New York, NY: Guilford.

Suldo, S. M., Gormley, M. J., DuPaul, G. J., & Anderson-Butcher, D. (2014). The impact of school mental health on student and school-level academic outcomes: Current status of the research and future outcomes. *School Mental Health, 6*, 84–98. doi: 10.1007/s12310-013-9116-2

Suldo, S. M., Hearon, B. V., & Shaunessy-Dedrick, E. (2018). Examining gifted students' mental health through the lens of positive psychology. In S. Pfeiffer, E. Shaunessy-Dedrick, & M. Foley-Nicpon (Eds.), *APA Handbook of Giftedness and Talent* (pp. 443–449). Washington, DC: American Psychological Association.

Suldo, S. M., & Shaunessy-Dedrick, E. (2013). Changes in stress and psychological adjustment during the transition to high school among freshmen in an accelerated curriculum. *Journal of Advanced Academics, 34*, 195–218. doi:10.1177/1932202X13496090

Suldo, S. M., Thalji-Raitano, A., Kiefer, S. M., & Ferron, J. M. (2016). Conceptualizing high school students' mental health through a dual factor model. *School Psychology Review, 45*, 434–457.

Swiatek, M. A. (2001). Social coping among gifted high school students and its relationship to self-concept. *Journal of Youth and Adolescence, 30*(1), 19–39. doi:10.1023/A:1005268704144

Terman, L. M. (1925). *Genetic studies of genius: The mental and physical traits of a thousand gifted children* (Vol. 1). Stanford, CA: Stanford University Press.

Vickery, C. E., & Dorjee, D. (2016). Mindfulness training in primary schools decreases negative affect and increases meta-cognition in children. *Frontiers in Psychology, 6*, 1–13. doi:10.3389/fpsyg.2015.02025

Wimberly, T., Mintz, L., & Suh, H. (2016). Perfectionism and mindfulness: Effectiveness of a bibliotherapy intervention. *Mindfulness, 7*, 433. doi:10.1007/s12671-015-0460-1

Winner, E. (2000). The origins and ends of giftedness. *American Psychologist, 55*, 159–168. doi:10.1037/0003-066X.55.1.159

CHAPTER 10

Finding Gifted English Language Learners:
Professional Learning Designed to Change the Lens

Anne K. Horak, Beverly D. Shaklee, and Rebecca L. Brusseau

Introduction

The urgency, importance, and complexity of addressing equity in the identification of students for gifted programs cannot be overstated. Justice Sonia Sotomayor (2013) captured one layer of this issue when she said, "Many of the gaps in my knowledge and understanding were simply limits of class and cultural background, not lack of aptitude or application as I feared" (p. 135). All too often, children from underrepresented populations attribute their lack of information to a lack of intelligence, instead of understanding, as Justice Sotomayor did, when it is a lack of exposure. To address the lack of access and, therefore, the lack of opportunity for underrepresented populations, we created Project ExCEL (Experiences Cultivating Exceptional Learning; Shaklee & Horak, 2014). Project ExCEL is a federally-funded Jacob K. Javits project designed to find and serve high-ability, low-income English language learners (ELLs), using problem-based learning (PBL) as the curricular platform for universal screening. PBL is an inquiry-based method of instruction adapted from medical schools. According to Savery (2006), PBL is different from traditional instruction in that:

- instruction begins with the introduction of an ill-structured problem as the driving force for inquiry,
- students take on the perspectives of stakeholders in the problem and are required to be self-directed and self-regulated in their learning, and
- the teacher functions as a coach and facilitator of learning to develop metacognitive skills.

The purpose of the professional learning component of Project ExCEL is to not only teach teachers the pedagogy of PBL, but also transform their perspectives and perceptions of instruction and their beliefs about students who are ELLs or live within impoverished environments, so that teachers look more deeply at these students' potential and ways in which they manifest giftedness or potential. The Project ExCEL professional learning sessions take place in recursive learning-teaching-learning sessions and are characterized by modeling, collaboration, and video analysis for reflective practice. The flow of these sessions is described in detail later in the chapter. To begin, a description of the project model is provided.

Project ExCEL

The ExCEL Model (see Figure 10.1) contains three indispensable key elements: systemic approach, community of collaboration, and continuous improvement. Underlying these elements is that the foundation of the ExCEL Model is design-based research. Design-based research is distinguished from other approaches, based on these critical elements: (a) a particular component, such as curriculum, is designed in a naturalistic setting; (b) the designed intervention is adjusted as a form of experimentation; (c) the intervention is tested in rapid cycles of implementation and analysis; (d) theories that contribute to the larger body of theory are generated; and (e) the researcher demonstrates how design intervention adds value and impacts broader issues (Brown, 1992). The elements of the ExCEL Model's systemic approach include: alignment to the target districts' strategic plan, personalized professional learning with ongoing embedded support, and customized curriculum. The success of the ExCEL Model hinges on continuous improvement. This element of the model includes focused and clear goals, feedback to and from teachers, and rapid cycles of implementation

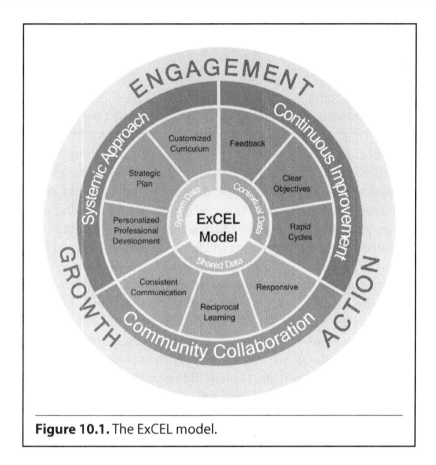

Figure 10.1. The ExCEL model.

and analysis of results. The third element of the model is community collaboration. Our belief is that learning is socially constructed; therefore, collaboration is an essential part of the process. The premise of the community of collaboration is that teachers and academicians have intersectionality as researchers and practitioners. This commonality reciprocally builds capacity and informs the research and practice of both groups.

The project takes place in two sequences, Find and Serve. These sequences occur over the course of two grade levels and a span of 2 years. The main objective of the first sequence, Find, is to implement PBL curriculum to create opportunities to observe students performing at high levels in order to identify gifted potential. The main objective of the second sequence, Serve, is to serve the identified students in advanced classes in order to understand their performance in terms of their achievement and engagement. From the school perspective (see Figure 10.2), the sequence of project activities begins with research approval in the district and continues with a session that begins the professional learning, followed by the first round of implementation and identification.

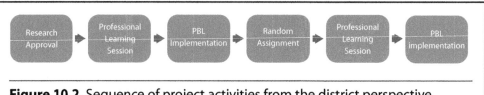

Figure 10.2. Sequence of project activities from the district perspective.

After identification, the students are scheduled for advanced classes. Teachers continue their studies with more advanced and extended sessions of professional learning, and the second round of implementation begins. The model continues with recursive cycles of professional learning sessions, curriculum implementation, and additional professional learning sessions. For the purposes of this chapter, we will focus on the professional learning component of Project ExCEL. The professional learning component of the ExCEL Model reflects the research work of Ermeling and Graff-Ermeling (2016) and the six criteria for professional learning outlined in the Every Student Succeeds Act (ESSA, 2015)—data-driven, sustained, intensive, collaborative, job-embedded, and classroom-focused—which taken all together positively influence change in classroom beliefs and practices. Archibald, Coggshall, Croft, and Goe (2011) provided further support for these elements, as well as modeling and video analysis used to promote reflective practice, as key criteria for effective professional learning.

Underrepresentation of ELLs in Gifted Programs

The underrepresentation of certain demographic groups in gifted child education programs has a long trajectory. Historically, multiple innovations have been used to try to address the obvious gap in services, including identification practices, placements, and curricular models, with limited success. Many program innovations have also included teacher professional development as an aspect of the intervention. Project ExCEL focuses on the intersectionality of teacher professional learning and curricular innovation, using PBL and intensive scaffolded support for implementation, with the goals of expanding teacher professional learning to find and serve historically underrepresented populations of gifted middle school students.

When Ford (2014) documented the underrepresentation of students from culturally and linguistically diverse backgrounds through the Relative Difference in Composition Index (RDCI), we understood how significant the gap actually is throughout the United States. The RDCI establishes a mathematical formula to determine the percent of underrepresentation in gifted programs, and the equity index (EI) is used to determine the minimum threshold for representation. Together, the RDCI and EI frame underrepresentation in terms of its mathematical relationship to statistical significance and the likelihood that identification policies, practices, and procedures are discriminatory, as opposed to due to chance. Using Ford's RDCI equation and national statistics, Hispanic/Latino students are underrepresented in gifted programs by 28%, and ELLs are underrepresented by 72% (Ford, 2014; Snyder, de Brey, & Dillow, 2016). In other words, the access to gifted education steadily decreases as age, cultural, and language variables increase. Therefore, an effective system of professional learning for teacher preparation needs to directly address the beliefs that drive these policies, practices, and procedures, and create conditions for change for a solution to a problem of this magnitude to have lasting impact.

Limitations of Current Identification Practices

Models of identification are often separated from the daily life of the classroom. Checklists, observation tools, testing, and other methods used to identify potential, capacity, or giftedness are neither job-embedded nor often part of the intensive professional learning of teachers. Even observations within a classroom are often bound by a short-term lesson or creative project that is used as a prompt. In some cases, the classroom teacher, resource teacher, or another stakeholder provides the evidence for identification. Project ExCEL challenges the notion of separation of identification from day-to-day classroom practices and teaching by using the PBL model as a dynamic means of engaging students in challenging curriculum. Thus, PBL actively engages middle school students in meaningful learning and provides a long-term opportunity for teacher learning about students' potential.

There is some urgency to finding equitable solutions for access to gifted programs. The population of ELLs, particularly from Latin America, is growing more rapidly than other demographic segments of the United States (Grieco et al., 2012; National Center for Educational Statistics [NCES], 2013). Nationally, data have documented that teacher observational tools are disproportionately relied upon as a part of the overall screening criteria (Mun et al., 2016). Yet, these scales contain indicators that are often challenging for language learners because they directly or indirectly reflect tasks more favorable to demonstrating English oral language skills and majority cultural values, rather than a capacity for thinking. For example, "asking questions," a descriptor found on many checklists, is typically intended to identify curiosity, which can be an indicator of potential. However, there are several cultural and language biases apparent in this indicator as written. First, the skill is one valued in the dominant Western culture. "Asking questions" is perceived as disrespectful of the teacher in some cultures. Second, "asking questions" is an indicator that relies heavily on oral language skills that an English language learner may be developing. Finally, we have long known (Flanders, 1961) that, during typical teacher-directed instruction, even students fluent in English may not have many opportunities to demonstrate this skill, due to the higher ratio of teacher talk to student talk in classrooms (Hattie, 2012; Walsh, 2002).

Through Project ExCEL, teachers are engaged in sustained and supported professional learning not only to change practice focusing on inquiry-based learning by using PBL, but also to examine their beliefs, experiences, and observations of ELLs who are engaged in challenging, meaningful curriculum. This process gives teachers a way to identify ELLs and impoverished students as having capacity and strengths.

Project ExCEL utilizes the implementation of a PBL unit as a dynamic curricular intervention to identify potential by using the model created by Shaklee (1993) for observational assessment of impoverished students. Shaklee and Viechnicki (1995) described four categories of identified gifted learners (see Table 10.1): Exceptional Learner, Exceptional User, Exceptional Generator, and Exceptional Motivation. The research was based on the premise that the attributes identified in the literature by Shaklee and Viechnicki (1995) might be evident, but they may manifest in different ways based on exposure, culture, and environment; there might be different ways that children could show what they know. Teachers learn to use reflective observation during PBL classes to identify exceptional potential. Documenting and debriefing about their observations allows teachers to expand their perspectives on the meaning of potential, giftedness, and development.

Table 10.1
Categories of Gifted Learners (Shaklee & Viechnicki, 1995)

Exceptional Learner	Acquisition of Information—memory, understanding, knowledge acquisition
Exceptional User	Application of Information—symbol systems, reasoning, problem solving
Exceptional Generator	Adapting Information—creative, self-expressive, nonconformist, curious, humorous*
Exceptional Motivation	Intense Desire to Know—perfectionism, intensity, initiative, inquiry, leadership

*Attributes are strongly influenced by environment

Throughout Project ExCEL, teachers observed students who emerged as having potential during the PBL experience, and teachers also indicated high confidence levels in their judgment in the identification of attributes related to Exceptional Learner and Exceptional User (Shaklee & Viechnicki, 1995). Teachers were often more uncomfortable with their judgments of giftedness when it was observed as a manifestation of Exceptional Generator and Exceptional Motivation. Interestingly, traits in these areas are typically not captured by ability tests.

Project ExCEL teachers indicated that their ELLs appeared to display potential when teachers observed performances of behavior mainly in the attributes of Exceptional Generator and Exceptional Motivation (Shaklee & Viechnicki, 1995). Teachers also indicated that they felt less confident in their evaluations. However, helping teachers look beyond the scope of academic traits and into generative traits, such as creativity or leadership, has given our middle school teachers a new lens through which to find potential. Further, we work closely with teachers to determine how these attributes are influenced by culture and environment. The ability to look deeply into culture and environment has helped middle school teachers move past dominant cultural orientations into valuing what students bring to the middle school classroom from their heritage.

Our discussions with teachers lead us to believe that the focus for many teachers continues to be student performance on state and local tests, few of which, if any, emphasize problem solving, creative thought, or leadership. In essence, if a student is not demonstrating performances associated directly with academics, teachers place less value on the attributes a student demonstrates. Highlighting this concern is the overreliance on oral and written vocabulary, asking questions aloud, and the differences between acquiring knowledge and using knowledge, which all skew identification away from the talents and abilities of children learning English. Thus, measures of verbal ability persist as a key identifier in current practices, and the movement toward multiple criteria may not go far enough to effectively respond to the disparity in identification.

We know that teachers and teacher beliefs are the most important variable in the classroom. Given the importance of the teacher and the teacher's professional learning, in Project ExCEL, we have invested in teacher learning and teacher judgment to uncover and nurture potential in middle school students who are ELLs. Our long-term research is grounded in PBL as an engaging high-powered curriculum, providing a dynamic environment in which to advance teacher understanding and student demonstrations to make a critical difference in their future.

The Influence of PBL on ELLs

The collaborative and inquiry-based nature of PBL is consistent with recommendations that ELLs, particularly high-potential ELLs, receive challenging instruction to support the acquisition of content and English language development simultaneously (Pereira & de Oliveira, 2015). In practice, PBL has been used to enhance achievement and engagement with ELLs at all levels, however, not for the purposes of finding talent or giftedness. Hussain, Nafees, and Jumani (2009) found that PBL was more effective than traditional instruction in increasing achievement of ELLs. PBL has been effective with ELLs with regard to student engagement, understanding the topic discussed, collaboration, and self-directed learning (Azer, 2009). Furthermore, ELLs indicated that PBL should be used in future courses (Azman & Shin, 2012). Findings from Project ExCEL have further contributed to the literature on PBL and ELLs, indicating that the achievement gap between ELLs and non-ELLs on content knowledge tests has narrowed—and, in some cases, closed—as a result of learning with PBL (Horak, Holincheck, Webb, & Nagy, 2017). Project ExCEL has had success with identifying potentially gifted ELLs at a significantly higher rate than traditional methods (Horak et al., 2017).

Effective Professional Learning Practices for Teacher Improvement

Effective professional learning is critical to the success of any change initiative. We have developed evidence-based support for transformative understanding, how the Project ExCEL professional learning aligned to this evidence base, and the implications of the outcomes of this effort. Although the evidence base for professional learning practices that helped teacher growth is thin, there is some encouraging evidence that reveals a much more complex relationship and provides support for a fundamentally different approach. As such, this work shifts away from a focus on designing professional development based on tinkering with quick-fix solutions, to professional learning centered on creating conditions that foster growth and are supportive of change.

To support transformative understanding, effective professional learning requires a different approach. One element of this is a shift in thinking about lesson planning. Ermeling and Graff-Ermeling (2016) noted that lesson planning in the United States commonly focuses on high-interest activities to increase student engagement. Yet, this focus leads to shallow lessons. Take, for example, a lesson aligned to objectives involving the Kennedy-Nixon debates during the 1960 presidential election. If the teacher's primary driver for the lesson were an emphasis on an engaging activity, then the lesson might unfold by having the students watch a clip of the debate and then engage in a gallery walk throughout the classroom, responding to meaningful questions intended to support analyzing and processing the video clip.

On the other hand, if the teacher's primary driver for the lesson were an emphasis on developing a coherent lesson storyline, then the lesson might unfold by having students take on the role of campaign advisors to one of the candidates. As a part of their job, students would advise the candidate on the best way to craft his media message for the audience. By doing this, students demonstrate a deep understanding of the political issues of the time and how the medium of television was adding complexity by increasing the influence of image on public perception. By placing students in this role, the teacher develops a storyline that guides students toward advancement in specific learning goals with increased depth. PBL is designed with this approach to lesson planning. Therefore, the professional learning should be designed to support not only the skill development of learning to teach PBL, but also the transformative understanding of why this type of curriculum is important and effective.

Project ExCEL Professional Learning Sessions

The challenge for Project ExCEL was to craft professional learning sessions that engage teachers in understanding: (a) the context of the underrepresentation problem, (b) the design of the PBL curriculum, and (c) the specific instructional methods and strategies needed to facilitate PBL. Further, our intent was to create an environment in which teachers can learn with fidelity. For the success of the project, teachers needed to understand that professional learning involved a systemic change in thinking and teaching. As such, the professional learning sessions were designed to support transformative understandings about curriculum, instruction, and students.

We use levels of service for progressive professional learning that show the inverse relationship between the number of teachers served and the investment of time and responsibility for implementing the ExCEL Model (see Figure 10.3). The professional learning is designed to progressively invest in teachers participating in the project as they develop expertise. Additionally, as teachers demonstrate increasing interest, willingness, and skill, the progressive professional learning is designed to support them becoming more engaged in effecting change and becoming experts and advocates for the project.

The Flow of the Project ExCEL Professional Learning

The Project ExCEL professional learning sessions take place in recursive learning-teaching-learning sessions, beginning with the Introduction session, then the Measures session, then the Reflection and Planning session, and then the Advanced session. Each session is structured by the team leaders (experts in gifted child education and PBL) to orient the objectives, based on a combination of topics identified to address the project priorities, as well as other priorities identified from feedback given by teachers and principals on areas of need and interest. The cocreated structure of the professional learning environment acknowledges the expertise and questions of our teachers and principals, while guiding their understanding of the elements embedded in Project ExCEL (see Figure 10.4).

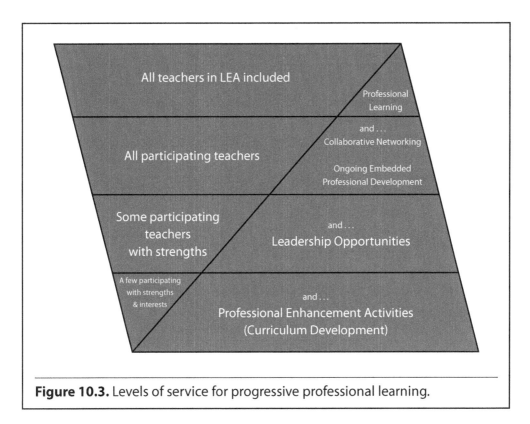

Figure 10.3. Levels of service for progressive professional learning.

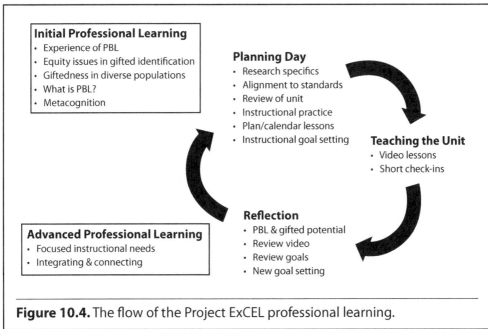

Figure 10.4. The flow of the Project ExCEL professional learning.

Introduction session. All teachers attend the introductory 2-day session prior to the first implementation of PBL. To build capacity and sustainability, this professional learning session is open to any instructional personnel whom the school leadership would like to include. The major objectives of this session are to (1) introduce the attributes of giftedness and giftedness in diverse populations, (2) model PBL and discuss its structure and benefits, (3) introduce the skills and tools for transition to the metacognitive coach to support PBL instruction, and (4) describe the teacher responsibilities as participants. An important element of this professional learning session is that the primary method of delivery is as a PBL experience of professional practice. This means that the session unfolds to the teachers as a PBL experience would unfold to students, except that the teachers work on a real-world problem of professional practice. The expert facilitator models methods appropriate to PBL instruction by moving through demonstrations of metacognitive coaching, organizing participants for self-directed learning, and instances of teacher direction.

Measures session. The Measures session focuses on the specifics of the administration of the measures, alignment to standards, incorporating assessment, balancing teacher-directed and student-directed instruction in PBL, the required lessons for the purposes of the research, appropriate adaptations and/or scaffolding, and pacing of the unit for a 90-minute or a 50-minute schedule. Emphasis is placed on collaboration for preparing to teach and best practice methods for PBL instruction. The Measures session is meant as a teachable moment when teachers are ready to ask about documenting achievement and successes of the PBL, typically prior to the implementation of the first unit.

Reflection and Planning session. The Reflection and Planning session takes place after implementation of the first unit and prior to implementation of the additional units. During this session, teachers have an opportunity to collaborate and plan. Project personnel conduct guided reflections using video analysis and the Cognitive Apprenticeship Rubric Tool (CART; Bland, Horak, & Xu, 2017), a measure developed for this specific purpose. The CART is described in more detail later in this chapter. From this video analysis, areas of need identified by the teachers are targeted for explicit instruction by the research team throughout the professional learning.

Advanced session. The Advanced session, a 2-day learning experience, takes place before implementation begins in the second year of the project. It begins with a review of the overarching topics and moves advanced teachers into more sophisticated understandings of the concepts related to giftedness and giftedness in diverse populations such as ELLs, instruction, and metacognitive coaching.

Alignment of the ExCEL Professional Learning Sessions to the Evidence Base

Through Project ExCEL, teachers participated in professional learning aligned to evidence-based practices to support transformative understandings and inquiry-based teaching reflective of the work of Ermeling and Graff-Ermeling (2016) and the six criteria for professional learning outlined in the ESSA (2015), as well as modeling and video analysis to promote reflective practice (Archibald et al., 2011). These practices, along with the subsequent research findings, are described in more detail in the following narrative.

Modeling

Modeling of PBL is an essential component of the Introductory session. Teachers take on the role of "learner," as an expert other—an experienced PBL teacher—takes on the role of classroom facilitator and metacognitive coach. The modeling sections of the session replicate the opening lessons that students will experience when teachers implement PBL experiences in their classrooms. The learners (teachers) receive several carefully selected initial texts that establish the stakeholder role, introduce an issue, and invite questions for further investigation. The learner-teachers work through the texts, contributing to a whole-group document called the Learning Issues Board (LIB; see Table 10.2). The LIB functions as a visual shared pool of knowledge. Here learners collect "known" facts inferred from the texts, as well as questions or gaps in knowledge. The LIB is also where students eventually prioritize questions for further research and plan for how the research will be conducted. The sample LIB shown in Table 10.2 is from a demonstration of *Fit to Print* (Gallagher, Plowden, & Townsend, 2017), a PBL unit about events in Cuba leading up to the Spanish-American War. In the unit, students take on the role of newspaper editors and grapple with the conflict of yellow journalism versus journalistic integrity.

Table 10.2
Sample Learning Issues Board From Modeling of *Fit to Print* During Professional Learning Session

What We Know	Learning Issues/ Questions	Plan of Action to Answer Our Questions
• The letter was written in October 5, 1897, which is before the Spanish American War. • We are Foreign Bureau Editors, and we are focused on Cuba. Editors decide what gets printed about Cuba. • We are talking about Cuba. Spain and America have a relationship with Cuba. • We have reference to stories from two journals, *The New York Times* and *The Journal*. • We are journalists, and we are in danger of losing our jobs because of possible downsizing. • We need to keep or increase our circulation. • We need to focus on the facts. • We need to be prepared to make a decision in the near future on whether the story is first page news. • We are only reviewing the stories from the past 2 months.	• What is true about the story of what happened to Cisneros? • Who is Cisneros? • Does that insinuate that the Journal is in cahoots (they are working together) with Cisneros? • What are the facts of this story? • Is our source at *The Journal* a reliable source? Is the document from Cisneros real? Who is our source? • What makes a story first page newsworthy? • What do our readers want? • What is our goal: increasing readers or to be influential? • How do we increase the readership and keep the integrity of the paper? Can we combine the two styles? Would changing the font, adding pictures, and creating a good title cause an increase in readership?	• Look in our storage room or archives to find the articles [referenced in the texts read by learners]. • Ask the Bureau Chief about what our role is. • Information on what is fact.

Informal conversations and formal interviews reveal that teachers repeatedly return to the experience of being a PBL learner during the modeling, as they prepare for instruction, respond to students during instruction, and evaluate the success of lessons. One teacher shared, "[the instructor] was amazing and I want to get to that level because it was exciting. I just kept thinking to myself 'Okay, you gotta remember to ask questions.'" In addition to resonating with teachers as individuals, the modeling is a shared source of pooled knowledge for sense-making among collaborative teams of teachers as they work through the process of implementing PBL at their specific schools. For example, during a recent planning day when a team of teachers debated various aspects of classroom and materials management, they collectively revisited the methods used by the expert facilitator that they remembered experiencing during the modeling. One teacher said, "I get the convenience of doing it that way [making a unit packet], but I liked how when [the instructor] did it, the papers only came as we needed or asked."

Collaboration and Embedded Follow-Up

Collaboration and embedded follow-up are intertwined and essential parts of the Measures and Reflection and Planning sessions. Collaboration lies at the heart and is facilitated by embedded follow-up. Collaboration occurs through two equally important dimensions. Project ExCEL staff closely collaborate with teachers to develop implementation timelines, collect data, develop curriculum, and sometimes to identify professional learning needs. One example of close collaboration is found in the curriculum development and refinement process. The buy-in factor from teachers supports student engagement, especially in the stakeholder role. Developing units that have high levels of teacher excitement or buy-in leads to higher levels of PBL fidelity; therefore, teachers are solicited for ideas and topics interesting to them and their students. Often, the submitted unit ideas undergo several iterations during the curriculum writing. The transformation from one idea into another is made as transparent as possible so that teachers recognize their idea submissions in the finalized unit. Once a new unit is available for teaching, the collaboration process continues, as teachers and teams pilot the new unit. Feedback from teachers is solicited throughout the unit implementation, regarding lesson sequence, content, student engagement, and accessibility to students. Changes are made to the curriculum based on teacher feedback. This process of cocreation serves as a professional learning experience for the teachers. As they work through the unit development process, they understand the complexities of the curriculum, and this, in turn, informs their teaching.

Project ExCEL staff also facilitate collaboration between teachers and teams as part of the sense-making process. One of the main barriers to implementation is the ability to translate the PBL model into the specific contexts of individual districts and/or schools, especially taking into account the district/school practices regarding standards and high-stakes testing. Therefore, collaboration between project staff and teachers is key in this area. During one or more of the embedded follow-up times, a project staff member facilitates a process in which teachers identify the standards that they wish to prioritize during the unit and then align lessons to those standards, while honoring the student-directed nature of the PBL model. This method of collaboration is intentionally oriented toward building capacity in teachers, instructional leaders, and administrators, so that they come to see PBL as viable model for serving gifted students.

Collaboration between project staff and teachers is accomplished through a variety of formal and informal follow-up contacts. In addition to formal data collection via focus group and individual interviews, staff remain in close contact with teachers during implementation (e.g., through e-mail, Skype, and phone). Additionally, staff will also often have brief reflection or debriefing conversations with teachers following lessons that are video recorded. The informal conversations that surround the follow-up contacts lead priorities for professional learning goals in the next structured follow-up session. Recent conversations with teachers combined with project staff observations during a video recording session highlighted the need for a more thorough exploration of why the PBL teacher must commit to modeling the stakeholder role. Subsequently, project staff are in the process of developing experiences to support teachers in learning this aspect of effective PBL instruction.

Continuous Feedback and Video Analysis for Reflective Practice

Project ExCEL prepares teachers to be metacognitive coaches for their middle school students during PBL implementation. As mentioned previously, during the learning sessions, the teachers engage in a coaching model and study lessons presented by an "expert" other in PBL. Teachers are video recorded implementing PBL lessons. At a subsequent Reflection and Planning and/or an Advanced Session, debriefing the video recordings becomes the focus. During the reflective conversations, teachers watch the videos of their teaching and videos of their colleagues' teaching. We ask teachers to indicate one thing that they did well, one thing that they thought might have been a missed opportunity, and one that thing they still have a question about or want to talk about more. From this conversation, we ask teachers to set a goal for teaching the next PBL unit. Over the course of a year, this cycle is repeated. This is also why taking this project on as a team initiative is so important. As teachers go through it together in cycles, they can offer different perspectives.

Metacognitive coaching is a key feature of PBL. Therefore, teachers were provided with the opportunity to reflect and mentor in order to become more proficient in coaching students. The Cognitive Apprenticeship Reflection Tool (CART; Bland et al., 2017) was designed to address two aspects of the PBL environment. One purpose of CART was to assess teachers' fidelity of implementation of PBL instruction, with a specific focus on metacognitive coaching by trained observers. A second purpose of the tool was to provide teachers with the opportunity to reflect on their application of metacognitive coaching and implementation of PBL as part of their professional learning. The goal of using the tool was to help teachers actively coach students more effectively, as students analyzed and considered how to solve an ill-structured problem (Powell & Stansell, 2014). The tool included criteria that addressed PBL facilitation strategies including:

- coaching,
- problem exploration,
- articulation and revoicing,
- scaffolding,
- use of open-ended and metacognitive questions, and
- summarizing (Hmelo-Silver & Barrows, 2006).

CART (Bland et al., 2017) was grounded by the theoretical framework of the Cognitive Apprenticeship Model (Collins & Kapur, 2015). Cognitive apprenticeship is defined as the guided learning processes on cognitive and metacognitive levels (Collins, Brown & Holum, 1991). This model was adopted for the theoretical framework underlying the development of CART because of its association with PBL (Dennen, 2004). A matrix of indicators reflecting the cognitive apprenticeship model and PBL facilitation strategies was created. Aligned items were selected for the tool. Using CART, teachers examine the degree to which they create a cognitive apprenticeship environment for students by cultivating students' cognition and metacognition within PBL to actively address an ill-structured problem (Powell & Stansell, 2014). CART (Bland et al., 2017) was chosen to ground the reflection because it is based on research and aligns with the PBL teaching model. The reliability and validity of CART is being established. A sample of some of the descriptors in this tool is included in Table 10.3. The descriptors of

Table 10.3
Sample of Cognitive Apprenticeship Reflection Tool (CART; Bland, Horak & Xu, 2017)

Methods	Items
Modeling	• Models open-mindedness and intellectual curiosity • Demonstrates reasoning at conceptual or global level • Evaluates ideas • Modeling students to record hunches, facts, learning issues, and action items on board
Coaching	• Probes for depth of understanding • Facilitates students to examine how new information helped clarify a part of the problem • Meets their knowledge needs through self-directed learning and social knowledge construction • Keeps the class focused on the problem/keeps learning process on track
Exploration	• Ensures all ideas get recorded • Leverages knowledge gaps as opportunities to learn • Supports students to identify new questions resulting from new information and decides what action to take when presented with new information • Explores accumulating evidence to support original hypotheses

the methods of the Cognitive Apprenticeship Model are listed in the first column, and the items reflecting the goals and strategies of a PBL facilitator are described by specific behaviors the PBL facilitator takes in the other column.

We ask the teachers to consider the extent to which they acted on or supported the items in the second column. Teachers are uncomfortable the first time that they reflect using this structure. They spend time worrying about distractors that are not related to the intention of the reflection, which is to focus on metacognitive coaching. But, when teachers return, they frequently request to—or, rather, insist to be able to—watch their videos again. One hunch we have about this is that rarely do teachers actually get the chance to truly reflect, using indisputable evidence, on practice. From this experience, we have found that metacognitive coaching takes more time than anticipated to develop. Teachers must integrate a lot of information.

This video analysis and reflection using CART seems to be pivotal for teachers. This is when we have seen teachers having insightful reflective moments about changing practice. When watching their videos, teachers will say things like, "[During the lesson] it felt student directed but when I watch it, it doesn't look that way." They can watch and rewatch for different purposes. For example, first a teacher may watch to count the number of times students talked in the classroom. The same teacher may rewatch the video to notice patterns in the types of questions she is asking or for patterns and trends in her responses to students. These data are a springboard for new understandings about where teachers' practice falls on the continuum of student self-directed to teacher-directed learning. Teachers will have difficulty considering themselves to have mastered student self-directed learning when they can count the number of times students talked in their classroom on one hand. For teachers who tend toward this type of instruction, however, the video helps to reveal the subtle changes that they can make to move them further along the continuum and reinforces the positive things they are doing, heightening their awareness of professional growth.

There is a significant relationship between teachers' openness to feedback and improvement and the number of observations a teacher receives and growth (TNTP, 2015). Teachers who have a strong alignment between their perceptions of instructional effectiveness and formal evaluation ratings have a steeper trajectory of growth than those who do not. This is why the loosely structured reflection protocol is important at this point in the professional learning. Teachers need to build their understandings themselves and set personal goals for the next round of implementation, but also have a structure or a guideline by which to rate themselves. To accomplish this, we guide them with a series of questions:

- What stood out to you?
- What is clearer to you?
- What is still unclear?
- What have you changed your mind about?

This rich base of yearlong scaffolded experiences provides what professional learning researchers refer to as transformative experiences, those that positively change the perspectives and practices of teachers. Some teachers reported reevaluating and redefining their role in the classroom. One teacher shared:

> We get bogged down by teaching the curriculum and the day to day. It's a good reminder to be on the lookout for the kids [ELLs] who are really trying to show you that there's something else going on in their brains and they are looking for that push. (Seventh-grade English language arts teacher, personal communication)

Other teachers reported how the continuous feedback supported new instructional strategies, which led to reconsidering the role of challenging curriculum in a classroom for ELLs:

> If you put them [ELLs] in a situation where there's enough structure, but a challenge, they will rise to it. Also, it was really interesting to see we have made our classroom a really safe place for them to be able to take chances. (Seventh-grade English language arts teacher, personal communication)

Although teachers' transformative learning manifests in a variety of ways, their changed thinking has positive implications for the ELLs in their classrooms.

Implications/New Insights

If you want to approach this kind of a model for change and identification, then these are the three elements that create conditions for change. The insights that come out of our research about the professional learning model can be categorized in these areas:
- teachers need time for sense-making,
- video annotation has been a meaningful reflective tool, and
- teachers respond to data.

Teachers Need Time for Sense-Making

According to Allen and Penuel (2015), sense-making is how teachers resolve discontinuity or ambiguity created by competing goals or changes. Teachers are professionals and absorb the information on an intellectual level efficiently. The majority of our teachers have been teaching during the age of accountability, focused primarily on competencies and on testing. This generation of teachers has less autonomy; thus, these teachers have little encouragement to be creative in their teaching. We have found that, affectively, there has been a longer learning curve than we expected. Rupturing and repairing beliefs about instruction has been more stressful and, in some cases, seemingly traumatic. As we worked with teachers, we would hear comments, such as, "I can't teach this. I don't know all the answers," or, "We start with a preassessment, teach, do a postassessment and reteach—how can we do PBL?" Both the affect and models of teaching being used in some classrooms were so structured that teachers literally could not see how they could ever use a PBL curriculum, much less allow students some autonomy and decision making in the classroom. To provide sustained professional learning, we started with reassurance and discussion of teachers' fears, moved to modeling the PBL, and provided onsite and online scaffolding for teachers through the process—thus, helping them understand that is natural and perfectly okay to be anxious with new content in a PBL experience, and that scaffolded teaching takes time to develop. We also found that using PBL requires a tolerance for ambiguity and emotional resiliency that needed to be developed and supported. To a certain extent, in this way, the teachers were on a similar trajectory as the students.

To support sense-making, we incorporated a demonstration of the PBL model by an expert teacher with years of experience in the model at the middle school level. The demonstration has been cited as central to the experience of the introductory session and is referred to repeatedly in teacher interviews. In order to have meaningful experience in the demonstration, teachers must be able to set aside their teacher lens and actively engage in the PBL experience as students. Using sophisticated curriculum, such as a PBL unit on the Black Death, was important. Teachers generally had a lack of experience or knowledge of this historical period; therefore, they could readily engage as a student.

To support sense-making, we also incorporated the teacher (see Table 10.4), the concept map, and the reflective questions that we used throughout the modeling experience to capture critical thoughts, as well as provide a visual means to collect information. These are similar tools used for students during the actual PBL experience.

Video Annotation as a Reflective Tool

Video annotation is a component recently incorporated into the sense-making cycle. We see it as a practice that extends the benefits of the video reflection and analysis to a larger audience. Previously, our process of video reflection occurred between a teacher and researcher, although, occasionally, teachers reflected in groups of two or three. The idea to annotate video, a common practice for preservice teachers (Rich & Hannafin, 2009), emerged as a way to give many teachers access to the thinking behind the teacher moves, or the strategic actions and adjustments taking place continuously, of teachers with strong PBL pedagogy. The video annotation process is straightforward. Project ExCEL staff use the teacher notes from the video reflection conversations to create textboxes (annotations) in commonly available video editing software.

Table 10.4
Sample Teacher Learning Issues Board

Observations	Reactions	Questions
• Students were engaged. • Never a denial of a question. • Did not hear affirmations. • Once she put up the LIB and started filling it in, we understood how to use it. • She highlighted and annotated the texts. • We keep circling back so it doesn't matter what order the group goes in. • There is no wrong answer. If it is student-led, then it is really not right or wrong, it is their perspective. • It can be scaffolded. It can be changed for us to meet the needs for our students. • We have students who may or may not engage for a variety of reasons.	• Impressed that she continued to use questions. • I wondered if I was I wrong. • The LIB lead the questions. I felt it was ok to ask questions. • I felt safe asking questions. • I didn't feel judged about the questions I asked. • The wait time causes you to reread everything. It makes you think of more things that you should be adding. • I'm torn. I am worried that students won't learn if (think alouds) isn't modeled. • I wonder if kids will be invested. • I'm concerned students will take advantage of the student-directed aspect of this. • I am concerned about having enough [understanding] about the content to teach this well.	• **Will all students participate by reading the material and talking about the content? (engagement)** • How explicit can we be with our instruction? Are we able to answer questions with statements? • **Can we model the thought process?** Think alouds? Can we use turn and talks? • How can we expect something that we haven't taught them? • How did you decide which questions to respond to or not respond to? • At what point do we shift from student-directed to teacher-directed without disenfranchising kids that are really into it? • Do the students fill out the LIB or is it a working document for the class? • How do you steer their research for credible resources? Is that important to the outcome?

Note. Bolded items reflect questions that teachers indicated as a priority.

Teachers Respond to Data

Unsurprisingly, given the generation of teachers with whom we work, they respond overwhelmingly to data. Qualitative and quantitative data are collected to determine:
- the effectiveness of identification,
- teachers' confidence level in their identifications based on the observations of students during a PBL experience,
- the increases in student content knowledge in English language arts,
- the increases in student motivation to learn and student engagement,
- the understanding of the attributes of advanced students and in particular advanced students from underrepresented groups,
- knowledge about how to teach PBL and fidelity to implementing PBL,
- the effectiveness of the professional learning, and
- teachers' beliefs over time about the attributes of advanced students and teaching PBL.

Further, we have offered data at many levels, including national, local, and school-based evidence, to support teacher understanding. Teachers new to the program find that teachers who have been through the program are more credible because of their experiences than the researchers. Likewise, teachers from schools that have been through the program are more comfortable at the initial professional learning session than teachers from schools implementing for the first time because of the evidence they have from their own school. However, their own classroom-based evidence from their own implementation of PBL has the biggest influence on their beliefs.

Summary and Concluding Thoughts

We started Project ExCEL intending to transform teacher perspectives and perceptions of instruction, as well as their beliefs about students who are ELLs or live within impoverished environments, so that teachers look more accurately at these students' potential and ways in which they manifest giftedness. To do this, we used a dynamic professional learning model with a living feedback cycle that is deeply reflective of identifiable teacher needs.

We learned that professional development does not change teachers, but professional learning can effectively create conditions that promote change—particularly around a focused objective, such as perspectives and perceptions of instruction, as well as beliefs about students who are ELLs or live within impoverished environments. Most importantly, this kind of transformative understanding is not accomplished independently through professional development, but rather with professional learning embedded in the context of a comprehensive model. Therefore, discussing how the elements of this professional learning model contribute to its success is important.

A Systemic Approach

The systemic approach of the ExCEL Model focuses on gaining support, including from stakeholders at the district, school, and classroom levels. Support on many levels means building awareness, knowledge, and excitement about the purpose and message—that this work has the potential to allow district leadership, school leadership, and teachers to see ELLs in a different way. By building systematic support on many levels, any individual at any time is empowered to remove obstacles and sustain the work.

Continuous Improvement

The research team needs to articulate a clear message about the overarching purpose of the work. The team must also check that the feedback on this message suggests that it is understandable. The message should be tailored so that all of the people that are a part of the system see themselves in the message, understand their role, and feel empowered by the message. The message also must be clear about what is beyond the parameters of the work—or, to put it another way, what is not in the sandbox. This is important because, as the work gains momentum and people see value in it, there can be a kitchen sink mentality, or a tendency to want to attach everything to it. Although this is actually positive feedback, the project cannot be all things to all problems. Education is complex, and there is no one silver bullet. Clarity on the overarching purpose and message is one way to maintain the focus on the goals of the work and keep the system in check.

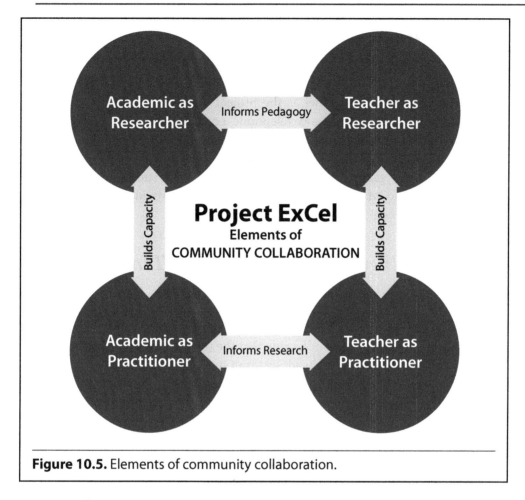

Figure 10.5. Elements of community collaboration.

Drilling down on this element, the continuous improvement cycles must be structured to be nimble enough to respond to needs in context, yet maintain the integrity of the overarching message and purpose. Equally important to consider is the fact that all systems experience stress. Friction and pressure may take many forms, and, without regular maintenance, their force has the potential to unravel the system. Thus, regular maintenance must be a part of the system to make certain that it can bear the stress of internal and external factors. This is why the living feedback cycle of community collaboration is so important.

Community Collaboration

The supports for the element of a community collaboration include consistent communication, responsiveness to the needs of the teachers, and reciprocal learning (see Figure 10.5). Essentially, we saw ourselves as functioning as two intersecting communities of practice learning from each other.

Communication

Members of the research team were in constant communication with district and school personnel as the project unfolded. In-person interactions, video conferences, and telephone consultations took place on a regular schedule. Our team reviewed our procedures and practices on an ongoing basis to ensure that communication was consistent, effective, and responsive. We gauged the degree to which we were successful with that by the extent to which feedback suggested we had provided a supportive, nonjudgmental environment.

Responsiveness to the Needs of Teachers

Maintaining a customer service orientation was one way we addressed responding to teachers' needs, as in "the customer is always right." If a team told us it "couldn't," we did not argue that the team members could or insist that they were required. Instead, we examined the root causes from their perspective. We collaborated to develop consensus on possible solutions and actions our team needed to take to support those solutions, ultimately following the lead of the teachers in terms of the direction for moving forward.

Reciprocal Learning

We diverged from the typical dynamic of many school environments, which is leadership at the top and teachers at the bottom. For our purposes, the intent was to leverage the teachers' knowledge and development to give them power over decision making and evaluation of student progress. To do this, listening was very important. The teachers needed to feel as though they had been heard. Hearing the teachers was not enough; we needed to articulate our understandings of what we heard and respond to the core idea that the teachers expressed. Feeling heard, in turn, developed resiliency for ambiguity, risk-taking, and problem solving.

We worked diligently through modeling language and scaffolding to flatten the hierarchy between our research team and our colleagues in the field. From this perspective emerged a precedent of open-mindedness and curiosity that, in turn, opened the door for the teachers to do the same. This is very different than coming in as an expert with the answer. This is changing the lens of professional development to professional learning and, together, building capacity for receptivity to change—a key factor in sustaining growth from professional learning.

Ultimately, every district, every school, every school team, and every teacher is standing in their own spot on the continuum. We saw evidence of teachers changing practices and beliefs, but rarely was it a smooth process. Rather, progress was in fits and starts. Professional learning must intentionally address this variability and reach teachers on an individual level. This is no different from the message we give our teachers when we tell them to differentiate for our students. Essentially, we are customizing professional learning in a standardized environment. This is why professional learning should strive to create the capacity and opportunity for growth by incorporating reflective experiences tied to data and practice. You do not get these outcomes by just "teaching the teachers to do PBL." You get these outcomes by putting into place a comprehensive system that creates the conditions for change. Transformative understanding, "changing the lens," is not just about professional learning; it is about all of the parts of the system working together to influence even a focused goal, such as perspectives and perceptions of instruction and beliefs about students who are ELLs or live within impoverished environments. The feedback from our teachers reflects the continuum of transformation that we are experiencing:

> In the era of standardized testing, we focus so much more on what our students can do and what they can't do versus what they want to be able to do. I was focused during PBL on those [ELLs] that wanted to be able to do. (Seventh-grade English language arts teacher)
>
> I value more curiosity versus knowledge [now]. . . . It's not about how much you know. Background knowledge definitely helps to aid curiosity. Curiosity shines here [in PBL]. (Seventh-grade English language arts teacher)
>
> The [ELLs] were all in to it. . . . Now, some of them, because they are scared of their accent, they just didn't participate that much. But they were really into it. They would pay attention. . . . Their background knowledge was being put to use, or their experiences were put to use. So they really thrive in that environment. It was really fair game. It was an even playing field, per se, for everyone. (Seventh-grade English language arts teacher)

As we reflect on how our capacity has been built and informed by the research and pedagogy through participation in the community of professional learning with the teachers, we have a vision for the evolution of this professional learning. Although modeling a PBL experience and student content objectives is an essential element of the introduction session, future introduction sessions will be grounded in modeling a PBL experience written to address a problem of professional practice. The intention is to immerse the teachers even more deeply into the professional learning experience. Using PBL to identify and serve ELLs in middle schools is only one part of the story of Project ExCEL. Equally as important to the success of this project has been the model of professional learning, utilizing the critical factors of sustained, job-embedded support and scaffolding; modeling; and collaboration between and among teachers and schools.

References

Allen, C. D., & Penuel, W. R. (2015). Studying teachers' sensemaking to investigate teachers' responses to professional development focused on new standards. *Journal of Teacher Education, 66,* 136–149.

Archibald, S., Coggshall, J. G., Croft, A., & Goe, L. (2011). *High-quality professional development for all teachers: Effectively allocating resources* [Research & Policy Brief]. Washington, DC: National Comprehensive Center for Teacher Quality.

Azer, S. A. (2009). Problem-based learning in the fifth, sixth, and seventh grades: Assessment of students' perceptions. *Teaching and Teacher Education, 25,* 1033–1042.

Azman, N., & Shin, L. K. (2012). Problem-based learning in English for a second language classroom: Students' perspectives. *The International Journal of Learning, 18,* 109–126.

Bland, L. C., Horak, A. K., & Xu, X. (2017). *Cognitive Apprenticeship Reflection Tool* [Unpublished measure in development]. George Mason University.

Brown, A. L. (1992). Design experiments: Theoretical and methodological challenges in creating complex interventions in classroom settings. *The Journal of The Learning Sciences, 2,* 141–178.

Collins, A., Brown, J. S., & Holum, A. (1991). Cognitive apprenticeship: Making thinking visible. *American Educator, 15*(3), 6–11.

Collins, A., & Kapur, M. (2015). Cognitive apprenticeship. In R. K. Sawyer (Ed.), *The Cambridge handbook of the learning sciences* (2nd ed., pp. 109–127). Cambridge, England: Cambridge University Press.

Dennen, V. P. (2004). Cognitive apprenticeship in educational practice: Research on scaffolding, modeling, mentoring, and coaching as instructional strategies. In D. H. Jonassen (Ed.), *Handbook of research on educational communications and technology* (pp. 813–828). Mahwah, NJ: Erlbaum.

Ermeling, B., & Graff-Ermeling, G. (2016). Every lesson needs a storyline. *Educational Leadership, 74*(2), 22–26.

Every Student Succeeds Act, Pub. L. No. 114–95. (2015).

Flanders, N. A. (1961). Analyzing teacher behavior. *Educational Leadership, 19,* 173–200

Ford, D. Y. (2014). Segregation and the underrepresentation of Blacks and Hispanics in gifted education: Social inequality and deficit paradigms. *Roeper Review, 36,* 143–154. doi:10. 1080/02783193. 2014. 919563

Gallagher, S. A., Plowden, D. L., & Townsend, S. (2017). *Fit to print: A problem about yellow journalism and the road to war with Spain.* Unionville, NY: Royal Fireworks Press.

Grieco, E. M., Trevelyan, E., Larsen, L., Acosta, Y. D., Gambino, C., de la Cruz, P., . . . Walters, N. (2012). *The size, place of birth, and geographic distribution of the foreign-born population in the United States: 1960 to 2010.* Retrieved from http://www.census. gov/content/dam/Census/library/working-papers/2012/demo/POP-twps0096.pdf

Hattie, J. (2012). *Visible learning for teachers: Maximizing impact on learning.* New York, NY: Routledge.

Hmelo-Silver, C. E., & Barrows, H. S. (2006). Goals and strategies of a problem-based learning facilitator. *Interdisciplinary Journal of Problem-Based Learning, 1*(1), 4.

Horak, A. K., Holincheck, N., Webb, K., & Nagy, S. (2017, May). *Empowering English language learners' academic potential through problem-based learning: Leading teachers with a lens for capacity.* Paper presented at the annual meeting of the American Educational Research Association, San Antonio, TX.

Hussain, M. A., Nafees, M., & Jumani, N. B. (2009). Second language learners' achievement in literature through problem-based learning method. *Journal of the Scholarship of Teaching and Learning, 9*(3), 87–94.

Mun, R. U., Langley, S. D., Ware, S., Gubbins, E. J., Siegle, D., Callahan, C. M., . . . Hamilton, R. (2016). *Effective practices for identifying and serving English learners in gifted education: A systematic review of the literature.* Storrs: University of Connecticut, National Center for Research on Gifted Education.

National Center for Education Statistics. (2013). *English language learners.* Retrieved from http://nces.ed.gov/fastfacts/display.asp?id=96

Pereira, N., & de Oliveira, L. C. (2015). Meeting the linguistic needs of high-potential English language learners: What teachers need to know. *Teaching Exceptional Children, 47,* 208–215. doi:10.1177/0040059915569362

Powell, J., & Stansell, A. (2014). Cognitive apprenticeship through problem-based learning. In J. Viteli & M. Leikomaa (Eds.), *Proceedings of EdMedia 2014—World Conference on Educational Media and Technology* (pp. 2256–2261). Tampere, Finland: Association for the Advancement of Computing in Education.

Rich, P., & Hannafin, M. (2009). Scaffolded video self-analysis: Discrepancies between preservice teachers' perceived and actual instructional decisions. *Journal of Computing in Higher Education, 21,* 128–145. doi:10.1007/s12528-009-9018-3

Savery, J. R. (2006). Overview of problem-based learning: Definitions and distinctions. *Interdisciplinary Journal of Problem-based Learning, 1*(1), 9–20. http://dx.doi.org/10.7771/1541-5015.1002

Shaklee, B. (1993). Preliminary findings of the Early Assessment for Exceptional Potential Project. *Roeper Review, 16,* 105–109. https://doi.org/10.1080/02783199309553551

Shaklee, B., & Horak, A. (2014). *Project ExCEL.* U.S. Department of Education, Institute of Educational Sciences, Javits Gifted and Talented Students Education Grant Program.

Shaklee, B., & Viechnicki, K. (1995). A qualitative approach to portfolios: The early assessment for gifted potential model. *Journal for the Education of the Gifted, 18,* 156–170.

Snyder, T. D., de Brey, C., & Dillow, S. A. (2016). *Digest of education statistics 2015* (NCES 2016-014). Washington, DC: National Center for Education Statistics, Institute of Education Services, U.S. Department of Education.

Sotomayor, S. (2013). *My beloved world.* New York, NY. Knopf.

TNTP. (2015). *The mirage: Confronting hard truths about our quest for teacher development.* Brooklyn, NY: Author.

Walsh, S. (2002). Construction or obstruction: Teacher talk and learner involvement in the EFL classroom. *Language Teaching Research, 6*(1), 3–23.

About the Editors

Angela M. Novak, Ph.D., is an assistant professor in Elementary and Middle Grades Education at East Carolina University, in Greenville, NC. She teaches undergraduate and graduate courses in education, focusing on assessment practices and gifted education. She also works with the University of Virginia as an adjunct instructor in its masters-level gifted endorsement series. Dr. Novak has served the National Association for Gifted Children (NAGC) in a variety of roles in the Professional Development Network, including Chair, Communications Chair, and, most recently, Program Chair. She has worked in public education in the gifted field as a classroom teacher, resource teacher, and central office support. She has also worked in the private, not-for-profit sector of gifted education as the Academic Director of the Summer Institute for the Gifted.

Christine L. Weber, Ph.D., is a professor of Childhood Education, Literacy, and TESOL at the University of North Florida, in Jacksonville. She instructs teachers in strategies for conceptual teaching and learning, assessment tools, and meeting the needs of gifted and diverse learners. She has been a member of the Editorial Review Board for *Gifted Child Today* since 1998. Under her leadership, the Florida's Frameworks for K–12 Gifted Learners was developed in 2007 and disseminated to all school districts in the state. Dr. Weber has published numerous articles and presented at state, national, and international conferences. She currently serves as the Representative Assembly for The Association for the Gifted, Council for Exceptional Children (CEC-TAG) and Chair-elect for the NAGC Professional Development Network. She previously served as Cochair of Awards for the NAGC Research and Evaluation Network. Her recent books, with coauthors Cecelia Boswell and Wendy Behrens, include *Differentiating Instruction for Gifted Learners: A Case Studies Approach* and *Exploring Critical Issues in Gifted Education: A Case Studies Approach*.

About the Authors

Janessa Bower is a doctoral student in educational psychology at the University of North Texas, where she studies creativity, advanced academics, and the amount of time required to truly think with depth and complexity. In addition to her work as a researcher, she spends her days teaching fourth-grade writers at a public school in Dallas, TX. Her passion is to instill the love of "why" in her students.

Lynette Breedlove, Ph.D., directs The Gatton Academy of Mathematics and Science at Western Kentucky University. She has served the needs of gifted and talented students in public schools as a teacher, gifted and talented facilitator, and central office administrator. She has been active in local, state, and national advocacy organizations, including the Texas Association for the Gifted and Talented, Kentucky Association for Gifted Education, National Association for Gifted Children, and serving as board president of The Association for the Gifted. She earned her M.A. in gifted and talented education from University of St. Thomas (Houston, TX) and Ph.D. in educational psychology from Texas A&M University.

Rebecca L. Brusseau, M.Ed., is a doctoral student at George Mason University and a graduate research assistant with Project ExCEL. Before beginning her doctoral studies, Brusseau taught elementary school. An aspiring teacher educator, Brusseau's research interests include teacher learning and culturally sustaining pedagogies. She can be reached at rbrussea@masonlive.gmu.edu.

Laurie J. Croft, Ph.D., is a clinical professor of gifted education in the Department of Teaching and Learning (University of Iowa College of Education) and is the Associate Director for Professional Development at The Connie Belin and Jacqueline N. Blank International Center in Gifted Education and Talent Development. She has made presentations at various state, national, and international conferences, and to parent groups, teachers, and school boards. She also has experience facilitating professional learning in gifted education for educators from around the world and has published chapters about professional development in several recent books in the field. Dr. Croft is responsible for coordinating the comprehensive program of classes in gifted education that allow both preservice and inservice educators to earn an endorsement in gifted education and serves as the Honors Advisor for the College of Education Honors Opportunity Program.

Joy Lawson Davis, Ed.D., is an independent scholar and educational consultant, holding two advanced degrees in gifted education from William & Mary. Dr. Davis is an active member of the National Association for Gifted Children. Dr. Davis has published numerous articles, technical reports, and book chapters. Her award-winning book, *Bright, Talented, and Black: A Guide for Families of African American Gifted Learners*, was groundbreaking, specifically addressing the advocacy needs of Black families raising gifted students. As an educational consultant, she has provided extensive services to school districts and presented at conferences in the United States, Trinidad and Tobago, South Africa, Turkey, and Dubai.

Terence Paul Friedrichs, Ph.D., Ed.D., has chaired the National Association for Gifted Children's first GLBTQ (gay, lesbian, bisexual, transgender, and questioning) informal group, Special Interest Group, and Network, and presently serves as the NAGC GLBTQ Network's Communications Officer. He was on the Minnesota Council of Gifted and Talented Board, and has published 20 works on gifted GLBTQ youth, including *Needs and Approaches for Educators and Parents of Gifted Gay, Lesbian, Bisexual, and Transgender Students* (2017). He has served for 40 years as a teacher, advisor, researcher, and public policy advocate for high-potential GLBTQ students and currently directs Friedrichs Education, an assessment, instructional, and college consulting center for gifted and special needs students.

About the Authors

C. Matthew Fugate, Ph.D., is assistant professor of educational psychology at the University of Houston–Downtown. He received his doctorate in Gifted, Creative, and Talented Studies from Purdue University. Previously, Dr. Fugate was an elementary teacher and gifted coordinator in Houston, TX. His research interests include twice-exceptional students and students from underserved populations. Dr. Fugate has presented to audiences nationally and internationally on topics, including twice-exceptionality, Total School Cluster Grouping, affective development, and creativity. He is an active member of the National Association for Gifted Children and the Texas Association for Gifted and Talented, and serves as associate editor of *Teaching for High Potential*.

Amy Graefe, Ph.D., is an assistant professor of gifted education in the School of Special Education at the University of Northern Colorado. She is also director of the Summer Enrichment Program, a nationally recognized summer program for gifted learners in grades Pre-K–grade 12 that focuses on the whole gifted child. In addition, she serves on her local school district's Gifted and Talented Advisory Council and on the Gifted Education State Advisory Committee for the Colorado Department of Education. Her primary research interests include secondary gifted education, creativity, and underserved gifted learners.

Anne K. Horak, Ph.D., College of Education and Human Development, George Mason University, also serves as coordinator for Project ExCEL, a federally-funded Jacob K. Javits grant. Prior to Mason, Dr. Horak taught middle school and served as program specialist for advanced programs. Her research focuses on underrepresented gifted students and problem-based learning, as well as teacher professional learning. Dr. Horak can be reached at ahorak@gmu.edu.

Claire E. Hughes, Ph.D., is an associate professor and Chair of Education and Teacher Preparation at the College of Coastal Georgia. Previously, she was faculty director of the Special Needs and Inclusion Program at Canterbury Christ Church University in England, and a Fulbright Scholar to Greece. She is active in the National Association for Gifted Children, and The Association for the Gifted (CEC-TAG) and Teacher Education Divisions (CEC-TED) of the Council for Exceptional Children. She is author of numerous books and chapters, and her research areas include twice-exceptional children—particularly gifted children with autism spectrum disorders, positivistic views of exceptionality, and international education.

Tracy Ford Inman, Ed.D., is associate director of The Center for Gifted Studies at Western Kentucky University and is active on the state, national, and international levels in gifted education. She serves on the boards of both the National Association for Gifted Children and The Association for the Gifted, Council for Exceptional Children. She has provided professional learning experiences for thousands of educators, taught gifted and talented children in the classroom as well as gifted camps, and counseled hundreds of parents. Dr. Inman has coauthored/coedited six books, four of which have won the Legacy Book Award from the Texas Association for the Gifted and Talented. She is also the parent of two gifted young men.

Chin-Wen Lee, Ph.D., has served on the Professional Standards Committee for the National Association for Gifted Children for the past 5 years. She also serves as an Educator Preparation Provider Annual Report Reviewer for the Council for the Accreditation of Educator Preparation (CAEP). She is a contributing author to *Using the National Gifted Education Standards for Pre-K–Grade 12 Professional Development* and *Teaching Gifted Children: Success Strategies for Teaching High-Ability Learners*. Her research interests include special student populations, educators' professional learning, and program evaluation that advances the profession of education.

Katie D. Lewis, Ed.D., is an associate professor at York College of Pennsylvania, formerly of Texas A&M International University. Dr. Lewis has 5 years of experience teaching in public schools, where she served as grade chair, lead science teacher, gifted cluster teacher, and mentor to student teachers. She is actively involved in the Texas Association for the Gifted and Talented Research Division, serving as Chair, and the National Association for Gifted Children Professional Development Network, where she serves as the Chair and Newsletter Editor. Her main areas of research interest include underrepresentation of gifted Hispanic students, teacher preparation, and writing to learn.

Ann Lupkowski-Shoplik, Ph.D., is administrator for the Acceleration Institute at the University of Iowa Belin-Blank Center for Gifted Education and Talent Development. She founded and directed the Carnegie Mellon Institute for Talented Elementary Students (C-MITES) at Carnegie Mellon University for 22 years. She coauthored *Developing Math Talent: A Comprehensive Guide to Math Education for Gifted Students in Elementary and Middle School* (2nd ed.), *Developing Academic Acceleration Policies: Whole Grade, Early Entrance, and Single Subject*, and the *Iowa Acceleration Scale*, and coedited the publication on academic acceleration, *A Nation Empowered: Evidence Trumps the Excuses Holding Back America's Brightest Students*.

About the Authors

Jennifer Ritchotte, Ph.D., is an associate professor of gifted education in the School of Special Education at the University of Northern Colorado. Her current research focuses on gifted underachievement, middle level and secondary gifted education, and the application of single-subject research design to support effective practices for twice-exceptional learners. Prior to this, she was a teacher of gifted and talented students at the middle and secondary levels. Through publications, conference presentations (state, national, and international), and workshops, she advocates for the needs of gifted students, especially students at risk for adverse educational outcomes.

PJ Sedillo, Ph.D., assistant professor of special/gifted education, New Mexico Highlands University, recently published two articles: "The T is Missing from Gifted/Gifted Transgender Individuals: Case Study of a Female to Male (FTM) Gifted Transgender Person" in *Journal of Education and Social Policy*, and "Why is There a Gay Rainbow Sticker on my 9 Year-old Child's Backpack?" in *Parenting for High Potential*. His book, *Solidarity Through Pride: 40 Years of GLBT Pride in Albuquerque 1976–2016* (ABQ Press), winner of the 2018 New Mexico-Arizona Book Award in the Gay/Lesbian (GLBT) category, chronicles Albuquerque's GLBTQ Pride movement. A Past-President of the New Mexico Association for the Gifted, Dr. Sedillo serves on the National Association for Gifted Children's Legislative and Advocacy Committee and chairs NAGC's GLBTQ Network.

Beverly D. Shaklee, Ed.D., College of Education and Human Development, George Mason University, also serves as Director of the Center for International Education. Her research spans some 25 years, focusing on underrepresented gifted students, teacher education and development, as well as issues of social justice. Dr. Shaklee can be reached at bshaklee@gmu.edu.

Elizabeth Shaunessy-Dedrick, Ph.D., is a professor in the Department of Teaching and Learning at the University of South Florida. She teaches courses in and coordinates the Doctor of Education (Ed.D.) in Program Development program and coordinates the Gifted Education program. She studies evidence-based interventions for promoting the achievement of gifted and advanced learners in schools, as well as stress, coping, and academic and emotional success of high school students in accelerated courses. She is coprincipal investigator on a grant funded by the U.S. Department of Education's Institute of Education Sciences to develop an intervention to prepare students in Advanced Placement (AP) and International

Baccalaureate (IB) classes for managing the academic stress inherent to learners enrolled in these accelerated programs.

Shannon M. Suldo, Ph.D., is a professor in the School Psychology Program at the University of South Florida and a licensed psychologist. Her teaching, clinical, and research activities pertain to promoting student mental health, primarily from a positive psychology perspective. She studies evidence-based interventions for promoting student subjective well-being and reducing symptoms of mental health problems; schoolwide strategies to identify youth without complete mental health; and stress, coping, and academic and emotional success of high school students in accelerated courses.